Religion after Postmodernism

STUDIES IN RELIGION AND CULTURE

Frank Burch Brown, Gary L. Ebersole, and Edith Wyschogrod, Editors

Religion after Postmodernism

Retheorizing Myth and Literature

Victor E. Taylor

UNIVERSITY OF VIRGINIA PRESS

Charlottesville and London

University of Virginia Press
© 2008 by the Rector and Visitors of
the University of Virginia
All rights reserved
Printed in the United States of America
on acid-free paper

First published 2008

1 3 5 7 9 8 6 4 2

Library of Congress Cataloging-in-Publication Data
Taylor, Victor E.
   Religion after postmodernism : retheorizing myth and literature /
Victor E. Taylor.
       p. cm.   — (Studies in religion and culture)
   Includes bibliographical references and index.
   ISBN 978-0-8139-2761-9 (cloth : alk. paper) — ISBN 978-0-8139-2762-6
(pbk. : alk. paper)
   1. Postmodernism—Religious aspects. 2. Narration (Rhetoric)
3. Thought and thinking—Religious aspects. 4. Religious thought.
I. Title.
   BL65.P73T39 2008
   149'.97—dc22   2008012924

For my parents
and
Judy and Joe

CONTENTS

In this book, as the title economically announces, I am concerned with the strange constellation of religion, myth, and literature—some would say the Borromean knot of the humanities. I refer to this constellation as "strange" because the apparent backdrop upon which these "celestial bodies" of texts appear, to foreshadow Robert Frost's "Stars," depends upon a critical nondisclosure within discourse or what Reiner Schürmann identifies more specifically as a prevailing "hegemonic phantasm," a presumed space beyond mortal thinking. Part 1 of the volume develops the problem of "hegemonic phantasm" in the context of ontology, oracular speech, and founding language. Part 2 brings the examination of hegemonic phantasm into a discussion of myth, with readings of Mircea Eliade, Claude Lévi-Strauss, Paul Ricoeur, and Slavoj Žižek. Part 3 takes up the issue of "hegemonic phantasm" as a problem of/for theoretical thinking, a theoretical thinking in relation to religious and literary works by such authors as Leo Tolstoy, Franz Kafka, and Christoph Ransmayr.

While the above paragraph schematically describes what this book is about, I should, to the best of my ability, trace its origins, something that, ironically, I will presently argue is metaphysically impossible. One "origin" is the late Charles E. Winquist, whom I knew as a mentor and a friend. The other "origin" is Slavoj Žižek, whom I do not know at all, beyond his writings and an interview I conducted with him in 2005. Let's begin with the first. Winquist, in many pedagogical situations, emphasized the importance of "levers of intervention," ways of disrupting the fixity of discourse. In this sense Winquist, a "postmodern theologian," can be understood as waging a war on totality in religious studies some time before Jean-François Lyotard made it generally permissible to do so with his groundbreaking study *The Postmodern Condition: A Report on Knowledge.* What is unique about Winquist's "theo-postmodernist" approach, an approach that sets him apart from, let's say, a typical academic manager of "religious" information, is his concern for the primacy of thinking—Winquist viewed "postmodernism," "deconstruction," "God," "psychoanalysis," and other scholarly devices for thinking as disposable utensils, things to be discarded after use and not things to which one would adhere dogmatically or affirm unconditionally. The concern, perhaps Tillichian, shaping Winquist's writings is a concern for nonfetishistic thinking. Thinking, in this regard, for Winquist is an "intervention" conditioned by liminality; it takes place in the powerful interval between the "given of actuality and the given of possibility."

It is easy or, one could say, easier to see the advantages of having the "given of possibility" always forthcoming, open, and never closed. It at least sounds good to the "postmodern" ear. However, the "given of actuality," which may be more difficult to accept, is also, in Winquist's understanding, not closed to critical inquiry; this nonclosure refuses "actuality" as an absolute origin or instance of overdetermination, exhaustible by any given metadiscourse. With the given of actuality and the given of possibility remaining open, Winquist creates a space, interval, or gap for thinking in which, through deracination, openness "clears a space for thinking," as he would say. So, in a manner of speaking, this book finds an "origin" in a lack of absolute origin and closure, in either the given of actuality or the given of possibility.

It must be kept in mind, from a Winquistian perspective, however, that this openness does not disintegrate into forms of political quietism and ethical paralysis; openness, for Winquist, is the paradoxical condition for thinking—the impossibility and the necessity of linking "event" and "response"; a thinking that manages this linkage too soon or that seeks to bring together, comprehensively, actuality and possibility in a totality of "givenness" will be a thinking that seriously "disappoints." This other, liminal thinking, while frustrating and not consistently demonstrable, then, is a "minimal thinking," a thinking that does not lay claim to or install a hegemonic structure or fold thinking itself into a specific actuality or a possibility. While thinking, here, may be minimal in nature and ultimately disappointing, but perhaps less so, this thinking certainly is not insignificant, especially as a theoretical concern. With its emphasis on interrogating discourse, even as a pedagogical praxis that is informed by a respect for difference, this thinking tenuously takes place in a general academic context in which ritualized submission to hegemony, no matter how obscenely repressive, is required to maintain the prevailing common sense of an age—or, as the nineteenth-century French novelist Gustave Flaubert would have described it, its "stupidity."

On to the second "origin" . . . Slavoj Žižek. Žižek's work, as Winquist would have described it, "exfoliates" problems. That is to say, Žižek doesn't build systems or provide old or new formulas to solve philosophical problems; he, as I understand his work, "re-marks" the problems, shows that each problem is more of a problem than one initially may have thought. In this regard Žižek's philosophical recalibrations are scattered throughout the book, especially the emphasis on "re-marking." Žižek's writings also are significant across a range of topics—film, philosophy, politics, and theology. Even across this comprehensive range of "expertise," however, "Žižek" here remains very much a "Kafkan Thing," an intellectual "Odradek" that resists being a figure reduced to a ground. In this sense "Žižek" is useful not for reaching a conclusion but for moving the analysis forward; "Žižek," for my purposes, is a "lever of intervention," not something to which one should adhere or that one should, necessarily, affirm.

Finally, *Religion after Postmodernism: Retheorizing Myth and Literature* attempts to "rethink," if not "re-mark," theoretical thinking in religious studies. Rethinking religious theory is examined in the context of literature or, as Derrida describes it, "literarity." Leo Tolstoy, for instance, attempts to rethink or re-mark Christianity with his *The Gospel in Brief. The City of K.,* a museum exhibition, attempts to rethink or re-mark Franz Kafka and the theological frames within which his works are placed. And Christoph Ransmayr attempts to rethink or re-mark ancient myth through Ovid's *Metamorphosis.* In each instance rethinking or re-marking achieves a failure, as it should. This "failure," as I will argue, is an openness to religious "theoretical" thinking, a maintaining of the interval between the "given of actuality" and the "given of possibility." With this in mind, a final turn in part 3 brings us to Franz Kafka's "The Great Wall and the Tower of Babel," in which thinking again occupies the space between ground and rising dust, dust that, like human nature, disperses in "all directions" [alle Himmelsrichtungen]. "All directions," therefore, may suggest Deleuzean lines of "flight" that assist in establishing the contours of a concept, or "all directions" may point to the process, perhaps futile, of drawing connections between the "given of actuality" and the "given of possibility." In either case it is the interval between the two that is of primary concern.

What is imagined . o o

I would like to express my gratitude to Dean William T. Bogart, Professor Dennis M. Weiss, and the Faculty Development Committee of York College of Pennsylvania for their partial support of this project. I also wish to express my thanks to Cathie Brettschneider and the staff at the University of Virginia Press for all their work. I am grateful to Professor Stephen G. Nichols and Dean Adam Falk for providing me with the opportunity to be a visiting scholar in the Department of German, Romance Languages and Literatures at The Johns Hopkins University. Also deserving of thanks is the *Journal for Cultural and Religious Theory,* which allowed me to publish revised essays in this book. I am indebted to Professor Clayton Crockett for his insightful reading of an earlier version of this text. I am most appreciative of Professor Gregg Lambert's many contributions to my thinking as I made my way through various "perplexities" during the writing. My tremendous debt to the late Charles E. Winquist needs to be especially acknowledged. This book, in many ways, begins and ends alongside his thinking. Finally, for their patience, my gratitude to S., B., and M.

Religion after Postmodernism

I

Vanishing Origins

1.1 Collisions and Intensities

Any discourse about primary process is heuristic and provisional. To think of it as foundational is a self-admitted irony. It is better characterized as a strategic initiative in the development of a hermeneutic tropology. Since whatever figurations represent the primary process are themselves simulacra, the achievement in the development of such concepts is not that we now have principles for grounding discourse but that we have principles for turning discourse. The concept of primary process thinking is a critical notation within a play of differences that the play of differences is incomplete and not capable of completion. It is a constant pressure within discourse to convolute its surface, space its achievements, and perforate its figurations.
—Charles E. Winquist, *Desiring Theology*

In the history of modern philosophy, the logic of "Whom do you believe, your eyes or my words?" found the strongest expression in Malebranche's occasionalism: not only is there no sensible proof for occasionalism's central tenet (according to which God is the only causal agent), this tenet is even directly contrary to all sensible experience, which leads us to believe that external objects act directly on our senses, causing sensations in our mind. When Malebranche thus endeavors to convince his readers to believe his words, not their eyes, the central enigma he has to explain is: *why* did God create a universe in such a way that we, mortal humans, necessarily fall prey to the illusion that sensible objects act directly on our senses? His explanation is moral: if we were to be able to perceive the true state of things directly, we would love God invincibly, through instinct, not on account of our free will and rational insight gained through liberation from the tyranny of our senses; that is, there would be no place for moral activity, for our struggle to undo the consequences of the Fall and regain the lost Goodness. Thus Malebranche delineates the contours of the philosophical position which explains man's epistemological limitation (the fact that man's knowledge is

limited to phenomena, that the true state of things is out of reach) by reference to moral grounds. . . . A certain radical ignorance is the positive condition of our being moral.

—Slavoj Žižek, *The Ticklish Subject*

I know of no other place than the one whereupon the waning century has
planted us. A slippery terrain, no doubt, in more than one sense. But what
could it mean to want to brutally leave this terrain in order to install oneself,
by eruption, on another one?

—Reiner Schürmann, *Broken Hegemonies*

The discerning, shared line of thought running through these diverse epigraphs ends in a forceful rejection of any exclusive instantiation of a mythic
totality, a "primary process," a "space," a "foundation," a "moral ground,"
a "master signifier," or a "terrain," that would seek to unify a subject and
object, an appearance and essence, and, more comprehensively, an event
and a response. The attempt to reconcile such separations, through an appeal to a "grounding discourse" or "foundation," as Charles E. Winquist
observes, only could come to fruition, if at all, as a "self-admitted irony,"
a simulacrum of ultimacy appearing as a Deleuzean "image of thought."
In this context "foundation," "grounding discourse," and "totality," from
Winquist's perspective, are merely tropes or heuristics that, figuratively
speaking, make a quarter or half circle merely seem whole.

Totalizing claims to ultimacy, claims suggesting that partial figures are
actually whole, are claims to be challenged by theoretical "thinking." Within this particular intervening context theoretical thinking should consider
that "truths are fictions imaginatively produced in a play of differences with
specific genealogies."[1] In this instance "thinking" could find that claims to
ultimacy are, finally, "fantasies of purity." If these claims to ultimacy are not
sufficiently engaged, a putative totality, free from the play of differences, as
the "ultimate" or the ultimate "grounding discourse," could be hegemoni-
cally imposed upon a universe of entities, forcing a foreclosure of theoretical inquiry and violently designating a point beyond which thinking could
not pass. Thinking-as-intervention, then, leads to an inquiry beyond this
impasse or a thinking that occurs in the absence of a grounding discourse;
this would constitute a strange thinking, a thinking, as Heidegger observes

in "What Is Metaphysics?," that defies limits through the power of "won-der": "Only because the nothing is manifest in the ground of Dasein can the total strangeness of being overwhelm us. Only when the strangeness of being oppresses us does it arouse and evoke wonder. Only on the ground of wonder—the revelation of the nothing—does the 'why?' loom before us."[2] For a post-Heideggerian investigation, as in the case of Winquist's writings, or, more generically, a theoretical study, a lack of intervention, a restriction on thinking, a suppression of Heideggerian "wonder," is, ironically, "un-thinkable." Even so, the unmitigated and countervailing force of "ground-ing discourse" in the humanities, while presumably unthinkable, is not un-precedented or without effect. In other words, "grounding discourse," with all its resources to foreclose thinking, is not a vague something of which to be wary, as if it were a frightful possibility looming on the horizon of a future yet to come; it is and has been, I will argue, one of philosophy's pri-mary problems, if not *the* problem.

Inspired by Heidegger's call to thinking "nothing," Reiner Schürmann astutely writes in *Broken Hegemonies* that "the history of hegemonic phan-tasms is the history of ultimate referents, which are, quite literally, 'nothing,' non-res."[3] These "nothings," however, for Schürmann, are not just innocu-ous, imaginary traces of an undisclosed *arché;* they are signs forbidding the further movement of thought—not only warning buoys beyond which in-quiry may not pass but, as we shall see, signs indicating a space in which thinking and wonder run the risk of annihilation. It is, then, this real pos-sibility of thinking's annihilation that demands a movement of thought, a tactical thinking against foreclosure or preemption. But what is it that stands in the way of thinking and wonder? Rodolphe Gasché, in *The Honor of Thinking: Critique, Theory, Philosophy,* complicates thinking's dependence on "wonder" by further raising questions about the need for thinking to, ac-cording to Heidegger, "unlearn" its limitations, limitations stemming from wonder:

> According to Heidegger, what is most questionable is the fact that we still do not think. Thinking, understood as the apprehension of being—that is, of that which alone provokes wonder—does not yet take place, first and fore-most because that which needs to be thought has turned away from human beings. Human beings will learn to think only if they learn to unlearn what thinking has meant hitherto. In short, thinking must still be learned in the

opening of oneself to what is the most astonishing (Being) for thought to be possible in the first place. If thinking does not yet occur, it is precisely because we have not yet begun to wonder. Thinking's task, in advance of apprehending Being in wonder, is for the time being limited to prepare the advent of what, according to Heidegger, is only a possibility of philosophy that still has not been actualized. . . . If there has ever been thinking, if it ever took place, it would have had to occur as a response to an unpredictable event so singular as to give rise to an equally singular act of thought, for thinking is truly thinking only on condition that meets an impossible demand. But what is the status of wonder in this impossible thinking? Is wonder, then, also something that cannot simply be presupposed, something whose condition of occurring links it—indistinguishably perhaps—to terror as much as to a promise?[4]

Thinking does not evolve from wonder; it, according to Gasché, comes from provocation, some encounter with an "unpredictable event." For Gasché, following Heidegger and Derrida, thinking and wonder do not necessarily or causally connect; that is, wonder "shares" a condition with thinking, rather than functions as thinking's condition.

So what is this condition? From the above passage one could say that the so-called condition is the "unpredictable event"—the meeting of a provocative "impossible demand." In this sense thinking and wonder derive from "nothing" or from no content, only a singularity. Gasché writes that "wonder, insofar as it is an event, whether it be determined as admiration, as perplexity, as horror, as anguish, as stupor, as nausea, and so forth, is something that comes upon us, that happens to us, and that imposes itself upon us in an unconditional manner."[5] Furthermore, Gasché notes,

> it is on the basis of the notion of such an unconditionality—which, for example, exists in that wonder that effects a breach with the regions of the visible and the transparent—that Derrida thinks thinking, that is to say, philosophy as originating in *thaumazein,* as the discourse of reason that, through the mode of calculation, makes judgments about conditionality, about limits, and about the possible. This thinking of thinking—not to be mistaken for a philosophy of philosophy—can no longer be said to have a single origin; it no longer begins with bare wonder alone.[6]

Thinking and wonder, therefore, in responding to an event, arise from an event with a "plural," nonhegemonic "origin." This plural, nonhegemonic origin, Gasché observes, is really no origin: "Thinking, no longer possessed of a single origin, no longer contents itself with simply unfolding that which announced itself in the very bareness or nudity of such an origin."[7] No origins are bare "nothings," if we return to Schürmann's Heideggerian observation. The problem, however, is that these "nothings" are passed off as something, some primordial condition; they come to rely for their existence on suppression and absences, absences that powerfully concretize, albeit through phantasm, the contours of reality by establishing, however tenuously, hegemonic, nonthinking, epochal, shadowy totalities—totalities that, as Michel Foucault famously concludes, harbor "not a timeless and essential secret, but the secret that they have no essence or that their essence was fabricated in a piecemeal fashion from alien forms."[8]

The material, historical, and, as we shall see, literary expression of these hegemonic phantasmic epochal totalities—nature/ancients, God/medievals, and cogito/moderns—is, as Schürmann indicates, amorphous, but one must bear in mind that this "nothing," paradoxically, is made visible and palpable in everyday life, with laws, institutions, ideological systems, and individuals speciously affirming a secret something to "nothingness," the paradigmatic Foucauldian "alien form."[9] This phantasmic, secret quality, the quality that defines totality in this instance, is hauntingly expressed by Franz Kafka in "The Problem of Our Laws": "The very existence of these laws, however, is at most a matter of presumption. There is a tradition that they exist and that they are a mystery confided to the nobility, but it is not and cannot be more than a mere tradition sanctioned by age, for the essence of a secret code is that it should remain a mystery."[10]

Whether it is the "Law" or some other discursive formation, it is clear that that which enacts or enforces these "ultimate referents" and their ultimate nothingness does so in the name of unquestionable authority, an authority that demands, as Schürmann further argues and Kafka presciently confirms, a "submission to some archaic figure, a figure that conditions but is itself unconditioned, one which may not be subsumed or submitted to a still more archaic thesis; it is an an-archic figure."[11] This, I should clarify, doesn't mean that one must psychotically break from the world and its customs. Laws have their necessary pragmatic function. The point is rather that while laws are necessary, "Law," that abstract metaphysical category, may have its own trajectories. My interest here, I should acknowledge then, is not politico-historical, although the implications of such an inquiry are certainly relevant in this regard. What is of primary concern in the following discussion of "ultimate referents" is not their cultural materiality or sequences in political history, although, as I have indicated, one cannot escape these effects, but the hegemonic condition of their "nothingness"—the alleged unquestionable conditionality of their condition and the subsequent philosophical prospects for thinking about and overturning, "turning," or "perforating," as Winquist writes, their philosophical, archaic power to establish a first order.

This concretized first order, this primary "an-archic figure," as a phantasmic figure, is simply, I'll argue, a hegemonic origin—an original, complete condition, to be more precise, that is assumed to be ontologically resistant to questioning, to submission, and to the acknowledgment of its own phantasmic "nothingness." Presented, historically and philosophically, as if it (origin) were "something" and not "nothing," this origin assumes an unquestionable hegemonic power over thinking. Because of this power, this origin, allegedly free from inquiry and purportedly without cause, these "alien forms," cannot be overlooked or remain immune from intervention. And, if this origin cannot be overlooked or unchallenged, following Schürmann's definition, then it also must not be left "unbroken."

There remains the question, however, of how to address the rhetorical, if not philosophical, power of such a configuration of "nothing-as-something" to act on thought, to limit thinking, especially a thinking that seriously and passionately challenges the authority of ultimacy. To begin, one, as Schürmann contends, needs to acknowledge the authority or ultimacy of the "referent," in this instance as it becomes visible as an "obligation we have—a ligature, a liaison—with regard to which there is no outside."[12] This "no outside" to which Schürmann refers, however, does not or should not imply that the "nothing-as-something" of "hegemonic phantasms" is without effects—that is, "nothingness" is not absolutely nothing. Clearly, "hegemonic phantasms" result in consequences that circumscribe thinking, and it is this ensuing curtailment of thought that is of primary concern as the issue of origins becomes more pressing as a matter directly related to the possibility of thinking.

To further clarify, this time by way of poetry, what is at stake in this problem of origin and the work of phantasm, especially hegemonic phan-

*transfiguration /
go beyond
boundaries
to
transgre[ss]*

tasm, I offer as a literary case in point Robert Frost's "Stars," a poem that on
one level, like Kafka's "The Problem of Our Laws," articulates the ineluctable issue of archaic ontology and the possibilities contained in transgressing the limits placed on thinking:

> How countlessly they congregate
> O'er our tumultuous snow,
> Which flows in shapes as tall as trees
> When wintry winds do blow!—
>
> As if with keenness for our fate,
> Our faltering few steps on
> To white rest, and a place of rest
> Invisible at dawn,—
>
> And yet with neither love nor hate,
> Those stars like some snow-white
> Minerva's snow-white marble eyes
> Without the gift of sight.[13]

More than simply expressing his peaceful sentiments as a "nature poet"
from the tranquil woods of Vermont and New Hampshire, Frost, in "Stars,"
offers a sharp, if not existentially disturbing, contrast between archaic
"something" and phantasmic "nothing." The poem's opening line, "How
countlessly they congregate," denotes the presence of a transcendent intentionality, a celestial consciousness that, as the second stanza indicates,
underwrites a purposeful stellar movement in relation to human life—that
ligature tautly stretching between the night sky and human existence. By
the third stanza, four subtly abrupt lines that shatter the possibility of
transcendent effect, these once hegemonic, sentient stars, these "watch-
ing" celestial bodies that seemed to move with a "keenness for our fate," are
nothing; they are phantasms that have neither "love nor hate." The stars, finally, according to Frost, are empty signifiers, not master signifiers, specks
of light with no secret to tell after all. Frost's final two lines—devastating,
strange lines that correspond directly to Schürmann's notion of hegemonic
phantasms—capture well the problem of origin and thinking. If the stars,
as the first and second stanzas indicate, hold our fate, then by the third
stanza they, like the "snow-white marble" eyes of the statue of Minerva,
that "archaic figure," "see" without the "gift of sight."

The stars, stripped of their intentionality, without the "gift of sight," like the cold stare of the statue, cannot credibly maintain their position of transcendent origin; they cannot "see," "think," or determine our fate. Understanding this, we must recognize that they, as ultimate nothings, cannot, as Schürmann notes, elude our inspection and keep themselves from failing the test of substantive ultimacy. Once this essential secret is exposed, the secret that stars "see" blindly, the space for our thinking, a thinking beyond origin, past Minerva, past hegemony, as Schürmann has described it, is opened for inquiry. These ultimate referents, which are ultimately phantasmic, as Schürmann describes them, in order to achieve their privileged status, rely on the illusion of a hidden, yet totalizing "beyond," a "nobility," or an essential secret; to return to Foucault, these "alien forms," for their validity, must then necessarily deny, make invisible, or cast into the shadows an untotalizeable "beyond of the beyond," an "outside." That is to say, ultimate referents, in order to remain ultimate, must refuse or delimit thinking, if by thinking one means breaching the limit of hegemonic conditionality.

Taking a similar philosophical approach as Schürmann to this particular problem of the "conditioning unconditioned," John D. Caputo, in his essay "The Experience of God and the Axiology of the Impossible," citing "Johannes Climacus," resists the preemptive power of "hegemonic phantasms" to redact theoretical inquiry by placing thinking alongside a "passion of thought." This turn to a "full intensity of experience," Caputo notes, posits the "fullest passion" of thought as that which "is pushed to its limits, indeed beyond its limits, to the breaking point, to the point where it breaks open by colliding against what is beyond its power."[14] This in effect is the first step in a long process of breaking "hegemonic phantasms" and revealing their nothingness. One could rightly observe here that Schürmann's and Caputo's emphasis on the "beyondness" of the beyond recaptures Heidegger's concern for thinking, expressed in his "Letter on Humanism": "It [thinking of Being] exceeds all contemplation because it cares for the light in which a seeing, as *theoria,* can first live and move. . . . Thus thinking is a deed. But a deed that also surpasses all *praxis.*"[15] For Schürmann and Caputo, Heidegger, indirectly, and "Johannes Climacus," directly and paradoxically, prepare thinking for that which "cannot be thought," a thinking that escapes the horizon of hegemony.[16] The question, then, is how to force a collision, a break between thinking, or a "passion of thought," and an ever-imposing limit: How does one break the horizon of the hegemonic with the "passion of thought"? How does one break, as Schürmann observes, phantasm? How does one, remembering Winquist's concern for finding transformative discourse, actually "turn" discourse? For this we must return to the issue of limits and the philosophical, if not theological, desire to effect the vanishing of origins.

To the extent that origins are presumed to lay claim to "ultimate" authenticity, they are assumed to exist, as we have discussed, in their most basic form, beyond question, and subsequently to exercise their authentic power thoroughly immune to moderate, not to mention radical, alteration, which thinking necessarily would provide if given the opportunity. Origins, in these instances of secreting themselves, do more than simply protect and advance the implications of their own hegemonic interests, however; origins, embedded in the phantasm of their ontological stability, also shield a search for meaning from the destabilizing force of "excess" or the possibility of colliding with a "beyond the beyond," as Caputo aptly describes it. In this sense origins are discursively designed to insulate thinking from excess; or, as one may argue, origins protect thinking from itself, its reflective, "provoking," or "passionate" critical capacity to return to its own self-authenticating source.

It is not just Kierkegaard (Johannes Climacus), as noted by Caputo, who occupies an honored place in history for his affirmation of thinking the "unthought." One finds this duty to thinking across the history of philosophy and most poignantly, as we have mentioned, in Heidegger's work, a body of texts certainly informing Schürmann's concept of "hegemonic phantasms" and Caputo's analysis of "passionate thought." With Heidegger, as with Kierkegaard, one finds a critique of "origins" that attempts to derail a (fore)closure of thinking, pressing, I would argue, past Kierkegaard's "passion":

> But as long as the truth of Being is not thought all ontology remains without its foundation. . . . It [thinking] strives to reach back into the essential ground from which thought concerning truth of Being emerges. By initiating another inquiry this thinking is already removed from the "ontology" of metaphysics (even that of Kant). "Ontology" itself, however, whether transcendental or precritical, is subject to criticism, not because it thinks the

Being of beings and thereby reduces Being to a concept, but because it does not think the truth of Being and so fails to recognize that there is a thinking more rigorous than the conceptual.[17]

The question surrounding Heidegger's place in the history of philosophy as the truly "last metaphysician," and the hesitation that his philosophy merely replaces one foundation with another more foundational foundation, are always open to debate. In fact, Schürmann's entire oeuvre is an attempt to radicalize Heidegger's phenomenology in an effort to make Heidegger's thought genuinely postmetaphysical. With this in mind, Heidegger becomes a highly charged or dubious figure in the discussion.

It is important, nevertheless, to keep in mind that the result of his inquiry is not necessarily equal to the aim of it, and if one is generous to Heidegger, it becomes apparent that he is striving for "passionate thought," a thinking, as he describes it, that is "more rigorous" than (read "*not* limited to") the conceptual apparatus of cognition: "The task of thinking would then be the surrender of previous thinking to the determination of the matter for thinking."[18] More will be said on this topic later, primarily in a return to Rodolphe Gasché's *The Honor of Thinking: Critique, Theory, Philosophy,* but for the time being it is important to note that overcoming or vanishing origins hinges on rethinking, passionately, conceptual thinking as an "unrigorous" thinking determined by limit and grounded in the wayward belief in the necessity of grounding itself. Passionate thinking, in the Kierkegaardian, Heideggerian, or Caputoian sense, therefore stands in opposition to a monolithic, self-protective, hegemonic origin—one that is readily accessible, that operates rhetorically and politically, without question, to control the production of meaning that forcefully issues from it. By colliding "origin" with a "passion of thought" in this way, one opens a space for a discussion of new possibilities, possibilities that escape what is now conceptually available: the Derridean "future to come" illustrates the tension. This desire for possibilities outside possibility or availability in many ways is a continuing concern in philosophy and one, as I will argue, that is still worth addressing, especially in the wider context of postmodern, postmetaphysical philosophy, which very much bears the residual traces of original power, a power, as Caputo remarks, that must be brought "face to face with its own impotency."[19]

Any "beyond" or "excess" in possibility creates a whole host of traditional problems for philosophy. First, following the requirements of metaphysics, one must explain what this "beyond" or "excess" is; that is, one may be required by the discipline of philosophy to provide a further explanation of its ontological reality. And second, one must then account for its "beyondness" or "excessiveness" in the context of the perennial divide between unity and diversity. Is the "beyond" or "excess" continuous with "Reality," or is the "beyond" or "excess" radically separate from it, distinguishing itself from that which lies prior to the limit quantitatively and qualitatively? These questions all fall within the larger question of difference and identity—the problems of spirit and matter, Being and being, self and other, and more broadly the universal and the particular. Solving or attempting to resolve these issues would mean accepting the problem at face value, which is in many respects more fundamental to the problem than the problem itself.

In postmodern theology, as an example, this issue of identity/difference is central to the problem of origins. One can point to the early work of Mark C. Taylor as representative of this wider concern in the history of philosophy to reconcile the limit of the "limit." In *Altarity* Taylor, a scholar whose work (then and now) moves through the complexities of Hegel, Kierkegaard, and Derrida, situates the problem of "limit" within the historical tension between identity and difference, with identity as the historically dominant term. Rather than repositioning a simple "alterity," a reinscription of the tension within already demarcated lines of inquiry, Taylor invents "altarity," a multivalent term, similar to Derrida's *différance,* that draws together "altar" and "alterity," causing a series or "web of associations" collapsing the divide between identity and difference. "The word suffers crisis when a difference that is not the opposite of identity and an other that is not reducible to same draw near. The ceaseless oscillation of 'altarity' implies the proximity of a difference and an other that call into question every word and all language."[20] Not only does "the word," as Taylor notes, experience a "crisis," but "origin" suffers a crisis too. What does it mean, then, to think the "altarity" of origin—something beyond or in excess of identity itself? This question creates severe intellectual tasks for religious, philosophical, and, I'll argue, literary thinking.

This fundamental engagement with a profound metaphysical problem, however, has not resulted in a grand resolution to the question of limit as much as it has a willingness to see the problem of limit across numerous situations—art, architecture, economics, language, photography, and digital culture. Where Taylor and other theorists keep the question open (theory's aim), others in the past have tried but ultimately failed, as Caputo puts it, to collide the "passion of thought" with a limit. Of course, these are by no means easy tasks, and even the renowned historian of comparative world religions Mircea Eliade, as we shall see in the following section, with all of his well-meaning sympathies for a plurality of experience generating from a religious origin, accepted only one, monolithic origin, which, as he understood it, would perpetually stand guard against a radical difference ("altarity") threatening to decimate the power of the sacred. This is the problem—the twofold redactive, limiting, and defensive work of origin. To engage this problem of origins and thinking adequately, one needs to better ascertain the nature of excess under redaction. Is it, one can ask, an excess that results in too much being added *to* something, a text? Is it instead too much that results in an excess *of* meaning—an abundance internal to a hermeneutic process that proliferates meaning ad infinitum? Or is it another form of excess—one that offers a different possibility? In the context of religious theory, this problem in the first two instances traditionally presents itself in two ways: as a unity beneath the diversity of the sacred (Eliade) or as a diversity underlying the unity of the sacred, a saturating diversity that leaves no trace of a monolithic authority in an origin (Derrida). As we shall discuss in the context of contemporary religious theory, the third configuration of the problem of excess lies in the reconceptualization of the problem itself, which may or may not provide direct answers to the metaphysical requirements posted above.

1.2 Possibilities of Excess

The mark (or *margin*, or *march*—in the sense of "boundary"—all of which belong to the same series of words) as re-mark is that particular infrastructural feature that prohibits any diacritically constituted series of terms, concepts, traces, or marks from ever closing upon itself. This impossibility of totalization or of self-closure is not due to an infinite abundance of meaning, which a finite consciousness would be unable to master; on the contrary, it hinges on the existence of a certain nerve, fold, or angle on which, as we shall see, this impossibility is structurally based.

—Rodolphe Gasché, *The Tain of the Mirror*

The presence of excess, in any formulation, is the condition or event for "thinking," a thinking that opens the radical possibility that a search for meaning actually could move beyond hegemonic origin and boundary; this thinking would enable at least two distinct lines of inquiry: (1) an innovative thinking that posits a multitude of creative possibilities that extend an identifiable limit of narrative from the *inside* and *outside;* and (2) the possibility of an entirely different, radically paradoxical and inventive *internal/external* "re-marking" of narrative—one that is incongruous with and resistant to the reading apparatuses preceding any available unifying point of view—that is, a truly new, "altered," or "unhinged" reading.[21] As the following section will develop, excess, *internal/external,* distracts from the comfortable limits generating from within a text, with its supposed enduring reserve of inherent, original meaning, or from within the attending subject, with his/her intellectual capacity to seize the transcendent original order issuing from words. In each of these instances the possibility for excess is supposedly foreclosed, anchored, or "quilted," in the Lacanian sense, within the confines of origin by the formal structures of narrative, ideology, or the discerning eye of the reader.

Excess, as an issue, appears again in Taylor's analysis of identity/difference, alongside Lacan's psychoanalytic discourse on the Real. For Taylor, breaking the limit of origin appears in Lacan as an "altarity" of the "real," and as Taylor notes, it is tied to notions of an excess of this "real," "[a] real [that] is *always* missing, *forever* lacking."[22] The "passion of thought" that drives Kierkegaard also, according to Taylor, is present in Lacan, for whom Kierkegaard represents the most acute "questioner of the soul" prior to Freud.[23] The aim of thinking then is not to recover what was never there in the first place—the unbreachable origin. Instead, as Taylor writes, "that which is 'originally repressed' signifies neither an original presence nor an original absence, but the presence of an absence that discloses the absence inherent in all presence and every present."[24] With this instantiation of Lacanian-inspired "altarity," it is possible to think against the limits of origin. The concept that allows a way through this bipartition of external and internal excesses, this "altarity," comes directly from Lacan's thinking of "extimacy," a key term that we shall discuss shortly.

Before addressing the impasse posed by the external/internal collision, it is important to recognize that without the marked limits keeping us in close proximity to the point at which things purportedly began, we would slide into a rift, a fissure in a once-unified, seamless origin. Here "hegemonic phantasms" assert their conditioning unconditionality and thereby set limits on interpretation and, supposedly, quell a "passion of thought." This, generally, accomplishes a very significant task: preventing an interpretive struggle from provoking thinking, reaching too far, leaving a remainder, and passing beyond hegemonic origin. Of course, the history of reading provides countless instances of failing to keep this promise, this pledge to contain and curtail thinking. Excess, or going "too far," in interpretation is not only a problem for narrative; it is the condition of narrative—an eternal "too much" that haunts all texts. This haunting, however, is not just limited to an apparition of the "too much" as a calculative "increase"; it also includes a "too much," an infinity, that effaces recognizable quantities—like Horatio's "reading" of the ghost of King Hamlet, who appears only as a "figure like" the deceased king, which means that there is some nonidentical remainder unaccounted for in his appearance.

This problem or promise of avoiding, containing, and eventually overcoming excess, as strange as that claim seems, sets up an expectation that reading practices are, in a manner of speaking, simultaneously restorative and excessive, with the latter, according to tradition, to be disavowed. "Restorative" or recuperative readings, relying on a metaphysical presence, as Taylor has described it, enclose excess and abide by the limits set forth by some origin, an origin to which all possibilities allegedly and ultimately return; restoration, in this sense, prepares the way for a critical practice that moderates a reach so as not to allow an overreaching of an assigned limit. Restorative reading also includes a diverse set of critical practices, from formalist stylistics to historicist text-period corroborations. In each and every instance, regardless of methodology, the goal of restoration is to render the "to be" interpreted object as an object of cognition—something issuing from an origin or from a discernible metaphysical reality that limits the projection of meaning to a set of determined possibilities within a shared

Restorative approach to reading

economy of rules and contexts. This distinction, I should point out, is not intended as a reinscription of René Wellek's "intrinsic" and "extrinsic" division of literary study, although I would place Wellek's two categories firmly within the territory of "restoration." Perhaps to clarify this distinction, a turn to J. Hillis Miller and the problem of reading in literary studies is required.

Miller, citing poetry, refers to this restorative approach as criticism that returns, inevitably, to the "center": "Most concepts of form in poetry presuppose covertly or overtly the existence of a center outside the play of elements in the poem. This center is at once the origin of meaning and at the same time the control over meaning. It keeps the meaning from having an indefinitely expanding resonance of implication initiated by the give and take of words within the poem. In our tradition this center has taken the names of *source, end, consciousness, God, the Word* and so on."[25] The "center," as origin, maintains the limits of reading, truncating the expanse of implication. More to the point, every "expanding resonance" is determined by this center, making "expanse" simply "ambiguity," resolvable ambiguity. This methodological return to "center" is what Roland Barthes describes as managing the "ambiguity of content," which is distinct from reading "stereographic plurality." To put it more simply, the formalist, the ordinary language philosopher, and the historicist—all metaphysicians of texts in certain respects, a category that also would include Wellek—disagree on the various uses or feasibility of any particular method of interpretation but, I will contend, agree on the final "unmitigated" fact that texts have "traceable" meaning, especially meaning that is settled (perhaps incompletely for Wellek) by a reconciliation of ambiguity to "a" center; this shared characteristic alone distinguishes all of these interpretive approaches from those of the deconstructionists and their arguments regarding the play of signification, "stereographic plurality," and excess "as" textuality.

final meaning based on an origin.

endlessly circular meaning internal referents.

Restorative methodologies, one must not forget, also share a much more general practice of showing that dispersed or fragmented elements actually belong to a unified, hegemonic whole, which is universal, thematic, political, or historical. "Excessive" readings, on the other hand, depart from limits, abandon intention and definition, leave or delve deeply into the body of the text, abandon its objecthood, and disrupt the systems of the narrative itself to form totalities. In other words, what restorative readings seek to

Mystery of the dance.   *Meaning in Dante not settled: disseminated: unsettled.*

unite through presence, excessive readings keep apart through aporetic difference or Barthesian "stereographic plurality." More specifically, excessive
readings posit an untraceable excess beyond and, paradoxically, within the
terms of the narrative.

Excess, as an age-old interpretive nuisance, the more than the "more
than," runs along two axes, the ambiguous and the stereographic plural. It
is within this conflict between two distinct and incommensurate fields of
inquiry that a Lacanian concept such as "extimacy" becomes vital. The concept of extimité, in its formulation of excess, not only threatens to dissolve
ambiguity and meaning but works to obliterate the "real object," meaning.[26]
More importantly, as Slavoj Žižek explains in The Sublime Object of Ideology, extimacy represents the possibility of an "obliteration of the signifying
network itself."[27] In this sense, and as it is applied to critical interpretive
practices, excessive readings permit systemic obliteration, while restorative
readings, still embracing the need for unity through hermeneutic inquiry,
never allow a metaphysical critique of excess as a guiding concept. This
then forces the question: What are the possibilities of excess? What happens, to return to Caputo's quest for a passion of thought, after the intense
point of "collision"?

The idea, then, of transforming exteriority and interiority within the
context of extimité points out two distinct modes of excess, with the first
taking the form of a quantitative increase (the "many" that obeys limits)
and the second, as "plurality," appearing as a radical alterity, perhaps "altarity," and obliteration. This duality maps onto the restorative and excessive valuation of reading in which the former remains within the narrative
body, "inherently," and the latter "obliterates" the body entirely. Jacques-
Alain Miller defines it in the following manner:

> Extimacy is not the contrary of intimacy. Extimacy says that the intimate
> is Other—like a foreign body, a parasite. In French, the date of birth of the
> term "intimacy" can be located in the seventeenth century; it is found for
> instance in Madame de Sévigné's Correspondance, a model of intimacy, from
> which comes this sentence: "I could not help telling all this in detail, in the
> intimacy and love of my heart, like someone who unburdens herself to a
> maid whose tenderness is without parallel." Is it not charming that one of
> the first occurrences in the French language of the term "intimacy" already
> has a relation to a kind of confession of the heart to someone full of tender-

ness. . . . There are several covers of this point of extimacy, one of which is the religious cover. Thus Saint Augustine speaks of God as *interior intimo meo,* "more interior than my inner most being." "God" here is thus a word that covers this point of extimacy that in itself has nothing likeable. This implies the schema—where the circle of the subject contains the most intimate (*intime*) of its intimacy the extimacy of the Other. In a certain way, this is what Lacan is commenting on when he speaks of the unconscious as discourse of the Other, of this Other who, more intimate than my intimacy, stirs me. And this intimate that is radically Other, Lacan expressed with a single word: "extimacy."[28]

As a concept "extimacy," prefiguring Taylor's postmodern "altarity," seems to avoid the immediate burden of metaphysical explanation insofar as it exists as a paradox—the interior that is more interior by virtue of its exteriority. In devising the concept in this way, Lacan, as noted by Miller, rejects the oppositional requirement placed on a "passion of thought" and gives new possibilities for our thinking of excess; that is to say, "extimacy" contains and reconfigures the problem it supposedly is meant to solve—the difference between the internal and the external.

It is worth briefly noting the significance of this concept to poststructuralist theory. *Extimacy,* as a term, functions similarly to the prefix *para,* a linguistic antecedent that I have discussed elsewhere.[29] On this point it is useful to return to one of the earlier discussions of *para,* by J. Hillis Miller: "In borrowed Greek compounds 'para' indicates beside, to the side of, alongside, beyond, wrongfully, harmfully, unfavorably, and among. . . . 'Para' is an 'uncanny' double antithetical prefix signifying at once proximity and distance, similarity and difference, interiority and exteriority, something at once inside a domestic economy and outside it, something simultaneously this side of the boundary line, threshold, or margin, and at the same time beyond it."[30] *Extimacy* and *para,* while not absolute equivalent terms, similarly address the problem of excess in terms of limits; that is, excess need not be pure interiority or pure exteriority. This notion of exclusionary difference or bipartition is shown by Lacan and J. Hillis Miller to be an unnecessary limit placed on thinking that, as a matter of thinking, discloses itself as false division, with interiority paradoxically *containing* exteriority. Mladen Dolar, in "I Shall Be with You on Your Wedding Night: Lacan and the Uncanny," describes "extimacy" in the following psychoanalytic terms: "All the great philosophical conceptual pairs—essence/appearance, mind/body, subject/object, spirit/matter, etc.—can be seen as just so many transcriptions of the division between interiority and exteriority. Now the dimension of *extimité* blurs this line. It points neither to the interior nor to the exterior, but is located there where the most intimate interiority co-incides with the exterior and becomes threatening, provoking horror and anxiety."[31]

The relationship between extimacy and horror can be seen more clearly as a conflict between the interior and the exterior, with traditional psychoanalysis offering a resolution through a strengthened and reinforced bipartition of opposites. If extimacy represents a "passion of thought" that breaks the limit, then any thinking that simply reinscribes the separation of interior and exterior by way of origin is a "thinking within" the limit. Moreover, thinking within the limit, or "passionless thought," only permits a set of choices—essence/appearance, mind/body—conditioned by the power of origin. In the case of psychoanalysis one could return to Lacan's antagonistic "source" and view Freud's "archaeology" as the paradigmatic attempt to restore the authenticity of origin to diversity, recuperating any excess or beyond into the unity of identity or the unconscious.

Malcolm Bowie, for instance, in *Freud, Proust and Lacan: Theory as Fiction,* describes this "archaeology" as a method of revealing "ultimate referents": "Archaeology and psychoanalysis are, then, both concerned with burial and excavation, with the making present of a previously lost past. In the life of the mind, the primitive sexual desire or traumatic event is inhumed by repression and may be exhumed within the analytic dialogue."[32] The putative "cure," or archaeological sought-object, in this instance, results from containing, by exhumation, an excess or beyond, aligning it with that which is most primary and unalterable—the lost past within memory.

The issue of "extimacy," like "altarity," becomes more apparent in this tension between the "inhumed" and the "exhumed" origin. The "Wolf-man" and "Katarina" case studies, as brief examples, with the latter understood as more of a chance encounter in the mountains, represent a transition from ailment to well-being by way of discovering, layer by layer, a unity in origin—a unity that is other than it appears. The "Wolfman," by way of synopsis, comes to see his neurosis as generating from his own "genesis," which is to say his confrontation with his origin in the image of his parents engaged in sexual intercourse. In this interpretation, which neglects the much more accepted "castration" reading, the "Wolfman" sees his "origin" as the origin of his condition, leaving him caught between the external act (as simulation) that culminated in his existence and the internal recognition of that existence as being beyond or in excess of his actual being. What was once an impasse in the form of neurosis seems to vanish as the "Wolfman" accepts the "memory/origin" of his trauma—a unifying origin as his own private myth that settles, as far as one is able to access, the diversity of his psychic life.

Similarly, "Katarina" experiences a series of memories/origins as she confronts her asthmatic-like neurotic symptoms. As she attempts to arrive at the principal origin of her anxiety, she hesitates on at least two "false" moments in her memory. Once "Katarina" learns that she can tell a doctor "anything," she begins to locate more precisely the place of that "original" memory. The "turn of the screw" comes, as Freud tells us, when it is discovered that the so-called primary memory merely functions as a disguise/trigger for an earlier, more original experience—the originary moment of the neurosis. In both instances the origin/memory is "contained" within and excavated from the neurotic matrix, and the process of analysis merely lifts that hidden memory into view as a settled diversity of experience: asthmatic attacks, heart palpitations, and fear of dogs are, metaphorically speaking, dusted off and transfigured into the unity of origin. As "readers" of their own symptomology, "Wolfman" and "Katarina" remain largely circumscribed within these unifying confines of origin, taking an early experience, real or imagined, as the founding, authentic moment of illness and, in its restoration to memory, cure. This is much more significant for "Katarina," in that her "analysis" is impromptu and without any meaningful duration. The recovery of an original memory is nothing less than miraculous, and Freud's literary manipulation of the facts speeds the reader and "Katarina" to a full reconciliation of the gap existing between an interior and an exterior.

The case-study examples, however schematic, demonstrate that restorative interpretation must, as a first imperative, seek a unified origin, which "Wolfman" and "Katarina" do, and then it must be guided, as a second imperative, by that origin to a reconciliation of excess—the neurotic symptom. In this regard each interpretation or cure is the result or instance of an "archaeological" restoration—a synthesis of what is posited as diversity or difference in experience. It is this relationship, however, between the diversity of experience and its synthesis in origin that undergoes a significant transformation once origin loses its unifying force. In each encounter Freud, through his revisionary footnotes and commentary, expresses his suspicion about the "origin" that is supposedly revealed at the time of analysis. At least for "Wolfman" his cure comes as a "phantasm" of memory—some *arché* that presents itself as the ultimate or as the unconditioned condition that he accepts. Just as "Wolfman" and "Katarina" confront their respective fears by undertaking a journey into memory or memory as origin, so too do other patients of Freud. More generally, however, the search for a "cure" through the voluntary or involuntary uncovering or "exhumation" of an origin is the de facto template of many conflicts, real and, as we shall examine, literary. The troubling question, however, regarding these searches for origins seems to go unanswered. Is it an origin, an *arché,* or is it merely a phantasm? An answer may reside in a turn to literary figures, whose artificiality and more involved (narrator-driven) descriptions of their "symptomatic readings" may reveal in more detail the problem of ultimate referents.

If one is to deal with the issues of Freud, memory, and origin in literature, Marcel Proust is unavoidable. What is *In Search of Lost Time* if not an extended "exhumation" leading to an "inhumation"? Roger Shattuck, for instance, in *Proust's Way,* draws Freud and the twentieth-century French novelist together through their respective understandings of memory, a memory that functions in the curative process:

> In *Beyond the Pleasure Principle,* Freud speculates that the elements of experience that enter consciousness do not leave memory traces. Consciousness provides a "protective shield" against stimuli—or at least a kind of bypass for them. Only things we do not become conscious of make an imprint that may be remembered. I find it a dismaying yet arresting theory. Is Proust saying something similar? Does the obscure mechanism or muse that activates our receptivity to impressions and reminiscences operate only when working surreptitiously, free of observation? Does any effort on our part to influence its working shut it off and float everything up into the dessicating air of consciousness?[33]

Involuntary memory, which is what Shattuck is referring to he
fact be a corollary to Freud's understanding of the unconscious
it represents an authentic reality, one not susceptible to the vagai
scious thought.

This rather traditional rendering of Proust's literary exploration of memory stems from Proust's remarkable closeness to Henri Bergson, who, in trying to steer a middle path between idealistic and realistic versions of reality,
offers memory as the complex effect that defies an easy reduction to either
end of the philosophical spectrum. The close connection between mind and
brain, according to Bergson, is more than a "coat hanging on a nail." Involuntary memory, then, becomes in this context restorative memory, a site
upon which a diversity of experience is synthesized into a totality that is
in effect greater than the sum of its parts. Of course, Deleuze's reading of
memory in *Proust and Signs* topples this conclusion by emphasizing the work
of signs (world, love, and art) over simple memory as the space of remembering. Nevertheless, as Shattuck observes, involuntary memory as a close
approximate of the unconscious sets in motion a search for "origin." The difference, however, is in viewing consciousness "not as a protective shield but
as a mysterious vital process."[34] This "vital process," as Shattuck describes
it, also leads him to posit that "the book hinges on the resolve Marcel wishes
to discover in himself."[35] I would only add to this summary by noting that
Marcel seeks to inhume himself through the dissipation of a self.

In Search of Lost Time, then, shares a great deal with the previous two
Freudian case studies, including a theory of development through restoration as a form of reconciliation. At times, however, these seemingly linear
progressions toward self-awareness fold back on themselves, creating literary searches for "origin" that in many ways defy a cure. In the realm of
modern literary aesthetics, if we see Sigmund Freud as an "author" giving
us memory as a way to the objective essence of things, then we certainly can
view Marcel Proust as taking all of that away. In addition to their divergent
goals, perhaps, one can find compelling similarities. For instance, Bowie
describes Freudian and Proustian language as an "unstable medium":

> The writings of Proust and Freud invite comparison at so many points that
> the avoidance of comparison by those critics who have been willing to link

their names must be accounted a thing of wonder. For Proust and Freud culture informs and is informed by sexuality, and both write urgently and at length about the manifold forms of sexual desire that meet and compete in the moral, artistic, and intellectual spheres. For both of them language is the hugely unstable medium in which desire is socialized and in which constant failures of that socialization occur: language is at once a retreat from, and a surreptitious return route to, the libidinal substratum. Add to this a willingness on the part of each to disclose the desiring impulses and gambits that underlie his own productions and the two writers begin to seem irresistibly, perhaps even cloyingly, comparable.[36]

In pursuit of the "libidinal substratum," Freud and Proust invest in "literary" archaeology, and this search for an origin, while maintaining hope for a recovery of the lost object in Freud, is for Proust thoroughly inverted in *In Search of Lost Time*.

As we shall see, this inversion removes the unifying force of origin from a theory of lived experience, giving literary, imaginary characters a much greater potential for instability than their so-called real counterparts. The breaking of limits, more abstractly, occurs in Proust as a literary-philosophical deconstruction of memory, the canvas upon which reality is rendered. Utilizing Bergson's theories of memory and, more generally, a new metaphysics, Proust shows time and time again the "phantasm" of origin. He does this most directly by presenting the reader with an excess that does not yield to synthetic unity; this is the "creative" work of writing that Deleuze associates so strongly with Proust's texts. The beyond as excess is then, in Proust's work, completely defiant of origin's redactive power—its ability to bring creativity, diversity, and difference under the rule of a hegemonic authority.

Typically, one would offer an analysis of Marcel to illustrate this point; however, Swann, a better figure in this regard, living under the rule of a phantasm (his love for Odette), finds himself, not unlike "Wolfman" and "Katarina," facing a fear and seeking an origin as a restorative "cure" for his emotional anguish. The problem with this therapeutic formulation, however, lies in the troubling absence of the type of unconditioned condition, as origin, one would expect to find in a "psychological" novel. Like Marcel, Swann too is wishing to discover some "resolve" in himself—something in him that is more than he is, that would rectify his sense of self.

While Marcel and Swann may be alike in many ways, there are, of course, many significant differences between Swann and, let's say, "Wolfman" or "Katarina." We obviously do not have a "real" person or therapeutic setting, nor do we have an analyst steering a patient through the painful "plague of fantasies" haunting his mind—only a narrator, which may make the turn to literature more relevant at this point. Nevertheless, Swann's predicament serves as a useful instance of this conflict between restoration and excess, and Swann, like the "real" patients of Freud, acts to confront the truth of his fear and, in so doing, presumes that he will find a cure in the revelation or excavation of a painful truth.

Swann's confrontation or collision with the fear that Odette is betraying him with some mysterious suitor takes him on a journey not just through memory but through interpretation as well. Swann, as we shall see, is a quintessential "symptomatic reader," an archaeologist of phantasms. Swann's journey through tormenting jealousy mirrors an academic's single-minded quest for the object of knowledge. In this instance jealousy and knowledge come to form an odd union in the novel. As Bowie writes, "jealousy . . . is the quest for knowledge in a terrifying pure form: a quest for knowledge untrammeled and unsupported by things actually known. It is a continuous journey towards a receding goal, an itinerary with no stopping-places and no landmarks; it is an appetite for knowledge, but knows nothing."[37] Swann's evolving suspicions, speculations, and certainties all point him toward an origin or truth that supposedly holds the promise of unity over difference.

Stanley Cavell, whose final analysis is somewhat different from the conclusions drawn here, in *Disowning Knowledge in Six Plays of Shakespeare*, correlates this quest for origin with philosophy's and literature's shared contention with skepticism. In particular, Cavell's Othello is very much like Proust's Swann insofar as both characters use jealousy as a means to purportedly gain knowledge and identity. Furthermore, Othello's demand for "ocular proof" of Desdemona's alleged betrayal fits well with Swann's late-night surveillance of Odette—an instance of "Seeing is believing," or "What do you believe? Me or your lying eyes?" More important, however, is the way in which both characters place a "finite woman in the place of God."[38] Desdemona and Odette function as originary points for identity, phantasms that seemingly secure Othello's and Swann's place not just within the social order but within the metaphysical order as well. This transposition, woman to God or origin, allows jealousy, in Othello and Swann, to function as an adhesive in identity formation—an identity that is predicated on the fidelity and existence of an other, of Desdemona and Odette. The difficulty, it should be noted, in securing knowledge and identity is that this demand for interpretative unity, which worked so well for Freud's patients, ultimately culminates in a betrayal of Swann and Othello. The presumed discovery of an origin as "truth" not only shows a lack of unity, a vanishing origin, but also presents Swann, our subject of study, with the possibility of radical difference, "altarity," or extimacy in interpretation itself. In other words, Swann has an "appetite for knowledge, but knows nothing," as Bowie has described.

Upon arriving at Odette's townhouse after a late evening, solo, at a banquet, Swann learns that his expectations of romance will be short-lived: "'No cattleya, then tonight?' he asked. . . . "No, dear, no cattleya tonight.'"[39] The euphemistic, botanical reference to sex shows Swann as seductive and suggestive—covert in the ways of love, or so it would seem. Odette's rejection of "cattleya" is met by Swann with a slightly humorous, if not passive-aggressive, "It might have done you good, but I won't bother you."[40] This, of course, is simply a futile and indelicate request, a much less metaphorical last attempt at sex before resigning himself to spending the rest of the evening alone. With no other option available to him at the moment, Swann acquiesces to Odette's wishes, and literature's most famous "booty call," to use the vernacular, concludes with Swann putting out the light and drawing the curtains closed around Odette's bed before sadly departing. Despondent, he leaves, and there is nothing immediately to suggest that her refusal of "cattleya" is anything more or less than her not feeling well, as she explains. The problem, or what will be the problem, appears "about an hour and a half" later in the story, although no passage of time is marked, other than a reference to a watch. In the quietude of his return home, Swann is provoked to spin a fantasy around Odette's rejection of his advances, and this leads to an interesting and delusional "archaeology" of signs.

"The idea," Proust writes, "suddenly struck him that perhaps Odette was expecting someone else that evening, that she had merely pretended to be tired, so that she had asked him to put out the light only so that he should suppose that she was going to sleep."[41] Swann speculates that Odette's feeling unwell and being tired were simply a ruse to shoo him away so that she might welcome some other "man who was to spend the night with her."[42] Swann, beside himself with fear and anger, ventures back to Odette's house in order to confront the "truth" of her infidelity. The question, then, is from where did this idea of infidelity rise? How did this linguistic excess enter into the situation? Is Swann's suspicion simply a conclusion based on Odette's questionable character? This is clearly part of it. More importantly, however, one could ask if this suspicion originated in the moment when figurative language supplanted literal language—at the introduction of "cattleya." If "Do you want to have sex?" can be transfigured into "Cattleya, then, tonight?," then what prevents "No, dear, no cattleya tonight" from meaning, "Leave, I am expecting someone else for sex tonight"? The answer is, nothing; there is no reason for it not to work this way—that is, once the figurative displaces the literal, any phrase, now unmoored from an origin, can mean anything, given the right conditions or "attunement." In this tension between interpretative registers, the question for Swann, then, is whether the right skeptical conditions exist for his speculation that Odette declined his advances in anticipation of someone else's.

Proust's description of Swann's late-night adventure to Odette's underscores the erratic, yet oddly focused trajectory of Swann's thinking. To borrow again from Cavell, what seems to be ultimately at stake in Swann's thinking is his identity, which is an identity desperately linked not to Odette, but to Odette's fidelity. In this sense, as Cavell observes in Descartes, "the integrity of my human, finite existence may depend on the fact and on the idea of another being's existence, and on the possibility of *proving* that existence, an existence conceived from my very dependence and incompleteness."[43] As we shall see, Swann's jealousy mingles with skepticism's challenge to knowledge. And furthermore, the scene, from the moment of rejection to the conclusion of the "confrontation," covers nearly five pages, five pages of seemingly desperate speculation in which Swann's sense of self is at stake:

> Amid the glimmering blackness of the row of windows in which the lights had long since been put out, he saw one, and only one, from which percolated—between the slats of its shutters, closed like a wine-press over its mysterious golden juice—the light that filled the room within, a light which on so many other evenings, as soon as he saw it from afar as he turned into

the street, had rejoiced his heart with the message: "She is there—expecting you," and now tortured him, saying: "She is there with the man she was expecting." He must know who; he tiptoed along the wall until he reached the window, but between the slanting bars of the shutters he could see nothing, only hear, in the silence of the night, the murmur of conversation.[44]

Swann is not just troubled by the thought of Odette with another man; he is "tortured" by the transfiguration of signs and symptoms surrounding his impromptu surveillance. The "light" coming from the window that once filled his heart with joy now, in his immediate experience, fills it with anger and jealousy. Just as "no cattleya tonight" can mean "I'm tired and unwell" or "I'm expecting another," the light, once a welcoming beacon, becomes another sign—a sign of infidelity.

As Swann draws closer to the "truth," he strangely shifts his focus from the emotional to the academic. The "torture" he experiences from the transfiguration of signs changes to an academic exercise in which the skills of textual interpretation preempt the feelings of despair described as he approaches Odette's window:

And yet he was not sorry he had come; the torment which had forced him to leave his own house had become less acute now that it had become less vague, now that Odette's other life, of which he had had, at that first moment, a sudden helpless suspicion, was definitely there, in the full glare of the lamp-light, almost within his grasp, an unwitting prisoner in that room into which, when he chose, he would force his way to seize it unawares; or rather he would knock on the shutters, as he often did when he came very late, and by that signal Odette would at least learn that he knew, that he had seen the light and had heard the voices, and he himself, who a moment ago had been picturing her as laughing with the other at his illusion, now it was he who saw them, confident in their error, tricked by none other than himself, whom they believed to be far away but who was there, in person, there with a plan, there with the knowledge that he was going, in another minute, to knock on the shutter. And perhaps the almost pleasurable sensation he felt at that moment was something more than the assuagement of doubt, and of a pain: was an intellectual pleasure.[45]

Swann's "intellectual pleasure," as paradoxical as it may first appear, describes a transition from one register of emotional experience, the one that follows trauma, to another, which seeks to reorganize trauma as a way to make the "problem with Odette" an object of cognition.

Swann's transfer to the "intellectual" can be seen as an attempt to overcome skepticism, to reassure himself, with "ocular proof," that his "being" is well maintained in Odette's fidelity. If he is betrayed, then, knowing and, furthermore, knowing that she knows that he knows—a spiraling epistemology in which he triumphs—will, Swann believes, at this particular point in his investigation, mitigate or at least soften the trauma of Odette's supposed indiscretion; that is, "disowning" the knowledge of her infidelity will somehow restore his sense of self, as if being played the fool is more damaging than being substituted for in the space of romance. The anticipated revealing of Odette's alleged infidelity, which ironically reverses his "drawing" her bed curtains closed, is likened by Swann to an intellectual activity in which his success is determined by his not being outwitted by Odette's alleged metaphorical assault on language, which is an instance of an excess of the truth.

The "collision" scene, while rich in interpretive possibilities, begins with a desire for truth, a paranoid truth that is manufactured by Swann. Proust, in providing increasing details, methodically places Swann (and the reader) on the path to some grand revelation. By the conclusion of the scene, the ridiculous "joke" is just as much on the reader as it is on Swann. After the heightened emotions, the remarkable imagined scenarios, and the anticipation of triumph over Odette and her alleged secret suitor, Swann, much to his dismay, builds his "plague of fantasies" around a plague of windows, in particular the wrong window! The entire sequence of associations and possibilities stems from the wrong sign, a mistaken identification that creates a string of impossibilities.

The introduction of this "antirevelation" is embedded in the language of textual analysis. Swann sees himself not as a betrayed lover, but as a "scholar" seeking the truth of a manuscript. His desire has been transformed into academic inquiry, with the truth of Odette's potential infidelity on par with the truth of textual exegesis. His "cure," he thinks, will come from or presumably arise from his paleographic acuity and philosophical commitment to truth, which in its presentation will, he believes, shatter all pain and doubt by restoring all things that are out of place to a place:

But his desire to know the truth was stronger, and seemed to him nobler. He knew that the reality of certain circumstances which he would have given his life to be able to reconstruct accurately and in full, was to be read behind that window, streaked with bars of light, as within the illuminated golden boards of one of those precious manuscripts by whose artistic wealth itself the scholar who consults then cannot remain unmoved. He felt the voluptuous pleasure in learning the truth which he passionately sought in that unique, ephemeral and precious transcript, on that translucent page, so warm, so beautiful. And moreover, the advantage which he felt—that he had over them lay perhaps not so much in knowing as in being able to show them that he knew.[46]

One of the emphases to be noted in this passage concerns the satisfaction of desire through truth or accurate "reconstruction." Swann invests in the archaeology of investigation, a process by which one removes layer upon layer of signs or symptoms to disclose the truth, "in full," as he says.

In addition to his "restorative" investments, Swann also feels a surge of pleasure as he contemplates purportedly the highest of intellectual achievements—knowing that one could show that one knew before someone else. To achieve this "scholarly" victory over Odette, Swann must unite or restore the signs or symptoms with an origin, which in this instance is Odette's imagined infidelity. Once that truth has been revealed, Swann believes, all excesses in signification will be contained, thoroughly recovered within the meaning delimited by an origin. The collection of excess will be so complete that even "no cattleya," with its new meaning bearing the sign of deception, will be restored to truth.

By the time Swann decides to knock on the window, the wrong window, he has very accurately restaged the problem of infidelity as a problem of interpretation, a problem, I will argue, of curtailing the effects of excess:

He raised himself on tiptoe. He knocked. They had not heard; he knocked again, louder, and the conversation ceased. A man's voice—he strained his ears to distinguish whose, among such of Odette's friends as he knew, it might be—asked:
"Who's there?"
He could not be certain of the voice. He knocked once again. The window first, then the shutters were thrown open. It was too late, now, to draw back,

and since she was about to know all, in order not to seem too miserable, too jealous and inquisitive, he called out in a cheerful, casual tone of voice:

"Please don't bother; I just happened to be passing, and saw the light. I wanted to know if you were feeling better."

He looked up. Two old gentlemen stood facing him at the window, and one of them with a lamp in his hand; and beyond them he could see into the room, a room he had never seen before. Having fallen into the habit, when he came late to Odette, of identifying her window by the fact that it was the only one still lit up in a row of windows otherwise all alike, he had been misled this time by the light, and knocked at the window beyond hers, which belonged to the adjoining house.[47]

The entirety of the episode, a scene that continues in painful detail, ends, like many of Proust's sentences, with an unremarkable fact—one many have claimed could have come much sooner in the narrative.

The importance of the mistake, however, lies not in its embarrassing depiction of Swann as an overzealous, pathologically jealous lover. Rather, the attempt to constrict a series of signs or symptoms to an origin is his failure; the scene demonstrates that archaeology, not jealousy, is a "misleading" endeavor. The question is, what makes it "misleading"? Is it simply an error? Was he a victim of architectural ambiguity? If the wrong window is an "error," it is an error before the fact of its discovery. Swann's "error" is made when he does not anticipate the possibility of finding a "window beyond hers"; in other words, he does not think about windows "allegorically," to recall Paul de Man. As passionate as Swann is in his attempt to expose Odette's supposed deceit, he fails to be "passionate" enough in his thought, which would have allowed him to consider the prospect not just of another window, but of considering possibility or allegory as a way through limitation. Swann, like "Wolfman" and "Katarina," embarks on a journey toward the truth with only one destination in mind, the hegemonic origin. The troubling fact, however, is that this truth, as a product of restorative practice, is monolithic and immune from excess or beyond. This literary example from a twentieth-century French novel provides a useful point of reference, as the question of limit and excess cuts across philosophical, literary, and religious discourse. Swann's failure, then, is Proust's success, insofar as the unitary nature of origin and its foundation for truth are re-

Excess of [?] and meaning.

vealed not as a window unto truth but as a mistaken window unto excess, an excess between windows.

The significance of excessive readings in philosophy, religious theory, and literature will be explored in more detail in part 3, with Leo Tolstoy, Franz Kafka, and Christoph Ransmayr. The point of Proust's Swann here can be found in the ways in which a search for truth, in this case Swann's suspicion or "jealous forgeries" of Odette's imagined (for the time being) infidelity, is complicated by excess, an excess that cuts across or breaks with the narrative possibilities delimited by the text. In this instance the "wrong window" never enters into Swann's search for truth—his thinking about the economy of signs leads to his single conclusion, not allegorical deferment. The "wrong window" breaks or, as we shall see, "short-circuits" possibility in two distinct ways. First, the "wrong window" completely disrupts the accumulation of signs in the confrontation scene, leaving the "wrong window" as a surprise to many, although one could argue that the bulk of the novel actually makes this outcome more predictable than Swann finding the right window; nevertheless, within the scene itself the "wrong window" functions as a disruptive excess. Second, the "wrong window" is significant at the level of possibility at an abstract level; that is to say, the "wrong window" paradigmatically represents the possibility that possibility, as knowable content, is always subject to a "passion of thought," an unaccounted-for allegorical excess as a *creative* possibility: Swann eventually discovers that he never really wanted what he thought he had desired, namely Odette. It is this second excess that deserves a more elaborate discussion for the simple reason that excess exceeds "quantity" in this theoretical space, which explains the importance of extimacy in theoretical analysis. The choice is more than just between a "right" window and a "wrong" window. There is another possibility that deals with the allegorical space between windows, which, as we shall see, is the subject of Slavoj Žižek's theoretical project.

The possibility of a space between "windows" and the further implications of Lacanian extimacy are developed in Žižek's critical analyses, although, with the exception of *The Sublime Object of Ideology*, the term *extimacy* itself does not frequently appear. In *Parallax View*, for instance, Žižek clearly relies on the tension between interiority and exteriority to make his case for the "short circuit," a critical perspective that calls into question the process of restoration. The section "Burned by the Sun," which appears in a chapter bearing the title "The Unbearable Heaviness of Being Divine Shit," seeks to "short-circuit" various approaches to the "Real Thing," the originary point through which all variables and differences are ordered—Swann's right window. The opening discussion includes a brief history of modern art and science. Science historically has sought the "real thing"; that is, science, with its formulas and instruments, has attempted to give us the truly, actually real. Art, with its servitude to mimesis, has attempted to give us appearances.

In Žižek's discussion the two, in modernity, flip. Science, perhaps under the conflicting paradoxes of relativity theory, quantum mechanics, and string theory, has in a sense given up on the truly, actually real and has instead satisfied itself with appearances. Modern art, not limited to quantification, however, has given up on appearances and has turned to uncovering essences: "Within the horizon of traditional metaphysics," Žižek writes, "art is about (beautiful) appearances with elusive and confused meanings, while science is about the reality beneath appearances. In a strange reversal, today's sciences focuses more and more on the weird domain of autonomized appearances, of phenomenal processes deprived of any substantial support."[48]

Modern art's pursuit of the "Real Thing" opens, for Žižek, a more fundamental metaphysical problem in this transit between appearances and reality. At one level the "Real Thing" can be that which lies beneath appearance; at another level the "Real Thing," following Aristotle, could be the appearance itself. There are other possibilities too: that there is no hegemonic "Real Thing," which would be the "Real Thing"; or that there is a "Real Thing" and we can't know it, which would be Kant's "Real Thing"; or that the "Real Thing" is the "gap" or "spacing" across appearances, "hegemonic phantasms." An attempt to choose among these possibilities requires an analysis of appearances and essences, with interiority and exteriority shifting primary emphasis.

Žižek's discussion of the myth of Plato's cave, which will be discussed in part 2, catalogs a variety of solutions to the appearance/essence problem:

> We should risk a different approach, and read Plato's parable as a myth in the Lévi-Straussian sense, so that we have to look for its meaning not through direct interpretation but, rather, by locating it in a series of varia-

tions: that is, by comparing it with other variations on the same story. The elementary frame of so-called "postmodernism" can in fact be conceived as a network of three modes of inversion of Plato's allegory. First, there is the inversion of the meaning of the central source of light (sun): what if this center is a kind of Black Sun, a terrifying monstrous Evil Thing, and for this reason impossible to sustain? Second, what if (along the lines of Peter Sloterdijk's *Spheres*) we invert the meaning of the cave: it is cold and windy out in the open, on the earth's surface, too dangerous to survive there, so people themselves decided to dig out the cave to find shelter/home/sphere? In this way, the cave appears as the first model of building a home, a safe isolated place of dwelling—building one's cave is what distinguishes us from the beasts, it is the first act of civilization. . . . Finally, there is the standard postmodern variation: the true myth is precisely the notion that, outside of the theater of shadows, there is some "true reality" or central Sun—all there is are different theaters of shadows and their endless interplay. The properly Lacanian twist to the story would have been that for us, within the cave, the Real outside can appear only *as a shadow,* as a gap between different modes or domains of shadows. It is thus not simply that substantial reality disappears in the interplay of appearances; what happens in this shift, rather, is that the very irreducibility of the appearances to its substantial support, its "autonomy" with regard to it, engenders a Thing of its own, the true "real Thing."[49]

This "true 'real Thing'" is nothing, a phantasm—only a moment of irreducibility of an appearance to an essence, an event to a response, or a sign to an ultimate referent. In the paragraph quoted above this is an instance of a failure, of an inability to effectively link a series of phantasms to the "right" window, as in the case of Swann, or symptoms to a condition, recalling Lacan. Gaps between different modes of "shadows," as opposed to different paths to origins, allow a refusal of a simple interior/exterior binary, with extimacy as the operative concept. Žižek's own rendering of the problem of Plato's allegory provides an example for traversing modes of shadows or breaking the limits of various hegemonies. This "short-circuiting" of an ever-present underlying metaphysics (one that attempts to overlook the phantasmic quality of the "Real Thing") sets the stage, as it were, for the possibility of excessive readings in religious theory, film, art, and literature, as we shall see in a later section.

1.3 Modes of Spacing

> Wagner's radically perverse idea was to "get Christ down from the Cross,
> or rather stop him from getting on it." . . . This is what Wagner ultimately
> has in mind by the "redemption of the redeemer": Christ does not have to
> die in order to redeem us. In Christianity proper, Christ redeems us by way
> of his death on the Cross, whereas for Wagner, the source of redemption is
> precisely that part of Christ which remained alive, which did *not* expire on
> the Cross.
>
> —Slavoj Žižek, *Tarrying with the Negative*

Žižek's analysis of Plato's cave through the concept of structural variation,
ending with a Lacanian "twist," deemphasizes a movement toward "substantial support," which is to say the setting of an appearance in an essence
or origin—Swann's right window. In the absence of substantial support,
the axis upon which appearance then turns becomes visible as "original
emptiness," a "phantasm-point" that is significant insofar as it shows the
distance between a master signifier and the place it supposedly occupies:
"The unmasking of the Master's imposture," Žižek writes, "does not abol-
ish the place he occupies, it just renders it visible in its original emptiness,
i.e., as preceding the element which fills it out. . . . [This] undermines the
Master's charisma, suspends the effect of 'quilting,' and thus renders visible the distance that separates the Master from the place it occupies, i.e.,
the radical *contingency* of the subject who occupies this place."[50] The same
"spacing" between modes is not just relevant to the "Master's imposture";
it equally applies to any situation in which the "radical *contingency*" of an
appearance is at work.

In *Tarrying with the Negative: Kant, Hegel, and the Critique of Ideology*, Žižek
brings this notion of "radical *contingency*" specifically into relationship with
Parsifal, the ignorant yet compassionate figure in Wagner's opera. The wider
context for the radical contingency of Parsifal is Wagner's Christ, the one
who does not need "to die." This "savior" is the paradigmatic instance of irreducibility—a surplus quality that transgresses the limitations of both the
bodily and the heavenly—the internal and the external. This Wagnerian
theological possibility, while, as Žižek notes, hauntingly pagan, offers a "parallax" moment in which a concept of Christ refuses a "substantial support"
and instead appears as a point of irreducibility, an instance of extimacy. In

this sense the Wagnerian account, as we see in *Parsifal*, leaves Christianity with an uncanny surplus, with the blood of Jesus, contained in the Grail, existing in an allegorical space between the bodily and the heavenly.

The point here, however, is not to enumerate various theories of Christ's nature—human, divine, other. Instead the present issue to consider relates to the problem of gaps, modes of spacing in which extimacy plays a critical role in addressing the irreducible. The figure of Parsifal, in this context, functions as a result of extimacy. Žižek writes that "*Parsifal is not feasible as a unique, psychologically 'coherent' personality:* he is split into himself and 'what is in him more than himself,' his sublime shadowy double."[51] In Wagner's opera one finds a Christ that need "not die" and an "ignorant, compassionate" hero in the character of Parsifal who is split against himself. In *Tarrying with the Negative* Žižek compares this surplus/extimacy to Hitchcock's "Norman–Mrs. Bates" transmutation.[52] While this comparison draws upon an analysis of gender in opera, it also opens onto a much more fundamental issue of "shadowy" doubleness that informs both *Parsifal* and *Psycho.* The primary problem that is brought forward in these instances can be described as one involving the traversing of "domains of shadows," which, as we have seen, is initiated by the phantasms surrounding an ultimate, empty signifier.

Continuing with Žižek's insights and the idea of gaps *between* "modes of shadows," or, in a Proustian sense, shadows between windows, a useful example of extimacy appears in a far less lofty example than the one cited by Žižek—Jared Hess's (*Napoleon Dynamite*) marginally successful comedy *Nacho Libre,* starring Jack Black. Far from the complex Proustian or Wagnerian characters that already have been discussed, Brother Ignacio, "Nacho," a seemingly flat antihero, will provide some useful material to the discussion. He is, on at least one level, comparable to earlier characters in his position as "pure fool." As we shall see, the film moves across various modes of possibilities, deferring the link between appearance and essence or meaning and interpretation. It is not until the end of the film that one sees the possibility of traversing modes as an instance of a "Real Thing," no matter how ridiculous.

Nacho, the morbidly overweight orphaned son of a Lutheran missionary and a Catholic deacon who, in failing to convert each other to their

antithetical theologies, decided to "get married instead," dreams about being a powerful and celebrated *luchador* (wrestler). His fantasy life, which
continues into adulthood, begins with a stubborn boyhood insistence on
dressing the part of a famous wrestling figure; his play-acting escapades
first land him in constant trouble with his Catholic caretakers, who find the
violence of wrestling immoral but the violence of poverty holy and, comically, acceptable.

One comes to see that this childhood obsession with light blue tights,
a red cape, and a mask has less to do with Lucho Libre—extravagant professional wrestling with flamboyant characters—and more to do with the
possibility of hope—a hope of transgressing the limits of his life. So far, as
any viewer of the film would certainly notice, *Nacho Libre* seems to be just
another silly film about overcoming adversity. While this may be finally
true, the film also offers other possibilities. The juxtapositions throughout
the film of wealth and poverty, worth and worthlessness, freedom and servitude, even as an expression of religious faith, are revealing; while the film
comically flashes back to Nacho's boyhood attempts to transcend his desperate circumstances in the Oaxaca orphanage, the trauma of his parents'
death undercuts the film's cheap laughs and the clichéd and hypocritical
admonitions against violence delivered by his caretakers. The grandiose
exploits of professional Lucho Libre, situated against the drab surroundings of the orphanage life, become, within the film's narrative, an auxiliary
space where fantasies of control, wealth, and triumph are vicariously lived
out by the younger and older Nacho; this dependence on fantasy, which
begins in childhood for basic psychological survival, continues into adulthood, when Nacho's hopeless situation and "grotesque" physique, constantly presented from the most unflattering camera angles, make him the most
unlikely candidate for the title of champion wrestler.

One of the film's opening scenes takes place in a graveyard, with the ro-
tund young Nacho playfully living out the heroics of a *luchador*. His imaginative life, however, is abruptly cut short when monks rip him away from
his fantasy, hose him down, and, finally peel away his vibrant blue and red
mask, replacing it with a simple brown robe. "Conscripted" into service first
as a "boy" cook and, later and only secondarily, as a monk at the orphanage,
Nacho is limited to the dark and dreary confines of the kitchen. After his

sudden induction into the culinary underworld of the monastery, the film leaps forward to Nacho's adulthood, which is oddly nothing more than a sad continuation of his traumatic childhood.

Nacho's Sisyphean existence seemingly comes to a crossroads with the arrival of a new teacher, Sister Encarnación (Ana de La Reguera). The stunningly beautiful nun, whose appearance is announced by the singing of a chorus, is the "miracle" causing Nacho to examine his life. The daily indignities he has quietly suffered at the hands of his "fellow" monks are made insufferable by the presence of Sister Encarnación. The humiliating and perhaps routine slap across the face he receives from a fellow monk while introducing himself to Sister Encarnación comes simply as the most recent reminder of his lowly status. Finding himself at the end of a long line of abuse, Nacho experiences overwhelming feelings of worthlessness, feelings that prompt a reinvestment in his childhood dream of being a *luchador*.

Little to nothing in Nacho's life is remotely rewarding. His work as a "cook" is limited to slop and nachos, which bring complaints from orphans and brothers alike. Can't we have a salad? one boy asks in desperation. Demeaned by his fellows and feeling defeated, hopeless, and disenchanted with monastic life, Nacho seeks out a "new duty," along with "chips," and ventures into the small village square, where he sees posters advertising Lucho Libre matches. While literally stopped at a crossroads, he sees "Ramses," the premier gold-masked *luchador*, who symbolizes everything Nacho desires—wealth, power, and respect. Predictably, the film's trailer leaves the impression that Nacho simply turns to wrestling in order to save the orphanage, which is consistent with the schmaltzy true story behind the film but not entirely the case as the plot develops. Brother Ignacio's unlikely transformation into "Nacho Libre," champion wrestler, is an exercise in material and spiritual excess—a Wagnerian dialectical reversal of the destitute condition of the life he experiences as a "man of the cloth."

Nacho, driven by feelings of worthlessness and a desire for "respect," realizes his dream midway into the film by becoming an amateur *luchador*. His secret career, however, turns out to be less than satisfying or successful, although as a wrestler he is able to provide some material relief to the orphans. When he discovers that he and his constantly snacking skeletal sidekick and wrestling partner, "Esqueleto," will receive a cut of the purse even if they lose, Nacho becomes disgusted and states that he wants to get paid for "winning," suggesting some wish for a restoration of order and honesty in his life. If the film were to remain at this level, these "themes," as narrative ends, would conveniently affirm the limits of reading; that is to say, reading the film as a fulfillment of these themes would count as restorative insofar as the interpretive ends appear to be predictably contained in the plane of ambiguity. While his "losings" pay for good food at the orphanage (produce for extravagant salads), Nacho yearns for something else, something that is actually in excess of his desire, which makes possible a reading beyond the limits of the narrative or, in this instance, beyond ambiguity. The film, then, offers two possibilities, in which the two members of the wrestling tag team, Nacho Libre and Esqueleto—polar opposites, *luchadors* who get paid for losing, the monk and the atheist, the "fat man" and the "skeleton"—both strive to reconcile desire with the possibilities of their existence, or to "re-mark" their desire in relation to some indeterminate excess. In order to achieve this type of re-marking, the film must be deconstructed to resist being reduced to clichés, which are ever present at the margins of the story. Excess, in this sense, represents a break with the narrative limits established by the "themes" of honesty and order.

As ridiculous as the film is in its portrayal of the "fool"/antihero, Nacho, it is at the same time not without a degree of complexity as various reversals unfold throughout the simplistic plot. Nacho's emotional speech upon having his secret discovered by his fellow monks takes the shape of a cliché, but with an ironic twist. His prayers for guidance, his exile in the wilderness (merely yards from civilization), and his misguided attempts to acquire the strength of an eagle by consuming a raw egg play with the notion of exteriority, excess, and redemption. Nacho, as one could easily predict, commits himself to discovering the "more" that is in him. The narrative unfolds in predictable phases: Nacho first wrestles for himself; then for his "love interest," Sister Encarnación; and then finally, as we will see, for some abstract notion of possibility.

After his exile from the monastery/orphanage, Nacho writes to Sister Encarnación, telling her of his upcoming match against the great Ramses for a prize of ten thousand dollars. Even though she probably "hates his guts," he writes, she is invited to the match and also, in an awkwardly comic way, to break her vow of celibacy with him, get married, and have many children. The letter ends with a cynical "whatever," as if any outcome is predictable, acceptable, and, ultimately disappointing, which is consistent with the pattern of Nacho's life and, ironically, with restorative reading practices. At this juncture in the film, the metaphysical correspondences between appearances and essences remain intact.

During the final match against the physically superior Ramses, Nacho Libre is embarrassingly tossed around the ring like a rag doll. To add insult to injury, Ramses's golden boot, the one that Nacho so coveted, finds its place firmly on Nacho's neck, leaving him squirming like a bug and unable to lift himself from the mat. As the referee begins the final count and all hope seems lost, Sister Encarnación miraculously appears on the stairway. This opens the possibility that the end will entail a "good" losing, a breaking of holy vows, romance, marriage, and children: *Rocky*. Thus, with a sad end apparently looming for Nacho, the viewer is suddenly led by Sister Encarnación's hopeful facial expression to consider another resolution: that it may be possible, however improbable, for him to win. Nacho Libre surely can muster the strength to force Ramses's foot from his neck and triumph over the evil masked hulking figure: *Rocky II*. These particular ends to the film would be "thematically" credible and entirely consistent with all the tropes of romantic comedy—love, literally in this instance, conquers all. Losing and winning both appear as perfectly reasonable resolutions to the ambiguity of content—even if one is less likely than the other.

Nacho Libre, however, seems to exceed the limits of ambiguity in this instance. A moment of excess at the finale "short-circuits" the metaphysical necessities of the narrative structure, a structure that comes to a unity through reconciliation and restoration. What is at first unknown to the viewer is that behind Sister Encarnación are the children from the orphanage, clothed in homemade versions of Nacho Libre's light blue and red costume. The orphans' appearance, one would surmise, will provide Nacho with the strength to overcome Ramses; this victory will "surely" come from God (as Nacho boldly predicts earlier in the film), his love of the children, and the desire to end their poverty—agape conquers all. But it doesn't work this way either. Surprisingly, neither form of "love" delivers Nacho from his impending defeat. Nevertheless, Nacho Libre does manage, against the odds, to lift Ramses's shiny gold boot from his neck, but not exactly because of Sister Encarnación or the children. In a series of "false" or interrupted

The Commedia [handwritten annotation]

endings, the film shifts among its restorative possibilities and its excessive possibilities.

So, for no predictable reason, Nacho Libre sees and "re-marks" the children's homemade light blue and red costumes, costumes that are identical to the one he made as a child. At this "screen memory" Nacho Libre is filled with "uninspired," transformative "eagle" strength and finds his way to victory. It is not love of the orphans, of God, or of Sister Encarnación that allows him to emerge as the champion. It is not a super-strength provided by "magic" either: it is the "miracle" of his weakness, one could argue, that gives him strength. All of these prior metaphysical correlations would be well within the system of restoration that the film, as I have argued, refutes. In the end the fulfilling object is not any "real object," but the possibility that was lost in childhood, a possibility of radically obliterating a "signifying network" that limited the condition of his life: he discovers that he doesn't really want what he earlier desired. With the vision of the costumed children as an invitation to radically depart from any cynical "whatever" that accepts the probability of available outcomes, Nacho Libre defeats Ramses, finally "flying" like an eagle over the ropes to pin him to the floor. This victory appears as a "miracle," a gap between modes of shadows, a "short-circuit" of the metaphysics of possibilities.

"beatific vision" [handwritten annotation]

Finding strength in eros or agape, two ways to reconcile ambiguity, contrary to the standard tropes of comedy, merely leads to disappointment and atheism. Let us, then, from the perspective of short-circuiting the mythical, review the plot to see the Žižekian "re-marking" of events. When Nacho asks for a divine sign, his robe catches fire, exposing his blue tights to the community of the prayerful. Revealed as a *luchador,* he tells his fellow monks that God will give him the strength to prevail against an onslaught of wrestlers and that he will win entry to the big match with Ramses. Nacho, with his secret revealed, is cast out. He nevertheless continues with his plan and, as a contestant, struggles to remain in the qualifying match until the end, when he is finally defeated with a "pile driver" and sent away in despair—abandoned by God and his community. Banished from the monastery, Nacho spends time—a day, more or less—in the "wilderness" and experiences the ravages of deprivation, eating cactus. This "exile" is meant to transform him, which it doesn't: the "backyard" relocation comically depicts the hero's estrangement from "home," his transformation, and his impending return, only Nacho's return has nothing to do with any metaphysical insight—the winner of the "mega-match" has a freak accident, and his championship bid defaults to Nacho.

The ever-present force of the ridiculous seems to guide the course of events. Nacho, abandoned by God and facing the prospect of being destroyed by Ramses at the start of the fight, turns to Esqueleto, the atheist believer in science, who recommends that they pray. Ironically, hopelessness leads Nacho to atheism, and fear leads Esqueleto to God. The idea put forward in this reversal is that simple transposition is ridiculous. Rather than any strict dialectical unfolding of "history," Nacho becomes by the final event a "vanishing mediator," driven by plain dumb luck and not some predetermined synthesis of antagonisms. The "final" end of the film, with Brother Ignacio dressed in a light blue robe and white boots, shows that the culmination of events was not strictly organized by an absolute dialectic of the narrative or any controlling logic. Nacho needed to obliterate all possible predictable outcomes deriving from the structure of his circumstances; in other words, the film finds excess in a "miracle," a ridiculous miracle, not a divine miracle from above.

Nacho Libre, then, ends with an emphasis on irreducible excess or, as Žižek would define it, a re-marking of a "gap." The final scene with Brother Ignacio "decked out" in his light blue robe, crucifix, and white boots, standing atop Aztec ruins with Sister Encarnación and the orphans, completes, albeit ironically, the "desire" he reveals in the letter—to be with Sister Encarnación and "many children." His return to monastic life is not a restoration of faith: God still abandoned him in his time of need, and it is this identification with "abandonment," perhaps in the person of Jesus, that allows him to devote himself to the orphans—those closest to God in that they are farthest from Him (we will see this developed in Žižek's atheistic Christianity). It is important to keep in mind, however, that his transformation is not the result of "fighting for God," but of fighting for the possibility of "obliteration." The orphans, then, are not just "real objects"; they are also "vanishing mediators" insofar as they, in their profound destitution, contain a real possibility for change.[53] Only through a radical obliteration of a signifying system can Brother Ignacio affirm his life in the world, a world liberated from determination and founded, at least for Nacho Libre, upon ridiculous dumb luck or, from a more philosophical perspective, the intimacy of the "re-mark."

The significance of the *Nacho Libre* example can be further detailed in relation to Žižek's early formulation of the Hegelian dialectic in *The Sublime Object of Ideology,* especially as it redefines the "Concept." In this instance Žižek presents an untotalizeable totality as a permanent or persistent fundamental condition at the heart of the dialectic. This means that the reconciliation of any contradiction, ambiguity, or alienation, as in the case of Nacho, simply disguises a much more powerful separation of any discourse from an origin that "resists symbolization, totalization, [and] symbolic integration."[54] The "impossible kernel," then, leaves the reader in the realm of excess—an excess that does not exist as some metaphysical reality waiting to be unveiled but as a fundamental rift that challenges the movement between figure and ground. Like the final scene in *The Full Monty,* which Žižek discusses in *The Ticklish Subject,* the final act in *Nacho Libre* is the act of a "loser," with "catastrophic loss" addressed in two modes: "insisting on the empty form as fidelity to lost content ('When there is no hope, only principles remain'); heroically renouncing the last vestiges of false narcissistic dignity and accomplishing the act for which one is grotesquely inadequate."[55] In each instance identity is marked or re-marked as a failure of the subject's ability to form a "positive self-acquaintance," a permanent instantiation of a "void" or "gap" that, ironically, is identity.

The amusing detour through *Nacho Libre* prepares the way forward to a more theoretical discussion of the relationship between ground and figure, a relationship posed as a problem of "suturing" the "original cleft" within the dialectic—that is, the assignment of an appearance to an essence or a symptom to an origin. The ending of the film shows an excess that cannot be easily restored to the condition of the narrative, and it is the excess of narrative, in general, that presents a complicated possibility for any interpretation, insofar as meaning, or at least interpretive response, does not fully generate from either an origin or an essence. The example of *Nacho Libre,* as limited it is, demonstrates the ways in which narrative resolution need not follow from a thematic or logical necessity. Excess can be a ridiculous miracle. In *For They Know Not What They Do: Enjoyment as a Political Factor,* Žižek describes this in Derridean terms as a "re-marking," a realignment of "ground" and "figure" that makes a new understanding possible:

Why must every mark (every signifying trace) be re-marked? Derrida's point of departure is the differential character of the texture of marks. A mark is nothing but a trace, a sheaf of features that differentiate it from other marks, in which this differentiality must be brought to its self-reference—in which every series of marks as semic (bearers of meaning) "must contain *an additional* tropological movement by which the semic *mark* refers to what demarcates the marks, to the blanks between the marks that relate the different marks to each other." In short, in any series of marks there is always at least one which functions as "empty," "semic"—that is to say, which remarks the differential space of the inscription of marks. It is only through the gesture of re-marking that a mark becomes mark, since it is only the re-mark which opens and sustains the place of its inscription.[56]

In addition to the "re-marking" in *Nacho Libre,* numerous examples from film and art are directly offered by Žižek. In the realm of art history, for instance, "re-marking" appears in Escher's work as graphic paradoxes in which a "basic procedure . . . of dialectical interplay of figure and ground, of gradual transformation of ground into figure, of retroactive re-marking of ground as figure, and vice versa," form unusual instances of extimacy.[57] The point of Escher's art here is not that one figure becomes another, but that a transformation takes place that cannot be accounted for within the text; that is, the moment of transition of, let's say, geese to field or stairways to landings is "vanishing." The "re-marking" is a gap, a "parallax gap," that is in excess of a restorative signifying system—the "short-circuiting" of a determining metaphysics that would unite appearances and essences.[58] To continue with this concept in the field of art, the work of American painter Mark Tansey, not mentioned by Žižek but nonetheless illustrative, reveals a similar Escheresque problem of transition and the vanishing gap that, I believe, more fully engages with this concept of extimacy.

Tansey's signature painting *White on White,* for instance, depicts a scene split down an imperceptible center, with Inuits, sled dogs, and swirling snow on the left and Bedouins, camels, and swirling sand on the right. Rather than discuss the painting's sociological content, with its focus on the slim degree of separation between the world's people, it is important to see the painting as a theoretical exercise in difference and discrepancy. A restorative and excessive reading of the painting would identify the major "rift" or "gap" occurring between "snow" and "sand"; each figure, as in an Escher drawing, seems to emerge from the same chaotic swirl. In other words, the discernible figures achieve their ordered presentation from undifferentiated "ground." The "re-marking" here is twofold—"between" two "realities" and "within" reality itself, which, I think, approaches the concept of the Žižekian "parallax gap" more closely. Visually, this concept is more accessible, which makes Mark Tansey's comment regarding the concept of the "rift" or "gap" critical to the discussion: "[A] picture might be coded by distinguishing rifts (contradictions, discrepancies, implausibilities) from resonance (plausible elements, structural similarities, shared characteristics, verifications). In fact, the notion of rift and resonance is fundamental to visual reception and the picture-constructing process as well."[59] Not being able to visually determine where the "sand" begins and the "snow" ends, or the point of transition within figure and ground, brings the viewer's attention to an unidentifiable space within the painting. Sand becomes snow, or sand and snow become figures imperceptibly, and the lack of substantive continuity or "substantial support," following Escher, heightens the significance of the rift or gap "at the center" of the painting. These "implausibilties" in Tansey's work, which are not ambiguities, appear as objects "morphing" into other objects or, more commonly, as a temporal, nonrecuperable anomaly. For example, *Purity Test* (1982) depicts Native Americans in traditional dress and on horseback observing Smithson's Spiral Jetty (1970)—a historical, temporal impossibility.

"Distinguishing rifts"—not just isolating fissures or ambiguities but raising them to a level of prominence—becomes not only the work of art criticism but the work of theoretical thinking in literature, philosophy, and religion. The visual tension "between" represented "realities," and within that reality itself, invites a more concentrated analysis of the temporal as another (nonvisual) "rift" or "gap" within painting. This nonvisual aspect of the work "appears" within the work as an effaced void. Rodolphe Gasché, in *The Tain of the Mirror,* describes this effacement as a wider process of deconstructive inquiry:

> By re-marking itself, the mark effaces itself, producing in this manner the illusion of referent. It effaces itself, disappears in the appearing of what is not—a proxy of itself. In affecting itself by the re-mark, designating its own space of engenderment, the mark inscribes itself within itself, reflects itself within itself under the form of what it is not. The mark is heterogeneous to

the mark. In marking what de-marcates it, the margin of the mark is turned into a mark that is heterogeneous to the heterogeneous space of its inscription. Infinitely re-marking that space by another semic mark, the mark renders the margin invisible. Likewise, it can be said that all the marks of a series are in the position of semic substitution for the spaced-out semiopening that makes them possible.[60]

Gasché's analysis of the Derridean "re-mark" brings to light several key aspects of reading against predetermined, hegemonic narrative frameworks. The "illusion" or "phantasm" or shadow of a referent, which is a major concept in Tansey's art, "appears" within a process of repetition and distancing. Each re-marking "effaces" the mark, which not only makes Tansey's painting visually implausible but introduces a space or void within the work. Tansey's pictorial examination of this problem of "rift" further develops the importance of seeing "transition" or "re-marking" as a process involving either an exteriority or an excess from within—something that does not predictably determine meaning or proper point of view from a narrative or pictorial space. Just as "re-marking" redefines the relationship between ground and figure, "rifting," as described by Tansey, amplifies the resonances within a signifying network and, at the same time, calls out to an excess of that system, obliterating it and leaving in its ruins new possibilities.

1.4 Words, Health, and Commerce

> Within the action there must be nothing irrational.
> —Aristotle, *Poetics*

Prehistoric man, in the various stages of his development, is known to us through the inanimate monuments and implements which he has left behind, through the information about his art, his religion, and his attitude towards life which has come to us either directly or by way of tradition handed down in legends, myths, and fairy tales, and through the relics of his mode of thought which survives in our manners and customs. But apart from this, in a certain sense he is still our contemporary. . . . If that supposition is correct, a comparison between the psychology of primitive peoples, as it is taught by social anthropology, and the psychology of neurotics, as it has been revealed by psycho-analysis, will be bound to numerous points of agreement and will throw new light upon familiar facts in both sciences.

> —Sigmund Freud, *Totem and Taboo*

When someone, driven by a desire that is no doubt obscure, but that we can always try to interpret, says untimely things, or attempts to privilege the untimely, that person is not seeking an absolute untimeliness—which, in any case, he would not find, even if he sought it. There is not that which is in conformity with time on one hand, and that which is absolutely unreceivable in time on the other. Each and every time, epoch, context, culture, each and every national, historical or disciplinary moment, has a certain coherence, but also a certain heterogeneity—it is a system in which there are zones of greater and of lesser receivability. And whosoever seeks the untimely attempts to recognize a certain receivability in zones of lesser receivability or conformity. I analyze in a context something that I feel is going against the current, but there is another current, as yet secondary, virtual, inhibited—it waits, pregnant with possible receivability. It is a matter of looking for something that is not yet well received, but that waits to be received.
    —Jacques Derrida, "I Have a Taste for the Secret"

Re-marking, a term derived from Derrida, points to a process in which the supposed hegemonic "completion" of a text is interrupted by the repositioning of "figure" and "ground" in such a way as to produce new interpretive or creative opportunities. This turn toward excess, however, is contrary to the demands of restoration, and the "more," which comes through the creative impulse, unfortunately comes to be understood as that pathogen that must be avoided. The philosopher-theorist Gilles Deleuze, as a related figure in this wider discussion of "re-marking," challenges the idea that creativity bears the marks of pathology with the line that "we do not write with our neuroses."[61] If humankind's creative endeavors are not just the results of "neurosis," then creativity or writing from a nonpathological excess introduces yet another possibility for understanding the concept of "re-marking." The problem, however, with carrying the significance of this line forward is in fitting the idiosyncratic nature of Deleuze's thoughts on literary production into the more familiar discourses on the function of narrative rules represented by Aristotle, Freud, and Derrida. In other words, Deleuze seems to see the actual paradox of "re-marking" as beneficial, while the others, at least in the first two instances, view it as a problem to be overcome with the inevitable and desired imposition of an excessless totality. Excesses as "neuroses," for Deleuze, are not strictly construed as pathologies; they are "blockages" or "interruptions" within the process of life, which extends, following Nietzsche, to a notion of narrative, of literary texts, as a matter of health and invention. It is the latter notion that is most intriguing here for the simple reason that "reading" or "thinking" always re-marks or reinvents the text, and this reinvention, as we shall see, opens a space that is in excess of both the text and the subject. Within the widest circle of similarity, the various epigraphs above point to something outside of or alongside literature, specifically something to be either avoided or embraced. For Deleuze and, to some extent, Derrida, the excessive idea that "literature is delirium" provides a point of departure that defines literature as something more than mimetic effort, more than its source, and more than just being about something.[62] The Deleuzean, and perhaps also Derridean, turn takes us past the text-centered and subject-centered resolution to the problem of rift. In other words, Deleuze and Derrida change the conditions of the inquiry by pointing to the ultimately unresolvable space between "saying" and "understanding," which places the issue of excess in language at the center of consideration.

Literature or, more generally, narrative as invention disrupts the rule of representation and pushes the "literary," as Deleuze states, to a "possibility of life," which is not a return to mimesis.[63] Peter Hallward, in *Out of This World: Deleuze and the Philosophy of Creation,* observes that "the work of art, understood along these lines, can have nothing to do with the process of describing or redecorating a reality external to it."[64] Furthermore, Hallward writes, "art doesn't expose truths or realities that would pre-exist it: it *makes* truth and participates directly in the creation of reality."[65] The two epigraphs from Freud and Derrida, with their corresponding emphases on something "neurotic," "untimely," and "heterogeneous," challenge Aristotle's exclusionary command prohibiting the "irrational," which limits creativity to the knowable, predictable, and rule-bound world. In fact, one can phrase it more starkly by saying that the excessive or "irrational" is the mark of seemingly "ruleless" sources; that this is exactly what Freud is searching for in his study of totems and taboos; and furthermore that the "irrational," as that which lies beyond or alongside "coherence," is the subject of Derrida's inquiry from the beginning, albeit for a different purpose.

In all three epigraphical instances, as complex as they are in their individual contexts, there is a shared concern that can be phrased as a question: what is the excessive "void" in the text? Or, from the nonepigraphical example of Deleuze, with and from what excesses do we write? Was "prehistoric man" neurotic, as evidenced by the ways in which "his" myths and relics seemed to order the world by invoking another, magical world? What of the seekers of untimeliness, as they are described by Derrida? Is their philosophical concern for heterogeneity or the enduring supplemental trace contained within any order simply "irrational" on its face? The earlier question of the ordering effect, I'll concede, is not strictly limited to the works referenced above or to their respective traditions. Narratives follow rules, and these rules lead to the unquestioned assumptions we recognize as sources. The relationship between these intervening rules and sources, then, calls one to question the linguistic nature of all texts that come to us as philosophical, religious, or literary.

Heidegger's essay "Language" makes the point that we are always under the rule of "speaking." We speak when we are "awake" and when we "dream," he writes.[66] This leads Heidegger to note that "language speaks," which forces the philosopher, the theologian, and the literary critic to think of language "itself"—language as captured in language. Before Heidegger's meditation on speaking, to which we will return later, there is an earlier philosophical recognition of this idea of language captured in language. It occurs in the founding dialogues of Western philosophy, which are concerned with not only the effect of order brought about by speech but with the nature of speech itself.

The nature and division of human and sacred language are central, for example, to Plato's *Ion,* a dialogue that is organized around the question of poetic ontology and a desire to interrogate both the effects and the nature of rhapsodic speech. A discussion of *Ion* in this context allows for an inquiry into the metaphysics of "literary" discourse and the significance of poetic interpretation, which is critical to an understanding of the relationship between governing rules and sources of speech. Giorgio Agamben, for instance, in *The End of the Poem: Studies in Poetics,* views this fundamental relationship between the two in the context of medieval Christian theology, in which "glossolalia" is understood as the "thought of voice."[67] The act of speech and the meaning of speech are separated by a concept of purity in which the "thought of voice" resides in some source, a primarily supercreative source, apart from human knowing, a knowing not subject to the rules of speaking. In the Greek context this "source" lies alongside the rhapsode's speech, and it is this "tongue" that permits the necessary emergence of a purported higher reality into the space of human life. Speaking, then, is either a gift, the effect of a divine moving, or a human communication:

> The gift which you possess of speaking excellently about Homer is not an art, but, as I was just saying, an inspiration; there is a divinity moving you, like that contained in the stone which Euripides calls a magnet, but which is commonly known as the stone of Heraclea. This stone not only attracts iron rings, but also imparts to them a similar power of attracting other rings; and sometimes you may see a number of pieces of iron and rings suspended from one another so as to form quite a long chain: and all of them derive their power of suspension from the original stone. In like manner the Muse first of all inspires men herself; and from these inspired persons a chain of other persons is suspended, who take the inspiration. For all good poets, epic as well as lyric, compose their beautiful poems not by art, but because they are inspired and possessed. And as the Corybantian revellers when they dance are not in their right mind, so the lyric poets are not in their right mind when they are composing their beautiful strains: but when falling under the power of music and metre they are inspired and possessed; like Bacchic maidens who draw milk and honey from the rivers when they are under the influence of Dionysus but not when they are in their right mind. And the soul of the lyric poet does the same, as they themselves say; for they tell us that they bring songs from honeyed fountains, culling them out of the gardens and dells of the Muses; they, like the bees, winging their way from flower to flower. And this is true. For the poet is a light and winged and holy thing, and there is no invention in him until he has been inspired and is out of his senses, and the mind is no longer in him: when he has not attained to this state, he is powerless and is unable to utter his oracles.[68]

Poetry, rhapsodic poetry, in Plato's view is irrational, delirious, and the poet literally "out of or in excess of his senses." This suspension of the rational within the rhapsode's art is necessary for the greater, sacred order to push through into human discourse. The poet becomes a "light and winged and holy thing" in which no "act" occurs until or unless inspiration suspends, if not displaces, the rational.

Again, as Aristotle, Freud, and Derrida observe, the rules of poetry, myth, and philosophy historically rest on an acceptance of two distinct yet corresponding "vertically" aligned fields, the sacred and the profane, with the former the ultimate object of inquiry. Ion, in this instance, becomes a suspect figure—one who makes outlandish claims about not only his proficiency in recitation but also his interpretive powers. It is the relationship or the lack of relationship between the two that draws Socrates's attention. How is it that the rhapsodic art, which requires a poet to be "out of his senses," includes the very "in his senses" needed for elucidation and interpretation? In other words, what are the rules of commerce between these two seemingly exclusive activities? Where does the Muse reside? Where is the elucidating human mind when recitation occurs? In each case, whether that of speech or that of interpretation, it is required that each have its "other" alongside it. The stakes of commerce are higher for Ion and for other so-called religious rhapsodes, writers, and hermeneuts, in that the order they claim to render is a divine order, and the effect of that order must be seen in a human world. Here it is worth noting the significance of an undeclared commerce between the "god" and the "human" in the production of texts, literary, philosophical, or religious. The power to render this divine intent, I'll argue, prefigures Socrates's concerns and, in fact, founds a "literary" beginning to philosophical and, more precisely, religious discourse.[69]

To return to the epigraphs, we see a burden developing specifically within the study of "religion," "philosophy," and "literature," which is the broader study of delirious, pathological texts—texts that "shadow" texts and texts that claim to bridge rifts, incommensurable planes, rational/irrational or sacred/profane. The "literary" or poetic, in this particular arrangement, is situated between two worlds, sacred and profane, and with seemingly contradictory purposes, mimetic or creative. If one accepts that the sacred order determines the profane order and that literature is the bridge between the two, then religious or philosophical "literary" studies is a relatively simply act of matching Order to order, restoring unity to a "broken hegemony." Furthermore, if this were the case, literature, subject to the greater disciplines of philosophy and religion, would function mimetically, distributing sacred-effects to readers without in any way shaping or, more cynically, distorting their purported truths. This, for the most part, has been the long tradition of studying religion, philosophy, and literature, with literature as the "example" of theological truth or as the "instance" or "illustration" of an epistemological, ethical, aesthetic, or metaphysical proposition.

The problem with this arrangement, in which literature is subservient to

other disciplines and practices, is that it overlooks the instability or otherness of the literary, its incorrigible nature that, harkening back to Deleuze,
continually opens onto new possibilities—one of which is that literature
doesn't represent anything "real" or that it is delirious by nature. This line
of argument follows the deconstructive turn in philosophy and linguistics.
Much of this argument can be sustained by a general theoretical insight
that texts exist between or across two registers of meaning, the literal and
the metaphorical. Paul de Man's early deconstruction, for instance, exac-
erbates the division or "gap" one finds in language's grammatical and rhetorical dimensions. This is not to easily suggest that ambiguity always is
the risk of reading, but that meaning, a whole meaning, is deconstructed
by two incommensurable frames of sense. Following de Man, it is important to distinguish between ambiguity and nonmeaning, with the latter
the result of rhetorical reading.[70] While deconstruction is better described
as deconstructions, the primary concern cutting across the figures named
above is with the assumption that language and, subsequently, texts harbor
a necessary meaning. We will return to this issue of the incommensurable
against the ambiguous, but for the present it is necessary to review the role
of the irrational or delirium in what I describe as sacred speech. For the
purpose of later clarifying the deconstruction of sacred speech, it is useful
here to return to a brief history of oracles in order to better understand what
is at stake in emphasizing the "gap" between figure and ground or, in this
case, speech and meaning.

1.5 Oracles and Apostles of Mourning

> How can man at the present stage of world history ask at all seriously and rig-
> orously whether the god nears or withdraws, when he has above all neglected
> to think into the dimension in which alone that question can be asked?
> —Martin Heidegger, "Letter on Humanism"

Philosophy, like all other creative endeavors, it seems, begins "out of its
senses." Alexander Pope asserts in "An Essay on Man" that "All Discord,
Harmony not understood."[71] "Discord" to "harmony," understood or not,
requires a moment of inauguration that is marked by a hegemonic, founding act of speech. This act of "speaking harmony," as we shall see, relies

on the force and effectiveness of "sacred speech" to dissipate the remnants of chaos, senselessness, and heterogeneity that antagonize, as Derrida observes, the rule of "coherence." Historically, these order-makers and their oracles have provided a necessary bridge spanning an alleged absolute reality that exists just beyond humanity's collective reach and the sensible, seemingly accidental, and discordant world of human affairs. This phantasmic bridge, were it to exist, would cover the abyss between a supposed absolute reality and the everyday world in which we reside. It is in this world that hegemony seems unbreakable. Sacred speech, which declares that it is self-evidently true, gives chaos an order and in so doing allows for a bipartition of reality and its unification. It is assumed that this act of speech, as a story-event that brings harmony to discord in the life of an individual and society, provides the foundation for all subsequent orders.

The history of Western philosophy and religion, as Schürmann notes, could be presented as a hegemonic series of attempts to reconcile a metaphysical misalignment or preempt the possibility of textual otherness. Aristotle, in his *Poetics,* makes clear that in stories a private reality and a public reality must unite and make sense or, in other words, be guided by that which is "rational." In this instance the sacred, while on some occasions disrupting the homogeneity of a rational world, actually inaugurates it. Stories then are by Aristotle's definition reasonable and ordered artifacts, which mimic for readers a common or shared world of experience.[72] This demand on stories to perform the work of coherence is not limited to the ancient world. Paul Ricoeur, for instance, holds the "narrative" to be a route to the "other" and to a wider interpretive order. One comes to see oneself and the world, he argues, through the text-other: "For us, the world is the ensemble of references opened up by the texts. Thus we speak about the 'world' of Greece, not to designate any more what were the situations for those who lived them, but to designate the non-situational references which outlive the effacement of the first and which henceforth are offered as possible modes of being, as symbolic dimensions of our being-in-the-world. For me, this is the referent of all literature."[73] This turn from the individual subject of life experience toward the communal or historical significance of experience places the focus on narrative's work in fashioning a "shareable world" or a rational, hegemonic world, a concept demanding that narratives assume a harmonizing function. Harmony, in this sense, comes from a rational interpretative action, as one finds in Ion's "theses" on poetry, while the "original" poetic act derives from some other extrahuman source.

From classical drama, to hermeneutics, to postmodern literature, sacred speech or its substitute has served as an instrument of regimentation, providing not only the content of stories but their rational structure, which encompasses the social dynamic. The difficulty in moving from the individual to the communal, however, presents itself in reading this *structure* or positing it in the first place. Sacred speech, a seemingly steadfast authority for any and all action, upon which so many individuals and civilizations have relied, today, in a postmodern era, seems to translate into ever-increasing and repeating interpretive possibilities that are far from the ethereal, inspired certainties of ages past. For postmoderns all "bridges" fail to reach the proverbial other side, and Muses are always mute.

If a belief in the past's access to the absolutely real is not actually true, it is at least what we wish to believe to be "historically" true. The ancients, for many, seem to have inhabited a transparent ontological order, and myth, since that glorious time, has functioned as a vehicle for occasional return. This shareable order, inaugurated first by myth, can be found in all historico-literary periods—the modern as well the ancient, with T. S. Eliot's "shareable" demiurge made manifest in verse, "Dayadhvam." Stories reveal sacred speech's endorsement and creation of a harmonious order to which private and public lives must conform. The history of stories, we easily can see, is a history of coherence. At the same time this particular history of coherence is unfolding, there is another narrative possibility—dissymmetry. As we shall discuss, every story of "chaos to order" harbors the alternative possibility of transforming any particular divinely inspired, universal harmony into something else, something it may not have anticipated or may not endorse.

While Aristotle may have rejected an appeal to the gods in his *Poetics,* the history of stories tells us that "gods" are a necessity. Deus ex machina may be bad for drama, but the general place of the "deus" in narrative is more difficult to judge. It seems that all stories must first find sponsorship within the absolutely real. In Plato's dialogues, as we have discussed, the rational is thought to supplant irrational fantastical stories—myths in which common-sense-defying events actually supplement, if not make possible, a rational dialogue. This dependency of the "rational" on the "irrational" comes to mark the birth of philosophy, and this "birth" is possible only in relation to a discursive journey through a mythical reality brought forward by sacred speech, myths, and oracular decries. Sacred speech, often with fabulist content, is taken to be an invocation of an absolute, ontological reality that informs, if not forms, the world as it is. While the intricacies of this act of divination may have altered over time, the logic of action that has derived from divination has not. The idolatry of our times, I'll argue, is the persistent attempt to follow in the footsteps of the past and "decode" an ontological order, revealing the order not only of that which was and is but of that which will be.

The problem, however, is that the hegemonic or harmonizing "Divine Will," which I mentioned earlier, never completely maps onto language and human experience, individual or collective. Even in the ancient past, it must be remembered, long before the wide acceptance of the nonconcept of *deconstruction*, which characterizes much of the philosophical sensibility of our times, myths and other forms of founding speech were not without their deferments and ambiguities, although great figures often overlooked this sometimes fatal characteristic. This is best captured by the famous predicament of Croesus, who failed to pay close attention to the nonspecificity of the Delphic response to the question concerning the invasion of Persia: "You shall destroy a powerful empire." The "powerful empire" that fell, of course, was, regrettably, his empire. While promising to disclose the unequivocal truth, the oracle, we find, often merely initiates a circuitous journey toward an unattainable divine intent that invariably ends in tragedy—which may have been the destination all along. These stories of divination are found across nearly all narrative traditions. And the powerful have not been the only recipients of these troubling oracular messages; others, less prominent, also have struggled with the equivocations from a putative divine space. Collectively, through great figures in literature, philosophy, and religion, all addressees of founding speech, high and low, struggle to find an ultimate meaning in ambiguous signs and distant events. While my study in this instance addresses speech and its relationship to oracles, it is worth noting Jacques Lacan's early emphasis on "foundational speech" or "votive speech" as a means by which all that a subject is is constituted by utterances in relation to others.

Shrouded in mystery, ambiguity, deception, or fantasy, these utterances are communications pertaining to a future to come. Oracles, we see in mythology and literature, bring this future to the shore of the present, often with dire consequences. The question, therefore, is not, what is oracular, sacred speech saying? Rather, the critical question is, how are we hearing this speech, and how are we constituted by it? In being attentive to the act of reception, we therefore are not able to ask, what does it say? Rather we are stuck with, what does it mean? Or, what does it mean for us? The point to keep in mind is that sacred speech is not necessarily posed as propositional language, and the mistake comes in treating it as if it were. This tension between "saying" and "understanding" requires a return to Heidegger's notion of dwelling in language:

> Language speaks.
> Man speaks in that he responds to language. This responding is a hearing. It hears because it listens to the command of stillness.
> It is not a matter here of stating a new view of language. What is important is learning to live in the speaking of language.[74]

Living in the "speaking of language" entails being suspended over an abyss, a space in which "stillness" or the unsayable preempts the fullness of speech. This is visually demonstrated in the postmodern artist Mark Tansey's paintings *Secret of the Sphinx (Homage to Elihu Vedder)* (1984) and *Interview (Secret of the Sphinx)* (1980), in which a well-dressed man with a recording device crouches before the lips of the Sphinx—presumably to capture a timeless secret via a microphone. The inspiration for the pieces is Elihu Vedder's 1863 *Questioner of the Sphinx,* which depicts a robed man with his "naked ear" pressed against the stone lips of the monstrous figure.

As we know, asking and the precision of how one asks, listening and the precision of how one listens, do not necessary result in actually receiving an untainted answer. If Croesus, for instance, had had a digital recorder to capture the oracle's response, however imprecise, it would not have changed his fatal "mishearing." It is also important to bear in mind Derrida's words of caution: "Each and every time, epoch, context, culture, each and every national, historical or disciplinary moment, has a particular coherence, but also a certain heterogeneity."[75] What better than sacred oracular speech to provide us with an example of something in excess of a "certain coherence," or something that repeats its own absence or, in a Deleuzean sense, its possibilities of "life"? Vedder and, more specifically, Tansey invite us to consider the quandary of reception, especially as it involves foundational speech. The issue within a postmodern era, which is distinct from Vedder's perspective, is one of the impossibility of disclosure. It isn't the case, therefore, that one needs to listen more carefully or more precisely (technology) to the "Sphinx." It is, rather, that the "Sphinx," like Frost's statue of Minerva or whispering scythe, has nothing to say that we can understand, which does not mean that something may not be heard. In this sense foundational speech or sacred speech is not a complete transmission; it is already incompletely spoken—written as a future possibility.

Nevertheless, for all who have a taste for the secret, Derridean or some other, the dual act of asking and listening produces a relationship not only with the secret itself, as it is portrayed in the paintings by Tansey and Vedder, but with our own desire to reconcile ourselves to it. If there is a secret, is it assumed that we can receive it? If there isn't a secret, we are left questioning why we crave one. As Derrida suggests, there is an impatience with our "taste for the secret," and this causes a forcing of oneself into the future, perhaps prematurely. It is necessary, in this instance of impatience, to see secrets and futures as joined philosophical problems.

John D. Caputo, in *The Prayers and Tears of Jacques Derrida*, writes that the "secret is the condition of the 'come!', the quasi-transcendental condition of its possibility and impossibility."[76] In one instance there is a "predictable future" (after this sentence I will go downstairs, have a glass of iced tea, and check to make sure the dog did not escape from the backyard). Within this "one instance" of the "predictable future," there is something entirely in excess of it—that is to say, a condition of the future that is not subject to projective thought—something that is "structurally unknowable."[77] Caputo, following Derrida, describes this "passion of non-knowing" as a function of an "absolute secret" that keeps the future "open, letting *l'avenir* be truly *à venir*."[78] The secret, in effect, is that the future is completely open, with no impossibilities, which may or may not be good news. Two theological implications are that God, for instance, is a future possibility and a future impossibility. We must wait and see, which seems to be the import of Derrida's thought for Caputo: "Jacques Derrida's secret, if there is one, lies on the textual surface, inconspicuous by its superficiality, without martyr to bear witness, without a revelation to unveil it, without a second coming or even a first. It is always to come."[79] In the wider context of religion, with an emphasis on secrets and futures, each step forward in time, under the aegis of sacred speech, requires some haphazard determination of the degrees of "predictability," "coherence," and "heterogeneity" contained within narrative. The future, then, is twofold, predictable and structurally unknowable, and by ignoring the accompanying "heterogeneity" in narrative "coherence," the listener or receiver of the "secret" places undeserved confidence in the completeness of sacred speech itself, inviting premature closures when openings or gaps abound.

In these impulsive instances those with a "taste for the secret," as Derrida and Caputo describe it, accept oracles as key to this would-be reconciliation. In this sense "coherent" speech, finally, would have the authority to command great figures to act in their present as if they knew the future, without qualification, which certainly is the theme, if not the route, of tragedy. In these instances it is not simply that the listener fails the test of accuracy. It is, rather, that the listener fails in his or her capacity to hear—that is, to attend to the heterogeneity or revolutionary possibilities within or alongside coherence and in the future that is structurally unknowable.

1.6 Language, Myth, and Interpretation

There is no religion unless God is tipped into language, or else he is frozen into an idol.

—Gabriel Vahanian, "God and the Utopianism of Language"

In Ernst Cassirer's *Language and Myth,* the opening chapter, "The Place of Language and Myth in the Pattern of Human Culture," begins with a vivid synopsis of Plato's *Phaedrus* in which Plato and Phaedrus "in the shade of a tall plane tree, at the brink of a cool spring . . . lie down; the summer breeze is mild and sweet and full of cicada's song."[80] This is, as Cassirer implies, philosophy with romantic scenes and literary embellishment. The tale of Orithyia being carried off by Boreas, the focus of the discussion, merges with Phaedrus being carried off by Socrates and thus prepares the way for a complicated assessment of myth and the closure of the irrational. Socrates's condemnation of the mythic elements in their conversation further points to a demand for coherence or rationality within discourse. Can one believe

such a story as Orithyia and Boreas or any story? While the myth has some
explanatory power, as Socrates concedes, it does not, in a manner of speaking, "cohere," which is to say the mythic elements invoke another sense-
making register into their dialogue. Myths traditionally demand that one
"believe" in them, not understand them. Socrates cannot believe, yet as
Cassirer notes, "he is not at a loss of its significance," which can mean its
power to persuade.[81]

One could argue that this "persuasion" follows the same path as his dialogue, but with one exception—it irrationally coheres. This "irrational coherence," as oxymoronic as it sounds, is a departure from knowledge and
invites the listener, in this case Phaedrus, to drift into a fabulist world.
Socrates's sharp rebuke to this wandering away from the realm of knowledge, however, subtly reinscribes an act of irrational coherence. Just as
Socrates excuses himself from such "pretty enough" interpretations, he invokes the inescapable presence of myth when he alludes to his own predicament: "But I have no leisure at all for such pastimes, and the reason, my dear
friend, is that as yet I cannot, as the Delphic precept has it, know myself."[82]
This isn't, as one could argue, a "reason" for not attending to myths in general; it is, in fact, a preemption of one myth by another. In other words,
Socrates is not really dismissing myths as much as he is attending to his
own "mythic problem." While the story of Orithyia and Boreas may be un-
believable, the Delphic message about "knowing himself" somehow is not,
and for Socrates his dismissal of myth as "artificial" and "tedious" belies
his own tedious preoccupation with "myth" as it comes from the oracle: "So
it seems absurd to me that, as long as I am in ignorance of myself, I should
concern myself about extraneous matters. Therefore I let all such things be
as they may, and think not of them, but of myself—whether I be, indeed, a
creature more complex and monstrous than Typhon, or whether perchance
I be a gentler and simpler animal, whose nature contains a divine and noble
essence."[83] The task in front of Socrates in the *Phaedrus* can be described
as future oriented (filled with im/possibilities) and within the space of religious thinking.

The interpretative obstacles or subjective void—whether the "I" is divine
or monstrous—that Socrates will encounter leave the reader reluctantly
concurring with one his predecessors, Heraclitus, who made the ineluctable observation that "the Lord whose oracle is at Delphi neither speaks

nor remains silent, but gives signs."[84] Ultimately, as we learn in the *Apology*, this appeal to interpretative undecideability becomes Socrates's final defense: what is death but an interval between an event and a response we cannot fill? In ancient times these moments of neither silence nor speech led mythical figures to step toward their respective futures or cosmic destinies. Neither silence nor speech also directed these classical figures by suggesting to them that they could escape the "structurally unknowable," as Derrida describes it, which was an error in understanding the conspiring elements of fate and interpretation as they tend toward sudden reversal.[85]

On these literary and philosophical occasions, one must be careful to distinguish between improper hearing and inattentive listening in which accuracy is not in play. The oracle's speech, as we find across Greek myth and drama, for instance, appears to us today as "unreceivable" as a complete, clear message; oracles, from a postmodern vantage point, simply conveyed news of an undisclosed promise, but this merely worked in the past to draw the hopeful toward, as Derrida has described it, more meaningful "zones of lesser receivabilities," leaving the listener, as we have seen, perpetually suspended between a desire for a moment of plenitude and a mourning for its deferred, if not cancelled, arrival. Cupping one's ear against the Sphinx's lips, for instance, does not remedy the problem of heterogeneity in coherence that Derrida describes. In other words, the postmodern taste for the secret is never satisfied because, in an odd, perhaps cynical way, postmoderns really don't expect it to be, or perhaps, more positively, postmoderns are more accepting of "heterogeneity" in "coherence."

The issue we have with oracles of the past is not that they simply misspoke or withheld a truth, as traditional scholarship would have it. Rather, the central problem with sacred speech as oracular utterance is the nature of speech itself; or, speech as it appears as a fulfillment of a promise of meaning—speech that claims to "speak" a secret that should close and not open the future for us. Postmodern mourners of oracular speech, all those who embrace heterogeneity in coherence, forfeit this "secret" to an understanding of language's aporetic nature. These postmodern mourners, if we are to establish a contrast with ancient mourners, are not in compliance with a definition of language that would allow for a bringing of the good news; they are instead apostles of mourning, indebted to language construed much differently and that leads us then not to a fulfillment or loss of a hegemonic "Divine Will" but into a space of separation and mourning that is neither "now" nor in the "future," but somewhere else.

This somewhere else is not of course spatial; it is a textual space—one, as we shall see, of deferment and difference. This emphasis on the nature of language is merely one way to distinguish the ancient listener from the postmodern listener. We, as postmoderns, share an interpretive hesitation with our ancient and modern counterparts, but unlike them we entertain the likely possibility that the speech never meant anything "really" or anything in the first place.

For the postmodern writer this leads to interesting philosophical, theological, and literary possibilities. If literature, as an example of contemporary oracular speech, does not make manifest eternal verities, then what if anything does it disclose? This will be a question for a later section, but for now we can posit it as a series of implicating questions: What would it mean, for instance, to write a literary text that mourns the "secret"? More specifically, what does it mean when the subject of the narrative actually knows in advance, not discovering, that such a "secret" doesn't or never did or never will exist? Or one could ask, what are the implications of a narrative without a narrative voice—one diluted, as in the case of the experimental writer Alain Robbe-Grillet's *Repetition,* with varying perspectives and multiple, indeterminate points of view that keep the present and the future, as it were, from happening? Before the postmodern issue of mourning can be addressed more fully, however, one must investigate the act of secret-sharing that postmodernism rejects. For this we again turn to the problem of sound and speech.

Drawing the distinction, then, between a listener who accepts the possibility of sound bearing meaning, albeit encrypted, and one for whom there is only sound with no meaning, encrypted or otherwise, leads to a significant linguistic problem that can be described as a tension between intimacy, as restoration, and mourning, as excess. Meaning in sound, in this first instance, would restore voice to speech; without this restoration of meaning, however, voice, along with speech, is just sound. Mladen Dolar, in *A Voice and Nothing More,* describes the fundamental assumptions guiding an understanding of the voice/noise opposition: "What singles out the voice against the vast ocean of sounds and noises, what defines the voice as special among the infinite array of acoustic phenomena, is its inner relationship with meaning. The voice is something which points toward meaning, it is as if there is an arrow in it which raises the expectation of meaning, the voice is an opening toward meaning."[86]

The difficulty in assuming that the natural trajectory of voice is in the direction of meaning becomes apparent as one attempts to locate the point of difference between the "infinite array of acoustic phenomena" and the particular fullness of speech. Dolar, of course, is very much aware of this and offers the following complication: "It [voice] is, rather, something like a vanishing mediator—it makes the utterance possible, but it disappears in it, it goes up in smoke in the meaning being produced."[87] The voice as "vanishing mediator" allows Dolar to define voice as that which "does not contribute to making sense. . . . It is the material element recalcitrant to meaning."[88] A further complication, therefore, occurs when this "vanishing mediator," the voice, is presumed to be more fundamental, more original than the sound that produces it.

Although not discussed by Dolar, Robert Frost's 1916 poem "Mowing" can be read as a mediation of this tension between "voice" and "sound," with a final emphasis on the existential problem created when one collapses the two:

> There was never a sound beside the wood but one,
> And that was my long scythe whispering to the ground.
> What was it it whispered? I knew not well myself;
> Perhaps it was something about the heat of the sun,
> Something, perhaps, about the lack of sound—
> And that was why it whispered and did not speak.
> It was no dream of the gift of idle hours,
> Or easy gold at the hand of fay or elf:
> Anything more than the truth would have seemed too weak
> To the earnest love that laid the swale in rows,
> Not without feeble-pointed spikes of flowers
> (Pale orchises), and scared a bright green snake.
> The fact is the sweetest dream that labor knows.
> My long scythe whispered and left the hay to make.[89]

The first line of the poem isolates one sound from the "infinite array of acoustic phenomena," the sound of the scythe along the ground. This particular sound is described as a "whisper"—something more than noise and less than speech or, perhaps, something oracular. Representing that which stands for both more and less, "whisper," in its various grammatical forms, appears four times in the poem. It is situated as a form of "protospeech," something in-between noise and speech, as I've already indicated. Each use of "whisper" is also placed in tension not just with sound but with the lack of sound, or speaking: "And that was why it whispered and did not speak." The "long scythe whispered" because, one could argue, it either had nothing to speak or because what it had to "say" was in excess of language. The latter, metaphysical position assumes that voice "precedes" speech since meaning is something that is "captured" by sound as opposed to being actually produced by sound. The line "Anything more than the truth would have seemed too weak" appears as an odd reversal in this instance, haunted by the presence of a more sensible line, "Anything less than the truth would seem too weak." How is it, then, that in Frost's poem "more than the truth" is too weak? The "more," at this point in the poem, is the "more" of hegemonic projection or speculation, which seems to mean "more" as an excess of simply sound. What could the scythe whisper, after all, that was more than a comment about the heat of the day? The "more" in "more than the truth," the truth of physical sensation, pertains to the generic practice of attributing meaning to sound or, considering the discussion of oracular speech, making sound into voice, the voice of language. Frost's poem, as a presentation of the tension between sound and voice, closes with a reminder that neither voice nor meaning precedes sound: "My long scythe whispered and left the hay to make." The whispering scythe never achieves voice; it can only order the world by making hay, not by making meaning, which would be making sound into voice.

In the long history of the sound/voice opposition, one easily could invoke Paul de Man's famous explanation of Rousseau's "Marion," which, following the argument, was just a sound that he (Rousseau) made and not a name that he spoke. More recently, however, Slavoj Žižek has discussed this as a problem of language's false ontology, a confusing of the "in-itself" and the "for-itself" (form/content) dynamic of speech that, I believe, provides a fuller set of implications for this study:

> At the level of speech itself, a gap forever separates what one is tempted to
> call proto-speech or "speech-in-itself" from "speech-for-itself," explicit sym-

bolic registration. For example, today's sex psychologists tell us that even before a couple explicitly state their intention to go to bed together, everything is already decided at the level of innuendos, body language, exchange of glances. . . . The trap to be avoided here is the precipitate *ontologization* of this "speech-in-itself," as if speech in fact pre-exists itself as a kind of fully-constituted "speech before speech"—as if this "speech *avant la lettre*" actually exists as another, more fundamental, fully constituted language, reducing normal, "explicit" language to its secondary surface reflex, so that things are already truly decided before they are explicitly spoken about. What one should always bear in mind against this delusion is that this other proto-speech remains virtual: it becomes actual only when its scope is sealed, posited as such, in explicit Word. The best proof of this is the fact that this proto-language is irreducibly ambiguous and undecidable: it is "pregnant with meaning," but with a kind of unspecified free-floating meaning waiting for the actual symbolization to confer on it a definitive spin.[90]

Dolar, Frost and, more directly, Žižek warn us of the dangers in assuming that speech "preexists" itself. This so-called trap, however, has perils beyond just the temporal ordering or causal relationship of sound and speech. If speech does not preexist itself, as the three argue, then meaning does not preexist voice. The greater existential issue perhaps, the one posed by Frost, takes shape around the subject's access to truth and value. In the absence of "free-floating meaning waiting for the actual symbolization to confer on it a definitive spin," as Žižek describes it, the subject is loose in the world, detached from the Real. To return to Frost, those believing in a "fay" or "elf" and the easy "gold" of mythology do not have anxiety over the status of meaning—it is in the "gift of idle hours." Those who hear only the scythe's "whisper," however, are thrust into an anxious world of mourning, a world in which there is no ontological ocean of meaning crashing upon the shore of voice.

This Frostian insight, one could argue, touches upon Derrida's "Copernican" analysis of speech and writing in the history of Western philosophy. Readdressing, then, the distinction between "speech-in-itself" and "speech-for-itself," as Žižek notes, leads to a clarification of a central problem in language; that is, voice or speech does not preexist sound or noise. Further, confusing this relationship allows voice a metaphysical status that preempts any critical appraisal, especially of the kind Derrida was able to perform in his classic study *Speech and Phenomena.* The implications of this are quite significant not only as a matter of linguistics but also as a matter of meaning in general.

Dislocating the voice-origin or any origin from its supposed "actual symbolization" creates enormous potential, a potential actualized by the deconstruction of the 1980s, for thinking or rethinking some of the fundamental theoretical issues in contemporary studies of religion, philosophy, and literature. What are the consequences for these disciplines in losing the distinction between "speech-in-itself" and "speech-for-itself," as Žižek describes it? The ambiguity or the history of ambiguity of oracles may shed light on this question—for what are oracles if not ultimate instances of voice becoming sound, becoming the ultimate "vanishing mediator"? As Michael Wood notes in his densely referenced *The Road to Delphi: The Life and Afterlife of Oracles,* "an oracle answers our question, and we interpret the answer. That is, we match the answer to events or places in the world, and we feel, when the match is good, that the oracle knew what was going to happen, or what was the right thing to do."[91]

1.7 Of Ambiguity and Oracles

When one is talking to living people it would be absurd, and professorial in the bad sense, to cling to the fiction that one can express pure thought, and one must do one's best, following one's own innervations, to make things clear to the people one is talking to. This does, however, have the disadvantage that when people like you come to listen to a person like me, you will almost inevitably be disappointed, as you will expect from what I write to hear something much more pithy than is possible in a spoken lecture. In short, one is, in educated language, in an aporia.

—Theodor Adorno, *Metaphysics: Concepts and Problems*

There are several historical, critical perspectives on this topic of the oracle as "vanishing mediator" and oracular equivocation, and Wood's observation that the human application of the divine message as the site of trouble captures key elements of the so-called divination process. While the oracle presumably provides us with access to the Divine Will, a moment of unity, it all too often places the burden of interpretation alongside the vagaries of desire, which, as we know all too well, tend to lead us to see signs not as "sign" but as a promise of desire's fulfillment. The literary tradition, for instance, insists not only on the play of desire but on the unreliability of "oracles" or other messengers bearing information concerning future events. The intent to deceive on the part of the oracle, in addition to deceiving oneself, is considered to be inherent in its function, with complicity between the oracle and a malevolent force forming the unraveling of fateful events. The oracle or soothsayer, in these instances, misleads by speaking in half-truths: Shakespeare's Macbeth, for example, does assume the throne as foretold, but his reign is brief and miserable, which was not the future he had desired or envisioned: "Infected be the air whereon they ride, / And damn'd all those that trust them!"[92]

Whether or not oracles or messengers always lie or sometimes lie or are mistaken is further complicated by the historical accounts in which oracles, as "public servants," seemingly told the truth.[93] These oracles of history, those that attempted to accurately tell the future, have a related, albeit separate function from the equivocating oracles of myth, literature, philosophy, and religion. In these instances the "divining agent" functioned more as a political consultant, and the advice given pertained to a practical situation of state. While Wood's study addresses the important historical and political role of oracles for the state, it is necessary to note that oracles of the humanistic tradition play a much larger role than their historical counterparts, as they speak not to the foreseeable future but to the "unforeseeable" future, a future with existential and mythological consequences. These oracles, then, come to serve a literary purpose.

Richard Kearney in *On Stories,* for instance, describes the ways in which mythic narrative "mutated" over time, leaving two distinct branches. The first is historical narrative, in which "storytellers like Herodotus and Thucydides in Greece strove to describe natural rather than supernatural events, resisting the Homeric license to entertain monstrous and fantastic scenerios."[94] The second branch or mutation is the "fictional." Distinct from the "historical" narrative with its basis in real events, the "fictional" narrative, as Kearney writes, "aimed to re-describe events in terms of some ideal standard of beauty, goodness, or nobility."[95] The significance of this move away from traditional mythos lies in the notion of the "as if," according to Kearney. Stories, within this departure from the more traditional mode, did not simply report events; they created them or re-created them within a larger framework of beauty, goodness, and nobility, as Kearney describes.

These oracle-stories, which differ from oracle-events, produce moral intrigue, as the principal characters of myth and literature delicately weigh the plurality of possible actions. Michael Wood refers to this as the "haunting point," the poetic necessity of an oracle being neither completely right nor completely wrong. What is of interest here is the human interplay of hope and dread as it surrounds the message:

> In oracle-stories the promise or the prediction needs only to have a chance of having been right, needs only not to have been unequivocally wrong. Faith, enthusiasm, and ingenious interpretation will do the rest. . . . Oracle-stories characteristically not only center on equivocation as part of their plot, the way they make the oracle come out right. They are *about* equivocation. They need the oracle to be both right and wrong; they need more than one outcome to lurk from the start in the oracle's utterance. It is because the oracle could have been wrong in these stories that we are fascinated by the way it came out right. In the equivocation we see the rightness and the wrongness all at once: the story disentangles them, but the tangle is what we remember, what we return to, the haunting point of so many stories.[96]

The hermeneutic problems associated with oracles find a home in literature, myth, philosophy, and religion. Discerning the ultimate meaning of signs and events is at the heart of each area of study, with the communicative act the object of intense investigation. Is the oracle truthful? How does one fully disclose its message?

These questions are framed within the overarching epistemological crisis attending all critical endeavors. Somehow, one assumes, the oracle's communicative act contains a discernible message, a knowable content. With this in mind the approach to oracles, prophets, or writers has been one involving the notion of interpretative remedy, a quest to discover the hidden truth, assuming that it is a univocal truth. Wood's "haunting point," then, is an interpretive choice, with all commitments essentially full of risk. Before we reconsider the epistemological problem of text interpretation, the way of understanding the most plausible or the most real, the ontological status of the communicative act must be investigated. Taking the oracle's speech to be representative of a reality places the "interpreter" in a precarious situation insofar as the choices for response are determined by a perceivable or receivable reality, a reality conditioned by custom or common sense or the limits of imagination. Language and world here allegedly unite in this hermeneutics of discernment, leaving the possibility that language and world are radically incommensurate outside the scope of inquiry. Any narratology—biblical exegesis, for example—partially takes this into account when texts describe actions or events that defy empirical reality. This empirical plane of understanding gives way to a symbolic plane—thus preserving a "truth" of faith or belief (*doxa*), while acknowledging an empirical or even logical impossibility. As a result "faith" or "belief" compensates for epistemological deficiency and allegedly bridges any disjunction between the empirical and the symbolic—this is the highest form of restorative reading.

Decoding a text or message begins therefore with a critical assumption—that there is some communicative content to be recovered, which is not always limited to some fact of the world. Political oracles reveal a supposed congruity between signs and the order of future events, implying a causality in which particular deeds completed on one day collapse the multiplicity of all future possibilities into a single, predictable sequence of events. Literary oracles establish a similar cause-effect dynamic between the deeds of today and the events of tomorrow. The difference between the two, however, is that the causality of the latter is much more subject to epistemic detour and symbolic interpretation. In other words, literary oracles, unlike their historically real counterparts, must obey the laws of fiction, not history, and collapse the multiplicity of the future into a plurality of choices, with each adding further weight to the existential burden of the characters.

It is at this juncture that the category of "apostles of mourning" becomes distinct from the categories containing politico-historical oracles, "apostles of the good news," or prophetic writers. Apostles of mourning withhold the possibility of a completeable communicative act; that is to say, "apostles of mourning" do not homologize the planes of futurity and language. Unlike the prophet or the modernist poet, the apostle of mourning removes the connective assumptions linking futurity, language, and reality. The process of mourning that brings together literature, philosophy, and religion then begins in the refusal of language to accept the possibility of a "Divine

Will" or "Divine Linkage." Contrary to the epistemological problem outlined by Michael Wood in his discussion of the "haunting point," my concern here is with the nature of the oracular message in a theory of language that calls into question a one-to-one correspondence between futurity and signs, event and history. Before we have interpretative choices, I'll argue, we must confront the ontological condition of language, or, the condition of such choices as they appear within competing theories of language. The interpretative choice, therefore, is an epistemological act, a decision to arrest a series of possible meanings.

In this instance it is assumed or argued to be the case that such a stoppage along the hermeneutic plane coincides with reality as it joins in unison a message, language, addressee, with an addressor. In retrospect it has been the oracle, politico-historical and literary, that has bound this hermeneutic plane to a collapsed linear procession of events. The apostle of mourning, as I will argue, makes no such attempt at synthesis. This will be illustrated in the later section on Leo Tolstoy, Franz Kafka, and Christoph Ransmayr.

1.8 Inside Words

In order to really understand where the power of the voice lies, and how metaphysics, philosophy, and the determination of being as presence constitute the epoch of speech as *technical* mastery of objective being, to properly understand the unity of *technē* and *phōnē*, we must think through the objectivity of the object. The ideal object is the most objective object; independent of the here-and-now acts and events of the empirical subjectivity which intends it, it can be repeated infinitely while remaining the same.

—Jacques Derrida, *Speech and Phenomena*

Oracular speech, as it presents hegemonic sacrality, appears as the paradigmatic example of language's untidy relationship to reality. In one sense—a very limited, traditional sense—language is a representative economy of sounds or marks standing for objects in the world or the qualities contained within objects in the world. The ideal object, as noted by Derrida, would assert its ideal objectivity in language, with its repetition infinitely being the "same." A basic or naive linguistics suggests a sign system with essential elements "in" words, with words, for instance, sounding like the objects they represent, a "sameness" that is transferred into or as words.

In the *Cratylus* Socrates, after an extended conversation with Hermo-genes, warns Cratylus that he should not invest too heavily in knowledge derived from "naming," even though "names rightly given are the likeness and images of the things they name."[97] It is better, we learn from Socrates, to pursue the truth of things "themselves," independent of language. Plato's epistemology, while offering words of caution, clearly extends this "like-ness" and "image" claim to include, more generically, the notion that some essence of the object resides in the word itself, just as the Form inhabits the sensible thing. The science of etymology is indebted to this linguistic theory, with the claim that ancient words are closer to the essence of the things they name—the field of onomatopoetics.

If this is true in the study of linguistics, it is truer still in mythology, in which the gods themselves are believed to give names to things. In the con-text of mythology Cassirer views this as an integral part the "mythmaking consciousness":

> Here in the realm of spooks and daemons, as well as in the higher reaches of mythology, the Faustian word seemed ever to hold good: here it was always assumed that the essence of each mythical figure could be directly learned from its name. The notion that name and essence bear a necessary and inter-nal relation to each other, that the name does not merely denote but actually *is* the essence of its object, that the potency of the real thing is contained in the name—that is one of the fundamental assumptions of the mythmaking consciousness itself. Philosophical and scientific mythology, too, seemed to accept this assumption. What in the spirit of myth itself functions as a liv-ing and immediate conviction becomes a postulate of reflective procedure for the science of mythology; the doctrine of the intimate relation between names and essences, and their latent identity, is here set up as a method-ological principle.[98]

The important issue raised by Cassirer addresses the relationship between linguistic theory and myth, with the name-and-essence relation providing the means to interpretation.

The mythmaking consciousness, then, involves an act of speech that brings into unison word and reality insofar as language bears the traces of an essential plane of order. This is why, for example, Faust, even though he is tired of "words, words, words," is able to conjure spirits—words offer up essences, even "spooks and daemons," as Cassirer observes. This is further complicated by extending the "name/essence" relation into time and reality by situating speech directly in line with an ontological order transcending or coinhabiting the world of sensible things. In oracular speech, for instance, one finds five distinct functions that compromise this unobstructed correspondence between name and essence. These include the request or petition, the content, the expression or transmission, the interpretation, and the retelling in "sensible" discourse. Within this process the content is futurity, and the expression or transmission can be understood as the actual "voice" or song of the oracle (sybil), with the priest providing interpretation and retelling in the form of a message.

The correspondence, it can be argued, fails to account for the simplest aspects of oracular speech, namely the petition-response. If words merely stand for objects and participate in them, then in what possible way could a petition-response, with its reference to the future, find a point of correspondence? This only would be possible if the "future" has already "happened" in some continuous reality. The "already happened" nature of the future takes us back to Wood's point in which the instance of word and object coalescences in petition-response, occurring both in the "future" and retroactively. More simply, the futurity of oracular speech is contiguous with the problem of prophecy—correspondence or fulfillment is confirmed or completed after the fact, not in the future. In other words, prophesy is, ironically, a function of retrospective gazing.

The point of the question is not to knock down an archaic theory of language or a more contemporary correspondence theory that unites words and things. More generally, and perhaps more simply, the question calls attention to any theory of language that entails reference to a reality, metaphysical or material. Oracular speech indicates a passage between the material petition (what could happen?) and the gods' intentions as they relate to human activity (that which shall happen).

The ambiguity that is associated with oracular speech, then, represents at least two precarious assumptions: (1) that the future can be directly referenced within a language system; and (2) that the plane of reference for the gods is linguistic, which seems implausible given what we know of mythology, since the gods are understood to inhabit a separate reality. The problem, therefore, can be posed as a question: what does language reference, if anything, in oracular speech? The remaining functions of oracular speech also challenge a theory of correspondence insofar as each function represents a degree of metaphoricity, which substitutes "similarity" for "essence" in words. From this one can dismiss the notion that words and things are metaphysically intertwined. If words and things are not on a metaphysical continuum, then what exactly is their relationship?

This question and related linguistic questions have been the concern of scholars from across the humanities and social sciences for centuries. If founding speech were in fact divine in nature, then there would no linguistic problem. The future would already exist, and oracular speech would simply provide a passage between the now and the future. The history of oracular speech, as described by Wood, suggests that this is not the case. The prevailing issue, however, is that the future, because it is the future, does not yet exist; or, the content of the future does not yet exist, and without content there is no object of reference. So the unresolved problem is twofold: what is language, generically, and what can be said of foundational speech or oracular speech, specifically?

In an attempt to come to some resolution, one could develop an anthropological or archeological or quasi-*CSI* approach to the question and attempt to re-create the development of language and the particular rituals surrounding oracular speech by recovering the physical evidence as if one were piecing together a puzzle.[99] A similar methodology could be developed within a historical analysis, which again would derive its conclusions from reconstructing available data in the form of documents or accounts. For instance, did human beings become sign-using creatures because of divine intervention or evolutionary "progress"? There are, of course, psychological elements to the question of oracular speech. Did the sybil or Pythia experience chemically induced hallucinations? Was "oracular speech" the result of trauma? Subterranean mind-altering gases?

All of these lines of inquiry, in their particular contexts, have contributed a great deal to exploring the twofold question. It is worth pointing out, however, that since all these approaches posit and understand the phenomenon differently, the various disciplinary results would not necessary contradict each other—just differ in defining the problem. The interdisciplinary approach that would synthesize these divergent analyses of the problem of oracular speech would be, at best, unwieldy. Nevertheless, several scholars of an earlier generation, primarily Carl Jung, Mircea Eliade, Paul Ricoeur, and René Girard, have explored the phenomenon of oracular speech and its relationship to myth through historical, anthropological, psychological, and to a lesser degree archeological perspectives. In this sense oracular speech exists within a framework that can be traced back to social, historical, or cultural origins. Whether it is the hero, the shaman, or the narrator, the "oracular function" of the speech remains intact as a coded message from a truth-giving source.

Now, within postmodern/deconstructive theories of language, the dynamic by which this speech materializes in any given context becomes the object of a type of interdisciplinary study. The nature of speech and what language is generically remains, I'll argue, a different problem within this framework, insofar as language and speech, while having a materiality within contexts, also have distinct and interrelated functions. The linking of the condition of the "materiality" of the sign and the nature of language is the concern of theory.

The central concern, then, arising from language's remainder is this interrelation and the disclosing power in the nature of foundational speech, especially oracular speech. The one-to-one correspondence theory of language, as I have shown, invites too many contradictions or nondemonstrable propositions at the level of speech—one would need to reveal the "essence" in a particular word in order to prove the theory. The failure of the one-to-one correspondence theory of language is just one example of the shortcomings of a general theory of language in which words refer directly to things, or, more generally, a theory in which language fully maps onto an empirical reality. This "mapping" leaves language as a secondary medium or simple recording surface rather than a site within which meaning is produced. Contrary to this, language doesn't simply capture meaning; it creates it, albeit apophatically.

This will be addressed in greater detail in subsequent sections, but it is worth noting here that in *The Trespass of the Sign*, the problem of linguistic reference is of great significance to religious theory. Kevin Hart's analysis of Derrida's deconstruction, for instance, allows for a reassessment of the problem with language before and after the Fall: "If the Fall introduced a gap between man and God, words and objects, thereby making signs the indispensable and imperfect vehicle for any knowledge, religious or otherwise, the economy of salvation was also worked out according to signs, specifically verbal signs."[100] With this, as Hart points out, we must return to the phenomenon of verbal signs as speech, founding speech.

1.9 The Linguistic Concern

Thus, at the moment when the question "How to avoid speaking?" arises, it is already too late. There was no longer any question of not speaking. Language has started without us, in us and before us.

—Jacques Derrida, "How To Avoid Speaking: Denials"

If we begin, as we have, with an acknowledgment of founding speech's alleged hegemonic, bridging function, we can turn to various theoretical discussions of language's epistemological and ontological elements. This philosophical consideration of theoretical discussions begins from a wide range of sources.

Geoffrey Galt Harpham's *Language Alone: The Critical Fetish of Modernity* begins with an overview of modern linguistic studies in the humanities and social sciences. By way of a comprehensive overview, Harpham focuses on a shared appraisal of language's relationship to culture by reexamining a widely misconstrued quotation by the Austrian philosopher Ludwig Wittgenstein that suggests that language and, subsequently, meaning are anchored in or indexed to cultural practice. Harpham writes: "'And to imagine a language means to imagine a form of life'. . . widely quoted and variously construed, this sentence suggests many things, among them the possibility that cultural forms may be inferred from language because the properties of a given language contain the culture's essential structures of feeling, its collective sensibility, the intelligible form of its otherwise inchoate character, the tools with which it constructs its sense of things in general."[101]

While noticeably absent from *Language Alone,* the insights of Stanley Cavell provide, if not support, an important perspective on viewing the various problems associated with "collective sensibility" or criteria for establishing, as Harpham notes, "essential structures of feeling":

What makes metaphor unnatural is its occasion to transcend our criteria; not as if to repudiate them, as if they are arbitrary; but to expand them, as though they are contracted. (The ordinary [or Wittgensteinian] grammar of "sun" must be preserved if the metaphorical application of it to Juliet is to carry; for example, the criteria for its rising and setting and its being obscured or eclipsed and its causing growth and thirst, and for its shining as something that, in creating day, hence night, lights the moon as well as the earth.) And metaphor transcends criteria not as if to repudiate our mutual attunement but as if to pressure this attunement (under which pressure certain of our attunements with others will fail; but with certain others the attunement will be intensified and refined). In the realm of the figurative, our words are not felt as confining but as releasing, or not as binding but as bonding. (This realm is neither outside nor inside language games).[102]

What is at stake in Cavell's brief description of figurative language, and in Harpham's insights into Wittgenstein's "forms of life," is the idea of contraction and expansion of meaning. The event or events that lead to such an intensification and refinement, according to Cavell, belong to a realm that is, as he describes, "neither outside nor inside language games," which, I believe, extends to Harpham's analysis of Wittgenstein's complicating of linguistic "attunement."

Following this, then, the modern turn "(in)to" language, as Harpham describes it, is divided suspiciously between a formalism (inside) and an externalism (outside), with each positing language as its central object of inquiry. The "misreading" of Wittgenstein noted by Harpham is thus revealing in many ways. First, as Harpham observes, this interpretation of "forms of life" is only possible as a "misreading" if, as he explains, one fails to read Wittgenstein's term in the overall context of the *Philosophical Investigations*: "Our confidence that we understand language is utterly misplaced; in fact, language is the site of a massive confusion. As he quotes later, 'we do not *command a clear view* of the use of our words.'"[103] The absence of this "skeptical" formation (a skepticism discussed thoroughly by Kripke) leaves Wittgenstein as an advocate for a foundationalism via "use," which clearly cannot be justified given the entirety of the *Philosophical Investigations*. Second—a point that Harpham does not discuss in great detail—there exists an unquestioned default assumption concerning the nature of language very much "prior" to Wittgenstein, which affirms that language *must* be in commerce with the world in general. And third, the privileged "misreading" of Wittgenstein exists in the context of the belief that philosophy is a subfield of the natural sciences, and this particular "measure" continues to develop an empirical standard for linguistic "interpretation."

These various "misreadings" of "forms of life," for Harpham, allow for an understanding of Wittgenstein as a foundationalist—a moniker that Harpham is eager to reject. By the same token, however, it is not entirely clear that Harpham prefers the notion of Wittgenstein as a "skeptic," as Kripke has described him. This place between these poles can be further clarified by Cavell's analysis of Wittgenstein and his reluctance to assign "forms of life" too easily to either philosophical category, foundationalism or skepticism. For Cavell and, to some extent, Harpham, "forms of life" does not simply mean that what we say is governed or determined by hard "rules" imposed either by grammar or by context. "Forms of life" represents a much more sophisticated, complex involvement with language. For Cavell any "one to one" correspondence between language and culture would be impossible given that new language games constantly enter into the economy of intelligibility, making a limiting totality of "rules" or "grammar" inoperative.

This observation advances Harpham's analysis insofar as it supports the idea of a gap between what is or can be said and what that saying means. In other words, saying cannot be reduced to grammar or context because it is precisely these boundaries that are contested by saying itself:

> We learn and teach words in certain contexts, and then we are expected, and expect others, to be able to project them into further contexts. Nothing insures that this projection will take place (in particular, not the grasping of universals nor the grasping of books of rules), just as nothing insures that we will make, and understand, the same projections. That on the whole we do is a matter of sharing routes of interest and feeling, modes of response, senses of humour and of significance and of fulfillment, of what is outrageous, of what is similar to what else, what a rebuke, what forgiveness, of when an utterance is an assertion, when an appeal, when an explanation—all the whirl of organism Wittgenstein calls "forms of life." Human speech and activity, sanity and community, rest upon nothing more, but nothing less, than this. It is a vision as simple as it is difficult, and as difficult as it is (and because it is) terrifying.[104]

The terrifying simplicity put forward by Cavell allows "forms of life" as "all the whirl of organism" to exist not as a lifeless bedrock in which meaning is anchored, but as a "living" process within which meaning is perpetually negotiated by speakers. The "whirl of organism," therefore, escapes the confines of both foundationalism and skepticism by rejecting the finitude or hegemonic limit of each category. For Cavell, to further elaborate, language "always [has] new contexts to be met, new needs, new relationships, new objects, new perceptions to be recorded and shared."[105] In this sense language never achieves a static existence, nor does it have a final appeal: "Language has no essence."[106]

This "excursus" on Wittgenstein opens the way for a wider analysis of language in the context of "premodern," "modern," and "postmodern" variations on linguistic limits. Harpham provides these frames of reference to better address the underlying problem of language across historical orientations:

> A "premodern" orientation, we might say, is signaled by a faith in the primacy of concepts on the one hand and the possibility of an unmediated observation of the material fact on the other. A "modern" orientation dispenses with both kinds of faith and pursues instead a rational inquiry into representation as the site of a reality that can be tested and verified. The modernist moment is achieved when the limits of language are seen as the limits of the world, and linguistic mediation itself becomes the object of observation. Both metaphysics and the "things themselves" are telescoped into "language itself," which becomes the one thing we can know, but the thing that will yield knowledge about all the rest.[107]

The division of the history of linguistic theory into three modes, premodern, modern, and postmodern, establishes a line of inquiry that views the "other" of textuality or the "alongside" of the literary as a critical factor in addressing the relationships among religion, philosophy, and literature, with the latter separating from its historical servitude to the former.

The "premodern orientation" is organized around "faith," in which the word mystically encompasses the concept and the object—a naive Platonic perspective. The "modern orientation," underwritten by a "faith" in science, offers the possibility that the world's order can be rendered knowable through rational inquiry. This investment in rationality makes a "science" of language critical to all disciplines, including the arts: "What distinguishes the modern emphasis on language from traditional humanism," Harpham writes, "is not just a more concentrated attention paid to language, but something more radical, a presumption that language could be studied as a thing apart from human beings and human behavior, and that it could therefore serve as the object of rational inquiry, even of the empirical sciences."[108] The analytic tradition embodies this notion of language as it attempts to find greater and greater degrees of linguistic clarity, even to the point of Donald Davidson's observation that propositional statements are either true or false "formally" and may or may not correspond to any fact of the world. The impulse to view language as nonreferential, however, is not unique to either the "Cambridge" or the "Oxford" linguistic turns of the twentieth century.[109] The object-dominated classical world that language supposedly referenced undergoes numerous qualifications, not the least of which is phenomenology, in which the world is "bracketed" and knowing becomes an internal process of mind.

The major implication of the "modern orientation," as Harpham describes it, does not, as one would assume, immediately involve phenomenology, however. The primary example that marks modernity's orientation toward language is, he affirms, in the history of painting. Harpham charts this move from the premodern to the modern with an analysis of representation in the arts: "Painting, music, dance, and literature become modern when artists divert their attention from the objects of representation, including the material world and their own subjective states, and devote themselves to a 'technical' exploration of representation itself, for which 'language' serves as a convenient synecdoche."[110] In art history figures such as Cézanne signal a break with the premodern "by decoupling the work both from the object painted and from the effect of the object on the perceiver in order to force a concentration on the painting, and even on the paint, itself."[111] Painting, like language, was thought to be an exercise in form, with referential necessity and viewer experience pushed aside, as they were in Carnap's "processing out" of the metaphysical excess and pseudoproblems of linguistics in general.

In literary studies one finds a later corollary in which avoidance of the "intentional fallacy" and the "affective fallacy" guides interpretation. The crucial difference with the New Critics, particularly Wimsatt and Beardsley, however, was that language, as much as it was the medium for linguistic art, also functioned to convey a universal sensory experience—one that maintained an exclusion of the "intentional" and "affective" impulse toward interpretation, while preserving the possibility of meaning to be found in the "work itself" or, as Walter Benn Michaels observes, the "public" sense of what the poet "said": "The New Critical reader's rejection of intention thus commits him not to thinking of the poem as a natural object like a rock but to thinking of it as a 'linguistic' object whose meaning is determined by a particular set of syntactic and semantic rules—by a language."[112]

Just as in Harpham's "Cambridge" and "Oxford" linguistic turns, the movement within a "modern orientation" is decidedly away from objective and subjective worlds and toward a world circumscribed by the "rules" of language or, later, the ordinariness of language—whether it's the "language" of philosophy, working according to formal structures; or of art, in which works have an internal integrity; or of literature, poetry, in which "words" are detached from the author and reader and thus find meaning in the syntactic and semantic rules of their public use. For painting and poetry within the "modern orientation," the law of mimesis is suspended in favor a new aesthetics in which "reality," empirical or transcendent, is not the default standard measure of intelligibility. Cubist paintings, for instance, do not look exactly like objects in the world; literary texts or experimental modernist texts, like *Finnegans Wake*, similarly do not offer a realistic linguistic depiction of human events. The earlier Wittgensteinian "misconstrued" invitation to see "forms of life," social and cultural, in language games systematically falls apart as one ventures into the linguistic theory of Harpham's "modern orientation." Language therefore does not provide the critical material of anthropological analysis. Instead language presents its own unique set of problems—problems that do not simply vanish under the magic wands of analytic philosophy's logical modalities, art history's "history," or literature's social or thematic realism.

The issue of language and representation as it appears across analytic philosophy, art history, religious studies, and literary aesthetics unfolds in a direction similar to Saussure's "structural linguistics." Harpham, after discussing the Wittgensteinian linguistic "turn" out of Frege, provides an equally concise and insightful analysis of Saussure's linguistic turn and its central role in defining studies in the humanities over the past several decades. The various linguistic turns that dominate the late nineteenth and early twentieth centuries appear within this wider context of the "modern orientation," an orientation, as we have seen, that generally is a rejection of choosing between either an objective- or a subjective-dominated reality. Saussure's significance, Harpham notes, comes from his standing as the "father-founder of the linguistics that most nonlinguists have preferred to call 'modern,' a linguistics, that is, that can be taken as a science by virtue of having *reduced its object to the manageable field of the system of signs.*"[113]

This "reduction" makes Ferdinand de Saussure's *Course in General Linguistics* the foundational text in "theory's" redefinition of language around the concept of a "linguistic turn." Since language within Saussure's analytic is a differential system with no "positive" terms, meaning is determined not by some outside reference to an objective reality but by a visual and phonic differential economy of signifying "images." Again, within the "reduction" words and things do not automatically coincide, as if each stretch of syllables attaches itself to the proper object in the world.[114] Language therefore comes before the fact of individual cognition. The antecedent and customary character of language as a structured set of relationships among sounds, graphic marks, and concepts becomes, for Saussure, the "object" of study.

This leads to a division of language into two related strata, *langue* and *parole. Langue,* standing for the diachronic character of language, bears the historical or sedimented meaning of a sign or its strong custom of association with a concept. *Parole,* on the other hand, refers to the synchronic character of a sign—its meaning at a particular point along the historical axis. This "scientific" approach provides a new "anatomy" of language, one that requires a new understanding of signs and their (non)corresponding meanings:

> Saussure regarded *langue* somewhat in the manner of a Durkheimian sociologist, as a "product of the collective mind of a linguistic community," a "social product stored in the brain." The linguist's task was to analyze this system as a "semiology," which meant "to define the units of a language, the relations between them, and their rules of combination." Paradoxically, *langue* referred both to a given linguistic system such as French or Italian, and to the universal or essential condition of language as such. Even more paradoxically, while a true linguistics could only study a *language,* it had to treat as "external" all factors peculiar to that language in order to focus on the universal conditions of systematicity and difference themselves. Only in this way could linguistics realize its destiny of becoming "Queen of the Sciences," a discipline that could stand proudly alone where previous linguistics had relied implicitly on natural history, anthropology, psychology,

physics, history, and various pseudo-versions of all the above. *"The only true object of study is linguistics,"* Saussure concluded with unusual emphasis, *"is the language"*—the system—*"considered in itself and for its own sake."*[115]

Saussure's quest, as described by Harpham, to reestablish a "Queen of the Sciences" in the form of linguistics depends upon the notion that nothing precedes language—or in other words, the notion that there is no ontological space prior to the space of language in which it is grounded; to present such a ground amounts to affirming a phantasm. Only with this in place can linguistics, like rhetoric today, as some would assert, announce itself as the metadiscipline of all disciplines.

Along with structuralism's "hermetic" or "in itself" consequence comes the exclusion of the speaking subject, in which, as François Dosse notes, "objectivity" depends on "banish[ing] from the Saussurean scientific perspective, the individual [who] becomes the victim of a formalist reduction in which he no longer has his place."[116] It is important then to recognize a reoccurrence in the discussion thus far—that is, the return of the (dis)possessed subject, a speaker, like the rhapsode, like the Platonic seeker of knowledge, and like the modern investigator, that vanishes before language. This dispossession anticipates the rise of the postmodern inquirer, who for Michel Foucault is "erased, like a face drawn in sand at the edge of the sea."[117]

Erasure "precedes" language, a language that renounces its relationship to the world of objects. More troubling for the "modern orientation," I will argue, is this language, a language of renunciation, set forward in the interest of preserving or advancing some metaphysical truth—whether it is religious, philosophical, or literary. This radical extension of the "modern orientation" and its reduction of language to formal or internal mechanisms open the way for a much more thoroughgoing critique of the possibility for sacred, founding speech that finds a variety of expression in postmodernism. The Foucauldian erasure of "man" is further explained in "Nietzsche, Freud, Marx" as an erasure of "beginnings," an eradication of any foundational space, not the least of which would be language: "There is nothing absolutely primary to interpret, because at bottom all is already interpretation, each sign is in itself not the thing which offers itself to interpretation, but the interpretation of other signs."[118] With Foucault's commentary on the suspect status of subjectivity and origins, one is confronted by the possibilities of having neither, in the sense that each was possible not only for the "premodern orientation" but for the "modern orientation" as well. The implications, then, of these two moments, erasure and nonorigin, become the concern of theoretical inquiry.

1.10 Postmodern Departures

Phrases obeying different regimens are untranslatable into one another.
—Jean-François Lyotard, *The Differend: Phrases in Dispute*

Reiner Schürmann, who is, as we have seen, hegemony's adversary, writes that "the explicit project of making the world uniform institutes the modern age."[119] For as long as this project of uniformity continued uninterrupted, one could argue that the postmodern or the "untranslatable" moment within the modern age could never have taken shape, but it has. The narrative detailing the rise of the modern age that we have explored demonstrates the important lines of filiation one finds across seemingly disparate traditions—traditions that were purported unified through translation across "regimens." Harpham's "wide net" of "premodern" and "modern" orientations allows us to view the shared, unifying concern with scientific inquiry in linguistics and philosophy, with literary studies following some time later in its mid-twentieth-century commitment to New Criticism. "Science," the method of empirical inquiry, turns language into a formal, objective structure, with predictable, translatable, and identifiable syntactical rules governing meaning. In this instance, as Harpham notes, Carnap, Wittgenstein, and Saussure, although the first two are separated from the third by discipline, are joined in a similar "modern," uniform enterprise.

One needs to be cautious in one's descriptions here, however, as the context of the "modern orientation" may seem to quickly expand to include all the historical particulars of a given age. William R. Everdell, for instance, in *The First Moderns,* rejects this seemingly all-encompassing width of the "modern orientation." The "modern" may in fact not exist as a coherent set of characteristics or, indeed, as a time, which invites a postmodern reappraisal of the modern: "The orthodoxy of the nineteenth century," Everdell writes, ". . . was called Positivism. Some called it 'modern,' but it had been invented in the eighteenth century, and had already passed its prime in England, France, and northern Germany. Positivism, sometimes called 'scientism,' was a philosophical program, drawn up in the belief that the problems of philosophy were all soluble if only people could resist the temptation to be mystical."[120]

Everdell's important mention of the historical limits of the "modern," while it does contain a variety of concerns and impulses, does not invalidate the long, philosophical view offered by Harpham. In fact, Everdell's "scientism" is necessary to an understanding of the "modern" as a project of uniformity, taking shape in relation to the Enlightenment and Romanticism. The question of timing, at least in Vienna, does not undo or make anachronistic the "modern's" movement toward a uniform objectivity, especially in the language-based disciplines of the humanities, for example, the logical empiricism of philosophy. The Vienna connection therefore, as cited by both Harpham and Everdell, allows us to return to Wittgenstein as the starting point for several linguistic "turns."

The first, as we have discussed, is the "Wittgensteinian turn" prompted by a "misreading" in which the world is invited into language—a cultural studies Wittgenstein. The second "Wittgensteinian turn" is the inheritor of Frege's philosophy of language, which reduces words to logical relations. The third Wittgensteinian turn, which we have not yet discussed, is the antecedent to postmodernism. This latter "Wittgensteinian turn" is to be found in the *Philosophical Investigation*—the work that provides the French postmodernist Jean-François Lyotard, as a case in point, with the basis for his version of deconstruction. This particular Wittgensteinian turn will be significant in the formation of Lyotard's attack on "grand narratives," especially science, and the strictly "modern" demand for uniformity, totality. Prior to Lyotard's rejection of "scientism" and earlier challenges to the totality of object-dominated philosophical and linguistic frameworks, there was another, earlier renunciation of scientism's march toward totality within the so-called modern: Friedrich Nietzsche's "gay science."

As one traces the various precursors to the linguistic aporia in modernity, it is necessary to view a second tradition in modern philosophy—that beginning with Nietzsche. If the underlying theme of the "modern orientation" is given as the need to sever language from the world, then Nietzsche's "gay science" stands as this need's most radical fulfillment. Nietzsche's antifoundationalism provides the most thorough unraveling of the Western metaphysical enterprise, with Heidegger's wish to view Nietzsche as the "last" metaphysician duly noted. Harpham, within his wide "modern orientation," places Nietzsche as a critical figure in philosophy's long progression toward linguistic objectivity:

> Certain features of the idea of language have long been attractive to ethical philosophers. Both language and ethics have been represented as counterinstinctual, something animals are incapable of, and yet at the same time as "natural" to human beings; both involve representation and judgment; and both are said to involve the exercise of freedom in the framework of custom, regularity, and law. Nietzsche exploited all these affiliations, but he also promoted a view of ethics that entailed a specific and controversial account of language. This account had not yet been formulated because Saussure had not yet thought of it. And yet, when once Nietzsche has chronicled the "tyranny of arbitrary laws" in moral thinking, when he has detailed the systematic and interlocking character of moral evaluations, when he has described morality as an historical phenomenon that produces at any given moment an apparently ahistorical system, when he has labeled morality as mere "*semeiotics*"—when all of this has been done, all that remains for Saussure to do is to gather these elements together and to label the whole business "general linguistics."[121]

The specificity of Saussure's project, of course, does not fall within Nietzsche's deconstruction (*avant la lettre*) of moral philosophy. The overarching deployment of the "arbitrary," however, does join the two intellectual endeavors, as Harpham argues, in the cause of dismantling metaphysics, linguistic and moral. The weaving together of these figures—Saussure, Nietzsche, Wittgenstein—with the thread of "arbitrariness" not only produces a historical context allowing us to better understand the "modern orientation" but also gives us a theoretical matrix in which the connections between word and world systematically become more entangled and subject to radical investigation from a postmodern orientation.

It is therefore not too difficult to imagine the enduring problems associated with naming the "postmodern." Its "family tree" becomes a "family rhizome," to recall Deleuze, forever stretching from and reaching into multiple spaces, historical, philosophical, and cultural. In this sense the "postmodern" has many beginnings and just as many articulations. It is preceded and made possible through Saussure's sign system with no "positive terms." It also finds a "father" in Nietzsche's antifoundationalism. In either case the "modern orientation," which Harpham defines in the context of postmodernism, cultivates a landscape for the paradoxical "rule of arbitrariness," a critical theoretical concept that changes the direction and nature of intellectual inquiry across the humanities and social sciences. With this radical change in the direction and nature of inquiry, we return to the earlier question of the ordering effect of rules, which is further complicated by the force of arbitrariness, configured differently in history, in language, and in metaphysics.

The paradoxical rule of arbitrariness, as we have viewed it, occupies two separate but related spaces, language and metaphysics. The two obviously are wedded in the long tradition of Western philosophy, but in the postmodern orientation they are estranged. Saussure's "general linguistics," as Jacques Derrida notes in *Of Grammatology*, flees from the world that it claimed for so long to represent. Once the burden of representation is lifted from language, metaphysics seems to collapse into muteness. The question, however, is, was there ever anything to represent in the first place? Anything more than phantasm? The implications of this question are far-reaching, chief among them the release of philosophical, theological, and literary inquiry from its collective and ultimate object of inquiry (Reality). Perhaps one way to approach this question in more detail is through the work of disciplines, as Harpham's book has already investigated. What role, one could ask, does this new inquiry, an inquiry that is not directed toward an object, play in thinking in a discipline or thinking with discipline?

Rodolphe Gasché, in *The Honor of Thinking: Critique, Theory, Philosophy*, situates the development of *theoria* in the history of Western thought as the critical variable in understanding the metaphysics of inquiry. This "theoretical" alternative to uniformity and objectivity marks a long contest between something ambiguously called "thinking" and philosophy, a distinction that is key in the writing of Heidegger. Gasché, writing in the spirit of Heidegger's concern, distinguishes between "Theory" and "theory," with the latter depicted as a North American "regional commodity."[122] "Theory," with its Greek origin in the fifth century BC, comes to us in numerous discursive and disciplinary forms—most powerfully in the modern age as German Romanticism, as Gasché discusses in his book. But first the Greeks. Gasché writes:

> What then did the Greeks understand by *theoria*?
>
> Traces of the idea of *theoria* can be found in Pythagoras. But it is with Plato's *Theaetetus* or *Philebos,* and in particular with Aristotle, that *theoria* effectively becomes a concept (almost) synonymous with philosophy. Let me note from the outset that the pristine religious connotations of the notion of *theoria* continue to shape the meaning of the term in philosophy. *Theoria* originally named both the festive embassy sent by the states to the holy games staged at the sacred places, the *theatron* on which the *theoi,* the gods, were celebrated under visible shapes, and the act itself of viewing the divine gods at these games.[123]

Theoria, as a viewing of the divine, becomes under Plato and Aristotle "spiritual contemplation," a "characteristic of philosophy."[124] Gasché adds that *theoria* is a "sort of contemplation that takes place for its own sake, detached from the immediate and bare necessities of life, and which, consequently, is *free.*"[125]

In this ancient context *theoria* allegedly separates itself from a material object, "freeing" itself to "think" the divine object, which means that *theoria* as philosophy "has its purpose in itself, this purpose becomes exclusively the bringing into view of what is (the whole of nature as that which points toward God as its divine cause), and as it shows itself in itself, that is, without the interference of utilitarian purposes, this is because philosophical contemplation comes closest to the absolute vision that constitutes the divine itself."[126]

There are two points to consider here. First, *theoria* stands with contemplation, an instance of "thinking" beyond the limit of the material. Second, *theoria,* as contemplation, directs itself toward the most fundamental question of reality—that of the absolute nature of the divine: "God is the first and most intensive realization of *theoria.* In *theoria,* as an *actus purus* of the spirit, God freely, that is, without any exterior end except the end of pure contemplation, looks at and enjoys himself in the pure bliss of absolute contemplation."[127] Each of these articulations of *theoria,* it can be argued, depends upon an understanding of theoretical contemplation as a materialization of totality: Gasché's "Theory," which later, as he notes, finds a powerful expression in Romanticism, comes into clear view with the writings of Schlegel.

Schlegel, in *Lucinde and the Fragments,* writes that "Theory" is the "piety of philosophers."[128] Gasché sees Schlegel's understanding of "Theory" as a version of Aristotelian theology, with religious thinking "trac[ing] and lead[ing] all concepts, that is, all merely *intellectual* syntheses, back to their originary *intutition,* to the singular and empirical contingency of their first sensible beholding."[129] Here one cannot escape the historical, philosophical, and, more importantly, theological implications of "Theory." "Theory" in this context is the mechanism by which, as Schürmann earlier notes, we see the "project" of making the world uniform. "Theory," with a capital *T,* returns thinking to discernible origins, and this maneuver, as we have discussed, is the obstacle that "thinking" itself must address, if not overcome. While this definition of "religious thinking" as a path in the direction of origin fits well with the notion of theory as "total-thinking," this particular Romantic version of "Theory" undergoes a radical revision in later twentieth-century theology, a "theory"-driven theology that resituated the primacy of uniformity and totality—a "theoretical" thinking that challenges the aim of totalization.

The transition from a modern "Theory" to a postmodern "theory" is clearly discernible in the humanities during the late 1970s and early 1980s. More specifically, the traditional disciplinary conflicts over language and metaphysics come to a point of convergence in a new field of inquiry, "religious theory," a field that began in the late 1980s as an extension—and to some extent a rebuttal—of the "postmodern theology" of the previous decade. In *Alchemy of the Word* (1979), republished as *The End of Theology* in 2000, Carl A. Raschke articulates a "new" theology that brings into conversation the rule of arbitrariness, continental philosophy, linguistics, and poetics. This turn away from the project of modernity and toward "theory," with a lower-case *t,* initiates a process of radical redefinition that leaves "Theory's" hegemonic quest for origin in ruins. Raschke's critical insight begins with a disavowal of totality and clear advocacy of the rule of arbitrariness within what was to become the theory of "postmodern theology."

The positing of "arbitrariness" against uniformity is significant for two reasons. First, Raschke's *Alchemy of the Word* was the first definition of postmodern theology as a "radical hermeneutics" and among the first discussions of religious studies in the context of early Derridean deconstruction: both Mark C. Taylor's *Deconstructing Theology* and the edited volume *Deconstruction and Theology*, compiled by Raschke, Taylor, and Winquist, were published in 1982. Second, Raschke's postmodern theology, which developed from his understanding of radical hermeneutics, linked the emerging interest in Derrida with previous scholarship in theology focused on Martin Heidegger and Friedrich Nietzsche, particularly the French "Nietzsche."

In the first preface (1979) Raschke correlates his interest in "ordinary language" philosophy with his interest in theological thought. Wittgenstein's linguistic "conventionalism," as Raschke describes it, finds a sympathetic disciplinary "ear" in the death of theology announced by Nietzsche:

> Wittgenstein's theory of discourse as a system of "language games" which can be reconstructed to show *how,* but not of *what,* we speak could not ultimately make intelligible the claim of traditional and modern theology that is somehow explicating a revealed logos, the so-called "Word of God." It could characterize the "logical behavior" of theological utterances, but it remained explicitly agnostic with respect to their ontological basis. . . . The customary manner of "doing" theology, even that contemporary mode which appropriated the neo-Wittgensteinian standpoint of linguistic functionalism and conceptual relativism, seemed to have reached a kind of senescence. And this senescence appeared to be a symptom of a deeper crisis of Western thinking which Nietzsche had poetically, and elliptically, tagged "the death of God." The specter of God's death loomed behind even the most ingenious and intellectually sophisticated defenses of the familiar religious and theological forms of language.[130]

This separation of the "how" and the "what" in speech invites a further consideration of the rule of arbitrariness in the "modern orientation," as Harpham describes it for general theoretical inquiry. For Raschke, however, the tension between the "how" and the "what" is not to be alleviated through a simple binding of the two through a transcendent reality that unites, through hegemony, all oppositions. In fact, the rules governing the use of language, in speech and text, and the referent of language place in question, as we have discussed, the ontological "basis" of texts.

In *Desiring Theology,* perhaps the last postmodern theological book, Charles E. Winquist, reflecting on the theoretical arguments of postmod-

ern theology, makes the following observation regarding the nature of se-
miotic systems that rely on some external regulation:

> Syntax in language is the normalization of combinatory forms through
> repeated usage and conventional agreement. In more exact semiotic sys-
> tems such as mathematics or logic, a project within the systems has been to
> bring the combinatory forms to explicit awareness and articulations. The
> failures of these projects have ironically led to important insights into the
> incompleteness of semiotic systems and the inability to fully rationalize sec-
> ondary process thinking even if we make the shift to quasi-transcendental
> analysis. The rules for the formation of discourse are always implicated in
> that which is other than the semiotic systems they regulate. A fissure mark-
> ing the complex of forces in primary process thinking keeps opening the
> secondary process of thinking, but what is available to be thought is always
> the surface display of differences.[131]

"Texts," sacred and secular, in this account are surfaces upon the play of se-
miotic differences. Theology or, more generally, religious studies finds this
troubling insofar as it must maintain the necessity of "God" in the "Word
of God"; philosophy, within the modern orientation, and theology, within
a postmodern orientation, attempt to curtail or provide semantic injunc-
tions in "how" one speaks about "Word" in the "Word of God." Earlier this
conflict between speech and referent became evident through a short history of oracular speech, which prefigures all discourse purporting to rest
upon a divine foundation. Added to the tension between the "how" and the
"what" of speech is, as Raschke makes clear, the "deeper crisis of Western
thinking" that is thoroughly Nietzschean. The "death of God," as Raschke
states, looms behind the "familiar religious and theological forms of language." The complications of linguistic-turn philosophy, with an emphasis
on the "Word" in the "Word of God," and the existential consequences of
Nietzsche's declaration open a new line of inquiry in which methods do not
seek objects or transcendent objects. With this Nietzschean move one sees
the reemergence of the problem of rules, particularly rules governing the
formation of narratives.

At this juncture it is useful to bring an important Derridean insight
into the analysis and, to some extent, draw into sharper contrast the shared
concerns of continental philosophy, ordinary language philosophy, and
religious studies described by, among others, Carl Raschke. The folding

together of linguistics, philosophy, religious studies, and poetics in the "postmodern" orientation seems a necessary next step to understanding the radical possibilities of Nietzsche's rule of arbitrariness or what Sarah Kaufman exposed as Nietzsche's "philosophy of metaphor." The significance of this will become apparent in part 3, as the link between religious theory and the literary imagination becomes more central. For now, however, it is worth recalling Derrida's "Des tours de Babel," in which questions of "translation," "universality," and "transferability" are critical to understanding not only the "how" and "what" of language but also the founding authority of speech itself.

Traditionally, the biblical Tower of Babel represents a lesson in human arrogance, a representation that is not altogether excluded from Derrida's "re-marked" reading. However, the departure from the traditional interpretation in Derrida's analysis is that in Derrida's "detour" through Babel the standard notion of God's punishment, as the destruction of the Tower, is only partly the result of hubristic overreaching. The emphasis on the destruction of the Tower, in the traditional view, also coincides with the destruction of "a Tongue," a single unifying language. It is as if God, in the myth, needs to preemptively destroy a foreshadowing of modernity, hegemony, or univocity by destroying the uniformity of language.

There is, however, another possible understanding of God's assault on univocity. Did God destroy a monolithic language? Or did God cause a confusion or "confounding" of language? Was "modernity" fundamentally displaced before it ever took root in Western thinking, when God disrupted the uniformity of total speech? This interpretive turn emphasizing "confusion" over "destruction" is elaborated by Daniel Heller-Roazen in his book *Echolalias: On the Forgetting of Language:*

> The nature of the punishment imposed on the builders remains equally obscure. The verses of the Bible leave no doubt that the construction and destruction of the edifice brought about the diversity of human language and, with it, the mutual incomprehension of speaking beings. Before the building began, we read, "the whole earth was of one language, and of one speech." When the Lord interrupted the architectural project, "scattering" the people, he "confounded the language of the earth," and for what would appear to be the first time, no one "understood another's speech." But how

was the divine judgment executed, and how exactly did the whole earth pass from one tongue to many? There is no discussion at this point of any act of divine creation. Strictly speaking, God does not produce the plurality of tongues that will henceforth divide the people of the earth: nothing, it would seem, is added to the "one speech" that precedes the tower to make it multiple.[132]

As Heller-Roazen points out, God did not "create" new languages as much as he "confused" a single language. He did not "add" or "subtract" from uniformity; God caused a moment of extimacy, an instance in which pure destruction was set aside for a "confounding" or confusing within language.

In other words, if we return to the myth, the punishment is, reading literally, the thwarting of the construction project. Symbolically, however, the Tower was an attempt by human beings to be as high as or higher than God. In this move from the literal to the symbolic, it would be expected of us to believe that God, seeing the progress of the Tower, decided that without some destructive or intervening gesture, the builders would realize their "elevating" goal. The second "destruction," not simply of the Tower but of the Tongue, appears as a secondary punishment for the hubris associated with auto-origination or, as Derrida states, a collective (the Shemites) making a "name" for themselves:

> What happened to them? In other words, for what does God punish them in giving his name, or rather, since he gives it to nothing and to no one, in proclaiming his name, the proper name of "confusion" which will be his mark and his seal? Does he punish them for having wanted to build as high as the heavens? For having wanted to accede to the highest, up to the Most High? Perhaps for that too, no doubt, but incontestably for having wanted thus to make a name for themselves, to give themselves the name, to construct for and by themselves their own name, to gather themselves there ("that we no longer be scattered"), as in the unity of a place which is at once a tongue and a tower, the one as well as the other, the one as the other. He punishes them for having thus wanted to assure themselves, by themselves, a unique and universal genealogy.[133]

The Tower and its destruction hold differing interpretative possibilities, especially as they are viewed as two related, but separate, acts of judgment.

First, if the Tower were engineered to reach or surpass God or to get God's attention, then, in a manner of speaking, it was a success—just not in the way it was initially intended. Second, as Derrida makes clear, the success of the Tower resides in a narrative of events in which God appears as "confusion." In this sense the Tower was a triumph insofar as it "reached" God's "unreachableness," as evidenced by the judgment of multiple tongues.

So while the mythical tower, the symbol of hegemonic desire, was destroyed, the uniformity of language was simply confused. The "what" of speech, to recall Raschke, coincides with the "how" of speech, as God stands in the narrative as complete confusion and nontransferability, the scattering force working against rules of coherence—architectural and linguistic. While the language of philosophy, with its inclination toward propositional phrasing, experiences disorientation when faced with biblical narrative, religious theory and its cognate discipline, literary theory, see God as "confusion" or see the eternal gap as an opportunity for further intellectual probing, with the purpose of augmenting the possibilities of "confusion"—the disruption of word, world, and God.

In *The Prayers and Tears of Jacques Derrida,* John D. Caputo describes this proliferation of languages as fundamental not only to theology but to faith as well:

> I mean a faith that is inhabited by the thought that the "name of God" gives way to translation, that it disseminates itself, that it multiples itself into other forms and figures, that the patent faith holds on this name does not give it exclusive rights, remembering, on no less authority than God himself, that when the Shemites wanted to make themselves a master name, God was on the side of dissemination. Is not the story of Babel God's way of urging that there are no master names, not even the name of God? Is that not even God's word?[134]

In ending with the myth of Babel, the initial problem of this inquiry remains—the end of the intimacy of hegemonic coherence in narrative and the mourning of its loss. This will relate to Franz Kafka's interpretation of the Tower of Babel, discussed in the final section.

For now the falling, "gaping," broken hegemonic Tower, as Derrida observes, coincides with a second fall into language, a language that maps not onto an ontological order of the real but onto the ruins of coherence and origin. While all this "falling" leads to more dissemination, more decon-struction, it is important to keep in mind Caputo's rhetorical question: "Is that not even God's word?" One could view Derrida's discussion of Babel as highly "religious," as a "re-marking," to preview Slavoj Žižek, of an ancient myth, a "re-marking" that not only forces new possibilities but creates new conditions for possibility itself.

II

"Re-Marking" Myths and Crypto-Commerce

2.1 Mythical Gaps and Deadlocks

Myth is thus the Real of logos: the foreign intruder, impossible to get rid of, impossible to remain fully within it. Therein resides the lesson of Adorno's and Horkheimer's *Dialectic of Enlightenment:* Enlightenment always already "contaminates" the mythical naive immediacy; Enlightenment itself is mythical, i.e. its own grounding gesture repeats the mythical operation. And what is postmodernity if not the ultimate defeat of the Enlightenment in its very triumph: when the dialectic of Enlightenment reaches its apogee, the dynamic, rootless postindustrial society directly generates its own myth. In what, then, does the break of modernity exist? Which is the gap or the deadlock that the myth endeavors to cover up? One is almost tempted to return to the old moralistic tradition: capitalism originates in the sin of thrift, of the miserly disposition—the long-discredited Freudian notion of the "anal character" and its link to the capitalist accumulation receives here an unexpected boost.

—Slavoj Žižek, "From the Myth to Agape"

The historical, if not institutional, context for examining hegemonic phantasms and the subsequent frayed relationship among word, world, and origin, as previously discussed, is myth. This particular multidisciplinary, founding role of myth in the humanities is an asset as well as a hindrance to contemporary theoretical inquiry and, I will argue, philosophical and literary studies in general, on which so much of theory depends. It has become customary that when one sees the term *mythology* in critical discourse the assumption, unfortunately, is that some argument for the existence of an eternal, primal, recoverable reality beneath the linguistic surface is crouching toward the interpretive horizon.

While such a use may not be far from how myth typically reasserts itself in contemporary studies, it is worth the time to consider other possibilities for investigating "mythology." Comparative mythology of the nineteenth century, with its folklorist emphases, largely set the stage for the perspective mentioned above. Somewhat consistent with this earlier "comparative" approach is the modern Western bias that *mythos* (irrational story) is a primitive, incomplete, or immature means of expressing *logos* (rationality). Additionally, Western classical "comparativists" of the nineteenth and early twentieth centuries increasingly viewed myth and folklore in particularly "eurocentric" terms, leading to charges that the "mythological" academic enterprise was thoroughly racist and politically suspect in its valorization of cultural progression, if not evolution.

There are other possibilities, besides the political, that become available when discussing or criticizing the use of mythology, however. One, I'll argue, doesn't necessarily need to abandon myth *eo ipso* or blindly follow the affirming or negating lines of inquiry stated above in order to make a strong case for studying mythology in the context of philosophy, religion, and literature. Similarly, one need not fully subscribe to the mystical innovations of the "wisdom traditions" and thereby create a separate world and epistemology so as to address the confusion of language captured, for instance, in the Babel story. "Mythology," like other discourses of origin, can be discussed in terms of theory or "broken hegemony"; that is, "mythology" becomes interesting for its structural "failure" to live up to its own claims to instantiate a hegemonic space.

Mythic narrative or, more generally, myth-related language within these more or less traditional approaches plays only a limited auxiliary role in the interpretation process. Grammar, rhetoric, and aesthetics are presumed to be preempted by the greater reality rising up from within the depths of the story. The ultimate goal sought by these particular suspect perspectives is the capturing of narrative excess within a discursive totality. Even within these prior approaches myths rarely fall neatly into interpretative categories. As any reader of myths knows, mythic narrative always has an initial problem to overcome—the empirical. In other words, the transition from a literal reading to a symbolic reading is a much more difficult task to accomplish than, let's say, the task associated with reading twentieth-century realist fiction.

Again, as discussed in the previous section, the "excess" of a narrative causes a rift between "figure" and "ground" or, more precisely, "saying" and "understanding." There are many ways to complicate this problem, and the first is related to the idea of temporality, a timing in which the present of a myth contains an eternality of meaning. Myth, in this conventional context, allegedly overcomes temporality by preserving a reserve of meaning that makes itself present independent of history. Myth, following this line of inquiry, is pertinent to the study of literature, philosophy, and religion beyond its historical polarity—*mythos* (irrational story) and *logos* (rationality). Myth or mythos, as Aristotle defines it, is not simply or merely plot. Myth does indeed contain self-affirming fantastical and, as we shall see, self-negating discourse—elements that provoke a critical assessment of its self-authenticating authority. Within this split or polyvalenced discourse, however, one can discern many other features and see, in fact, interpretive possibilities that challenge and exceed interpretive, hegemonic frames, past and present.

Rather than being seen as an overcoming of temporality by housing the "eternal," myth can be understood as being deeply divided by it—"remarked," in Derridean or Žižekian terms, by temporality itself. In other words, the traditional assumption that a "great" single, universal truth contained within mythic narrative actually reconciles all variations across time and culture is displaced by myth's multivalent properties. Derrida's Tower of Babel analysis is an instance of this issue of temporality and reveals in relation to this question of timing two simultaneous acts of divine confusion—Tower and Tongue. The destruction or confusion of the Tower, depending on how one sees it, or the myth of architectural catastrophe, dominates the history of interpretation regarding the biblical event. What Derrida offers, however, is a competing myth of confusion that is simultaneous with the myth of the "arrogance" ascribed to the ancient engineers. The competing myth is the myth of unity through language. Presented in this light, the act of divine destruction, as it culminates in linguistic confusion, actually opens a line of inquiry in which a new relationship among philosophy, religion, literature, and naming can emerge.

The point to consider here pertains to the ways in which a theme, in this instance human arrogance, becomes central in one myth and, through thematic migration, universal in other myths. If one were to remain exclusively within this traditional frame of reference, the Tower of Babel story acquires its mythic, hegemonic dimension only insofar as it confirms the power of God and the chronic waywardness of humanity. With Derrida's "Tower and Tongue" analysis, however, the problem of Babel extends beyond these mythic parameters and into an understanding of myth that does not demand interpretive uniformity, which, one could observe, in an ironic way, is the "point" of the myth in the first place. The result of this analysis is not to arrive finally at the original truth but to see that myths contain rifts, gaps, and subsequently proliferate temporally and interpretatively.

A further consideration of temporality in myth leads to the issue of mythic antecedents. In what ways do myths affirm or negate, as we have discussed, propositions regarding the exposition of truth in philosophy, religion, and literature? Mircea Eliade, for instance, in *Myth and Reality,* offers the history of myth as a way of contrasting archaic and modern societies, with the former understanding "myth" as "true story" and the latter positing it as "fiction or illusion."[1] We also know from Heidegger's story of Western philosophy, for instance, that the "Asiatic" mythological culture needed to be supplanted in order for Western philosophy, with its emphasis on *logos,* to emerge.

This perspective was long viewed by historians of religions, such as Mircea Eliade, as a second "fall," a further departure from the eternal truths contained in archaic, sacred texts. Heidegger, on the other hand, sees the departure from mythology as an ascension of humankind, a moving away from superstition toward the truth of "Being":

> In philosophy we can no more go back to Greek philosophy by means of a leap than we can eliminate the advent of Christianity into Western history and thus into philosophy by means of a command. The only possibility is to transform history, that is, truly to bring about the hidden necessity of history into which neither knowledge nor deed reach, and transformation truly brought about is the essence of the creative. For the great beginning of Western philosophy, too, did not come out of nothing. Rather, it became great because it had to overcome its great opposite, the mythical in general and the Asiatic in particular, that is, it had to bring it to the jointure of a truth of Being, and was able to do this.[2]

It may have been Heidegger's "myth," following Schelling and Hegel, that philosophy eclipsed myth, but one can easily see evidence of the opposite—

evidence that philosophy in many ways is entirely dependent on myth, as previously discussed.

The greater trouble with this, as Slavoj Žižek notes, is that myth was never fully eradicated from the beginning of the philosophical tradition—Plato clearly intersperses mythology throughout his dialogues, especially as a means of supporting basic tenets of "philosophical" thought: "The problem with the 'Western mechanistic attitude' is not that it forgot-repressed the ancient holistic Wisdom, but that it *did not break with it thoroughly enough*: it continued to perceive the new universe (of the discursive stance) from the perspective of the old one, of the 'ancient wisdom,' and, of course, from this perspective, the new universe cannot but appear as the catastrophic world which came 'after the Fall.'"[3]

More to the point, however, is the idea of myth functioning as a closed system within which all discursive elements are negotiated and rendered meaningful through this "Western mechanistic attitude." Babel, according to the hegemonic tradition, for example, is a myth *about* human overreaching that describes the relationship between God and humankind. This "universal" story as starting point, then, makes "sense" across disciplines. It is, one could conclude, "reasonable" from a philosophical perspective that God would raze the Tower—any reasonable, all-powerful God would have done the same thing. Myth here gives us the story and its meaning, while philosophy simply affirms it, makes it "reasonable." As Derrida shows, however, Babel has other mythic elements and themes that do not fully correspond to the destruction-of-the-Tower reading. The initial point here is that myths can and do "re-mark" their closings with a "Western mechanistic attitude" and come to function self-deconstructively by their failure to totally limit an interpretive process. Once again Žižek provides a useful exposition of this in his essay "From the Myth to Agape."[4]

Žižek's analysis of myth and *agape* begins with a retrospective commentary on the work of Lacanian Marxists of the late 1960s and 1970s. Drawn to Lacan's anti-Americanism, scholars of the day limited their critiques of literature, philosophy, and culture, according to Žižek, to a few mythemes, not seeing or perhaps ignoring other critical interventions. The "American way of life" myth, which was the focus of analysis at the time, circumscribed cultural phenomena with "false ideology" discourse. Žižek's point in mentioning this limited perspective becomes clearer as he continues to develop the concept of "re-marking" "mythical Fate" and further emphasizes other universal problematics and their aporias. In the first full section of "From the Myth to Agape," entitled "Hamlet before Oedipus," Žižek writes that "when we speak about myths in psychoanalysis, we are effectively speaking about ONE myth, the Oedipus myth—all other Freudian myths (the myth of the primordial father, Freud's version of the Moses myth) are variations of it, although necessary ones."[5] This monomythical reserve informing all Freudian discourse, Žižek observes, carries beyond the borders of psychoanalysis into literature, philosophy, and religion. As necessary as these submyths are to the general problematic of Freudian psychoanalysis, they additionally speak to a limit or boundary that inquiry supposedly should not transgress.

A transgression of the Oedipus-Hamlet boundary entails, as Žižek argues, a "short-circuit," a placing of Hamlet *before* Oedipus. How does this transgressing/short-circuiting/"re-marking" work? "Hamlet," Žižek writes, is, according to a standard psychoanalytic interpretation, a "modernized version of Oedipus [bearing] witness to the strengthening of the Oedipal prohibition of incest in the passage from Antiquity to Modernity."[6] This set of limits around death and incest leads to a pre-Lacanian "naive" psychoanalytic reading of the Hamlet narrative, with an emphasis on obsessional neurosis. Žižek further notes that this depiction of obsessional neurosis is distinctly a "modern phenomenon."[7] While it is certainly informative and useful, it conflicts with a myth or mythic theme that literally predates Oedipus: "The elementary skeleton of the Hamlet narrative (the son revenges his father against the father's evil brother who murdered him and took over his throne; the son survives the illegitimate rule of his uncle by playing a fool and making 'crazy' but truthful remarks) is a universal myth found everywhere, from Nordic cultures through Ancient Egypt up to Iran and Polynesia."[8] Not only could the field of mythology identify numerous pre-Oedipal examples of "revenge," but there is, Žižek observes, a "celestial" or astronomical dimension to the play that runs contrary to the "family narrative." While Žižek does not more fully elaborate on this particular astronomical aspect of the play, treating this observation as an aside, he does raise the issue of multiple interpretative perspectives. Regardless of which approach is dominant, revenge or stars, Žižek ultimately argues that "the Hamlet narrative IS earlier than the Oedipal myth."[9] With this proposition, which will have repercussions for religious discourse, Žižek opens the possibility for radical "re-marking" or "short-circuiting."

Is there any significance to this insight that posits Hamlet as an antecedent to Oedipus? What difference might Hamlet *before* Oedipus make in the study of myth, literature, philosophy, and religion? If one follows Žižek's argument, the implications are enormously significant, insofar as the entirety of Western civilization is predicated not on just the "one" Oedipal myth (incest and patricide) but on the whole of the Oedipus story in its affirmation of a new order (Hegel). What is at stake in this "re-marking" of Hamlet/Oedipus is a reorientation of some, if not all, of the fundamental assumptions guiding Western civilization. Derrida's analysis of the Tower of Babel, as a similar instance of re-marking, reorders the narrative around the destruction/confusion of Tower and Tongue, with the latter a more significant entrance of God into the world of human affairs—confusing a "unity" of language.

Žižek's focus on the distortion of the Hamlet narrative by the Oedipal myth reaches across mythology and directly into Judaism and Christianity, the most immediate foundational myths of Western culture:

> So, in the case of Oedipus and Hamlet, instead of the linear/historicist reading of Hamlet as a secondary distortion of the Oedipal text, the Oedipus myth is (as Hegel already claimed) the grounding myth of the Western Greek civilization (the suicidal jump of the Sphinx representing the disintegration of the old pre-Greek universe); and it is in Hamlet's "distortion" of the Oedipus that its repressed content articulates itself—the proof of it being the fact that the Hamlet matrix is found everywhere in pre-Classic mythology, up to the Ancient Egypt itself whose spiritual defeat is signaled by the suicidal jump of the Sphinx. (And, incidentally, what if the same goes even for Christianity: is not Freud's thesis that the murder of God in the New Testament brings to the light the "disavowed" trauma of the Old Testament?)[10]

Through a rapid series of commentaries on contemporary film, *The Bridges of Madison County*, and *Terms of Endearment*, Žižek develops the idea of "melodramatic reversal," a moment in a film or text, generally, in which some excess of knowledge is revealed to the principal character by some unassuming or "ignorant" figure.

This idea of textual excess yields an alternative line of interpretative possibilities that the tradition proper could not have engendered. For instance, in *Terms of Endearment,* Žižek writes, Debra Winger's character "tells her son (who actively despises her for being abandoned by his father, her husband) that she is well aware of how much he really loves her—she knows that some time in the future, after her death, he will acknowledge this to himself; at that moment, he will feel guilty for his past hatred of [her], so she is now letting him know in advance that she is pardoning him and thus delivering him of the future burden of guilt. . . . This manipulation of the future guilt feeling is melodrama at its best; its very gesture of pardon culpabilizes the son in advance. (Therein, in this culpabilization, in this imposition of a symbolic debt, through the very act of exoneration, resides the highest trick of Christianity.)"[11] Here Žižek brings together two lines of analysis as they relate to myth and reversal. The first, in connection with Oedipus/Hamlet, shows that founding myths "suture" narrative to the "Real of logos" and thereby cover up a more fundamental "gap" or "deadlock" in narrative.[12] In the second instance this covering-up of the "gap" or "deadlock" makes possible a dramatic reversal that is not simply an instantiation of a binary opposite. While its analysis twists and turns through Hamlet, Aristotle, and Marx, "From the Myth to Agape" eventually settles on its main concern—the concept of indebtedness and culpability that was first breached in *Hamlet* and contemporary film.

Hamlet's response to Horatio's sympathetic observation about Claudius's and Gertrude's wedding—"thrift, thrift"—is an ironic comment directed at the fact that the food from the funeral furnished the wedding banquet. The economic interpretation goes beyond the frugality of the new king and his sister-in-law bride; it represents another frugality—a failure to "pay" proper due to the dead King Hamlet.[13] This theme of indebtedness leads Žižek to his culminating discussion of Christianity *before* Judaism. Does "thrift, thrift" also apply to Christian theology? Does a Christian frugality always fall short of paying its debt to Jesus for paying humanity's debt?

The answer to these questions can be found in understanding desire and its relationship to consumption. Once a sacrifice is made "to [the] gods," Žižek writes, "the innermost part of the slaughtered animal (heart, intestines), we are free to enjoy a hearty meal of the remaining meat. Instead of enabling free consumption without sacrifice, the modern 'total economy' which wants to dispense with this 'superfluous' ritualized sacrifice generates the paradoxes of thrift—there is NO generous consumption, consumption is allowed only insofar as it functions as the form of appearance of its opposite."[14] In this context "thrift" is both a response to excess (Aristotle's moderation) and a result of excess itself (Freud's theory of fixation at the anal stage). The two possibilities for "thrift" are in effect deadlocked in paradox, just as the Buddhist desire to end desire becomes as obsessive as any coveting of commodity.

Žižek, on the other hand, sees an alternative to these options of "thrifty consumption":

> How, then, are we to break out of the deadlock of the thrifty consumption, if these two exits are false? Perhaps, it is the Christian notion of agape that points towards the way out: "For God so loved the world that he gave his one and only Son, that whoever believes in Him shall not perish but have eternal life" (John 3:16). One usually opposes here the Jewish rigorous Justice and the Christian Mercy, the inexplicable gesture of undeserved pardon: we, humans, were born in sin, we cannot ever repay our debts and redeem ourselves through our own acts—our only salvation lies in God's Mercy, in His supreme sacrifice. In this very gesture of breaking the chain of Justice through the inexplicable act of Mercy, of paying our debt, Christianity imposes on us an even stronger debt: we are forever indebted to Christ, we cannot [ever] repay him for what he did to us. The Freudian name for such an excessive pressure which we cannot ever remunerate is, of course, superego.[15]

"Christian Mercy," in the progression of mythical adaptation, seems to trump "Jewish Justice," with Jesus, as God, exacting His punishment on himself and thus releasing humanity from its obligation to pay for its own collective sins. From a Judeo-Christian perspective Jesus, as the proxy victim, incurs humanity's debt and in doing so transfers it to himself—the ultimate act of divine mercy that is at the core of the Christian transition from Jewish mythology.

The problem with this trajectory from Judaism to Christianity, however, is that it assumes that agape allows one to transition from mythology into a "Real." Rather than seeing agape or the divine act of mercy as a superseding of Jewish justice, particularly as Jesus's sacrifice forms the foundation of a "new" testament, it is important to recognize an important "re-marking" of the so-called Old Testament narrative. Again, Žižek writes that, far from delivering humanity from indebtedness, "Christianity imposes on us an even stronger debt: we are forever indebted to Christ, we cannot [ever] repay him for what he did to us." In this sense humanity is not relieved of its debt at all; instead the debt is "consolidated" into a higher state of indebtedness—one that, unlike the former Jewish debt, cannot ever be repaid: "Judaism is conceived as the religion of the superego (of man's subordination to the jealous, mighty and severe God), in contrast to the Christian God of Mercy and Love." Žižek continues: "However, it is precisely through NOT demanding from us the price for our sins, through paying this price for us Himself, that the Christian God of Mercy establishes itself as the supreme superego agency: 'I paid the highest price for your sins, and you are thus indebted to me FOREVER. . . .' Is this God as the superego agency, whose very Mercy generates the indelible guilt of believers, the ultimate horizon of Christianity? Is the Christian agape another name for Mercy?"[16] Žižek "re-marks" Christianity as a "line of credit" that will never reach a "zero balance"—a hyper-Judaism or, as we shall see, a reversal of Judaism's "enigma of God."

Critical to the "re-marking" of the Christian narrative is the concept of identification within belief, which appears to shift from Jewish indebtedness to Christian hyper-indebtedness. Christian hyper-indebtedness, unlike the indebtedness of Judaism, leads to a reconfiguration of the divine as an approachable figure, which is to say that Christianity, according to Žižek, allows a reversal of the Jewish God as wholly Other. In a somewhat ambiguous set of maneuvers, Žižek offers a version of Christianity that reverses the age-old predicate of "perfection," a concept of the divine that also applies to paganism.

When God becomes human, as Žižek describes, the Christian believer is set on a peculiar path on which he or she must come to identify not with the "enigmatic perfection of God," but with the very accessible "imperfection" of God in the form of Jesus:

> Is it not crucial to accomplish this move also apropos of the notion of Dieu obscur, of the elusive, impenetrable God: this God has to be impenetrable also to Himself, He has to have a dark side, an otherness in Himself, something that is in Himself more than Himself? Perhaps, this accounts for the shift from Judaism to Christianity: Judaism remains at the level of the enigma OF God, while Christianity moves to the enigma IN God Himself. Far from being opposed to the notion of logos as the Revelation in/through the

Word, Revelation and the enigma In God are strictly correlative, the two aspects of one and the same gesture. That is to say, it is precisely because God is an enigma also IN AND FOR HIMSELF, because he has an unfathomable Otherness in Himself, that Christ had to emerge to reveal God not only to humanity, but TO GOD HIMSELF—it is only through Christ that God fully actualizes himself as God.

Is this impenetrability of God to Himself not rendered manifest in Christ's "Father, why did you forsake me?"—the Christian version of the Freudian "Father, can't you see that I am burning?"? This total abandonment by God is the point at which Christ becomes FULLY human, the point at which the radical gap that separates God from man is transposed into God himself. The Christian notion of the link between man and God thus inverts the standard pagan notion according to which man approaches God through spiritual purification, through casting off the "low" material/sensual aspects of his being and thus elevating himself towards God. When I, a human being, experience myself as cut off from God, at that very moment of the utmost abjection, I am absolutely close to God, since I find myself in the position of the abandoned Christ. There is no "direct" identification with (or approach to) the divine majesty: I identify myself with God only through identifying myself with the unique figure of God-the-Son abandoned by God. This divine self-abandonment, this impenetrability of God to himself, signals God's fundamental imperfection. And it is only within this horizon that the properly Christian Love can emerge, a Love beyond Mercy. Love is always love for the Other insofar as he is lacking—we love the Other BECAUSE of his limitation, helplessness, ordinariness even. In contrast to the pagan celebration of the Divine (or human) Perfection, the ultimate secret of the Christian love is, perhaps, that it is the loving attachment to the Other's imperfection. And THIS Christian legacy, often obfuscated, is today more precious than ever.[17]

This lengthy excerpt details a series of thematic transitions in which Žižek completes a set of necessary "re-markings" that come not just from the logic of the narrative but from an internal paradoxical point that makes "re-marking" possible. God as a perfect impenetrable Other, even to "Himself," enters into a process of radical reversal in so far as God arrives at a moment in which "He" is completely accessible to "Himself" and humanity.

This, according to Žižek's "re-marking" of Christianity, is made possible through Jesus incurring humanity's debt of sin. It is important to view this "sin" not as "forgiven," as if there is some meta-accounting program that can merely assign a "paid in full" to a "bill"; this "sin," rather, has been assumed by another, in this case Jesus or God Himself, as the "lien holder." With "forgiveness" preempted by a "third-party" payment made on behalf of humanity, God must undergo a "full" transition into the human, as Žižek notes. The critical point, then, in the "re-marking" of the Christian narrative comes when God, as Jesus, becomes not wholly perfect but wholly imperfect—human.

Christianity, after this complete paradoxical transition, is a religion predicated not on God's perfection but instead on God's imperfection or limit, a limit that rests upon an eternal space between sin and payment. This is what John D. Caputo refers to as the weakness of God, an identification with the fully human Jesus, although Caputo is unwilling to follow Žižek into an orthodox atheism: "Žižek is only half right to say that the perverse core of Christianity lay in Jesus' being abandoned and that what we should learn from his death on the cross is that there is no Big Other to save us, so we should get on with our lives. The other half, what Žižek leaves out, is that in this abandonment there lies the weak force of God. . . . The power of God is not pagan violence, brute power, or vulgar magic; it is the power of powerlessness, the power of the call, the power of protest that rises up from innocent suffering and calls out against it."[18] Žižek's concept of agape may mitigate the difference between these two versions of Christian "weakness."

The ultimate "horizon" of Christianity, however, as Žižek argues, requires an abandonment of Christianity itself—just as God abandons Himself in the person of Jesus. Agape then may just be the "calling out" that Caputo demands. The radical "re-marking" here extends far beyond the "melodramatic reversal" Žižek presents in his film analysis. "Re-marking," as it relates to the Christian myth, takes shape only in "agape," which Žižek views as an identification with absolute abandonment; that is, as he writes, "when I, a human being, experience myself as cut off from God, at that very moment of the utmost abjection, I am absolutely close to God, since I find myself in the position of the abandoned Christ."[19]

This "re-marked" Christianity unfolds rather loosely at the conclusion of the essay; a more thorough elaboration appears as a book-length study that Žižek entitled *The Puppet and the Dwarf: The Perverse Core of Christian-*

ity: "When Christ dies, what dies with him is the secret hope discernible in 'Father, why has thou forsaken me?': the hope that there is a father who has abandoned me. The 'Holy Spirit' is the community deprived of its support in the big Other."[20] Deprived of the "big Other," Christianity becomes a social philosophy dedicated to an ideal of justice—not redemption, necessarily, and clearly not physical resurrection. "Re-marked" Christianity, which we will see in the later section on the novelist Leo Tolstoy, redefines the mythological authority behind "sacred" speech and language. The reversal of the Christ myth or narrative, which should not be burdened with an oversimplified association with fiction, does much more than simply provide yet another interpretation of the "Jesus-event." As previously discussed, "re-marking" alters the textual variables from *within* the narrative and, at the same time, offers the possibility, as Žižek explains, of a total "obliteration of the signifying network." In this instance the Christ myth becomes an interpretive "crisis," as the "Jesus-event," understood as a way to identify with the atheist Jesus, overturns an entire theological signifying network—traditional Christianity.

2.2 Myth, Symbol, Continuity in Eliade

For the past fifty years at least, Western scholars have approached the study of myth from a viewpoint markedly different from, let us say, that of the nineteenth century. Unlike their predecessors, who treated myth in the usual meaning of the word, that is, as "fable," "invention," "fiction," they have accepted it as it was understood in the archaic societies, where, on the contrary, "myth" means a "true story" and, beyond that, a story that is a most precious possession because it is sacred, exemplary, significant.

—Mircea Eliade, *Myth and Reality*

Before examining the fuller implications of a Žižekian "re-marking" or "short-circuiting" of myth, and more specifically the "comedy of Christianity," it is important to take account of three major fields in which myth or sacred speech has been defined. The linguistic focus that follows returns us to a wider discussion of language, with which we began; however, this attention to language of course has implications for history and politics, implications that, I believe, a final section on Žižek's concept of the "parallax gap" will address.

Mircea Eliade's "phenomenology," Claude Lévi-Strauss's "structuralism," and Paul Ricouer's "hermeneutics" show what is at stake in understanding myth as a "network," a network to be obliterated. The first figure to be considered is Mircea Eliade, the father of the history of religions. Eliade's theory of mythic language and his reliance on the concept of *coincidentia oppositorium* (coincidence of opposites) will be central concerns initially. Claude Lévi-Strauss and Paul Ricouer bring the analysis closer to issues of hermeneutics and post-structuralism, sharpening the focus on a Žižekian parallax view.

Invoking the sacred, as it is present in myth, provides a number of opportunities to view the theoretical limits of phenomenological, structural, and hermeneutical analyses. The "criteriology," as Paul Ricoeur would express it, of these approaches allows for a developed understanding of critical interpretation in religious theory as it appears today. While the methods that I have listed belong to a particular scholarly era, they do not remain within the confines of that era, and the issues that gave rise to these "conflicts of interpretations" continue to thrive on a series of engagements within and in opposition to a multiplicity of discursive fields. The writings of contemporary figures in religious theory rely upon the critical insights of these prior investigations, and a review of these will underscore the significance of contemporary theoretical concerns. Additionally, the primary issues relating to ontology, epistemology, and ethics that prompted these investigations are perhaps more pressing today than they were for a previous generation of thinkers. The common issue across the three fields (phenomenology, structuralism, and hermeneutics) is mythic language and the possibility of meaning.

Mircea Eliade's contribution to the formation of a new subdiscipline in the field of religious studies, the history of religions, is immeasurable and at times difficult to define. David Cave economically states that "during the sixties and seventies the history of religions largely rotated around his insights, orientations, and terminology."[21] In the early 1980s, with the rise of deconstruction, Eliade was heralded by many scholars as an "anti-Derrida," a protector of a "something" *hors-texte*. Eliade's own later writings and addresses culminate in a very strong case for placing him in this role—a role that also moves him into the "New Age" camp, with its idea of a revitalized "primitivism." As I have argued in another context, there is a way to read Eliade as a "postmodernist," although this requires an almost exclusive emphasis on his earlier work, especially *Patterns in Comparative Religion* (1967).[22] Simply—perhaps too simply—Eliade's body of work ultimately points to an understanding of reality as bifurcated, with one part sacred and the other profane. The meaningful aspect of this age-old division comes as Eliade develops a "religious philosophy"—largely Catholic, I would contend—that strives to show the ways in which these two distinct "worlds" encounter one another.

While the founding assumption of his work is rooted in a traditional religious and philosophical "common sense"—hence the simplicity—Eliade's larger theory of this dialectic of the sacred and profane is enormously complex and abstract, even to the point that his writings have been attacked for their perceived lack of methodology. For the purpose of explaining what is for the most part a mystical process, Eliade invents a comprehensive nomenclature that ties all the world's religions together under the concept of hierophany—the manifestation of the sacred within the profane. Religious rituals, objects, myths, and experiences all follow the same ontological necessity—to express the sacred in the midst of the profane. The underlying phenomenon of the religious is universal, according to Eliade; that is to say, the *same* sacred pushes through different rituals, objects, language, and experiences. To the extent that the world's religious traditions differ, they do so only at the surface level. The greater depth, the sacred, is completely uniform in its absolute reality.

For the phenomenologist or "historian" of religions Mircea Eliade, myth, in the context of archaic societies, means a "true story." Eliade takes these myths to be "true," which is to say, inherently meaningful, within very precise cultural and historical contexts. And while some myths may not be "true stories" for us, they nevertheless are "true" in some circumstances for others, or "true" relative to our myths. More important than a myth's veracity at face value is its "sacrality," which is to say the way it joins an ab- *perceived* solute reality with the everydayness of human activity. Eliade views myth not as a "problem" of interpretation but as the means of interpretation, with language functioning free from the "gap" or "rift" after the Fall. It is important to keep in mind that Eliade's theory of history, or phenomenology of history, allows for a division of the sacred and profane only under the condition that a dialectical inversion is not only possible but imminent. With this necessary condition myths are true insofar as they participate in the unfolding of a transcendent reality.

From the beginning it is important to point out Eliade's limitations on the issue of language. Unlike some of his contemporaries, Lévi-Strauss, for instance, Eliade did not spend his time working through a comprehensive, general theory of language, although Douglas Allen argues in *Myth and Religion in Mircea Eliade* that such a linguistic theory exists, albeit cryptically. The horizon of a transcendent reality, one could infer, provided for Eliade a remedy for any imperfection in language itself. One sees this most clearly in his understanding of symbolism, with the sacred "coming through" to the viewer as an original or ecstatic experience. Thomas J. J. Altizer, in *Mircea Eliade and the Sacred,* observes in the most concise and perceptive way to date Eliade's "linguistic theory" as an element of metahistory:

> For our history is rooted in absolute autonomy, it is enclosed within itself, wholly isolated from a transcendent ground, it is simply the product of human and natural powers. So likewise the language of our history is a language created by a profane consciousness, it has abandoned a sacred or transcendent ground, having been created by an immanent consciousness that is wholly absorbed in the immediate here and now of profane existence. Consequently, the language of the Sacred can be no more than a meaningless cipher to the language of the profane; and, for Eliade, the language of the sacred can have only a dialectical relation to the language of the profane: the sacred can become manifest only through a negation of the language of the profane.
>
> Quite simply the language of the sacred is myth, but what we moderns understand as myth only appears when the sacred has disappeared from our horizon. Eliade, along with other modern scholars, has taught us that myth dissolves the world of concrete time and space.[23]

Altizer's assessment of Eliade is, I'll argue, accurate and consistent with the general theory of the dialectic elaborated throughout Eliade's work. Profane language bears the burden of inadequacy when it comes to divulging the content of the sacred.

There are several reasons for this, and the first has to do with Eliade's resistance to what he defines as "reductionism." Citing Frazer and Tylor as the primary examples of the "confusionist" position, Eliade contests reducing religious phenomena to any profane discourse—history, sociology,

psychology, or science.[24] Ambiguously included among these profane discourses is the "literary," which Eliade views as having dual functions—empirical and symbolic. It is the latter that draws Eliade's attention, not so
much for the fact that he is a "writer" but for the fact that literature, because
of language, is able to preserve the "symbol"—the ideal and therefore un-
deranalyzed axis upon which the sacred and profane turn. Literature then
is distinct from myth when its language "dissolves the world of concrete
time and space."

The dissolution, however, leads Eliade into a methodological quandary,
with the ultimate mythological move toward the sacred confused by the
seemingly unexplainable transitions between profane "things" and sacred
"essences." One occurrence illustrating this appears in Eliade's journal,
in which he reports a discussion with an interviewer. When asked how he
came to a particular interpretation of a tapestry, Eliade replied that when
he looked at it, that is what he "saw." Under normal circumstances "Rorschaching" as a disciplinary endeavor is not permitted, but with Eliade it
is not only permitted but expected. The critical point here has to do with
"transition"—moving from the profane to the sacred. Žižekian theory
places this particular practice within the realm of "re-marking"; however,
unlike Žižek, Eliade provides little to no explanation of how this or any
reversal of the sacred/profane takes place—the coincidentia oppositorum remains a mystery.

One way of deciphering Eliade's philosophy of the sacred/profane dialectic is to investigate his understanding of language and myth. Douglas
Allen, in the opening chapter of Myth and Religion in Mircea Eliade, explains the issue of methodology in Eliade's work by way of his critique of
"reductionism," a process of rendering intelligible rituals, object, texts, and
experiences that, according to Eliade, strips phenomena of sacrality. The
remaining question, however, is, what is this "sacred" that escapes knowing? Clearly, the sacred for Eliade is a separate reality; whether it resembles
a Kantian noumena or a Hindu Brahma remains the "irreducible" in the
"reduction."

The principal site of the sacred, for Eliade, is myth, religious myth. His
fundamental "theoretical" assumption is that all religious myth (perhaps
all myth) brings forth the deepest levels of human existence. That is, for
Eliade religious myth, through divine language, makes present the sacred.

I place the term *theoretical* within quotation marks to suggest that Eliade's grand assumption is not necessarily rooted in a detailed elaboration of philosophy and religious studies. In fact, for Eliade much of the groundwork for these various terms and concepts comes from his "intuitive" engagement with religious phenomena. One wishes to be fair to Eliade and agree that many of his insights, especially as they regard the "symbol" and "archetypes," can be traced to figures such as Carl Jung and Ernst Cassirer. In many other instances, however, Eliade's "methodology" springs forth more as conjecture and creative "Rorschaching" than as exact analysis. Defenders of Eliade would hasten to add that it is his very separation from modern discourse and method that makes Eliade the great interpreter of symbols. Through this "antireductionism," as Eliade defined it, one discovers the great sacred "system" beneath all phenomena—this is in large measure the methodological beginning of "the history of religions" as a subdiscipline of religious studies.

If everyday reality is merely the play of surfaces situated on top of a greater reality, then myth is the space of commerce between the two. Unlike ritual objects that can easily vary from culture to culture, myth has the advantage of symbols and archetypes (real, eternal entities). These, Eliade and others, particularly Jung, believed, created a system within which ultimate meaning was communicated to individuals. This in many respects is a hyper-re-marking, to use a Žižekian term again. What an individual believes to be an ordinary object in a dream, for instance, is actually radically transformed into an archetype. So, for example, I could say that after gardening I dreamed about a "tree." This "tree," according to Eliade, is not just the residue of my day; it is a "cosmic tree," representing eternal renewal.

Given Eliade's antireductionism, any image or object appearing in experience, dreamed or otherwise, corresponds to some greater symbol or archetype that can be found in myth:

> In general it can be said that myth, as experienced by archaic societies, (1) constitutes the history of the acts of the Supernaturals; (2) that this History is considered to be absolutely *true* (because it is concerned with realities) and *sacred* (because it is the work of Supernaturals); (3) that myth is always related to a "creation," it tells how something came into existence, or how a pattern of behavior, an institution, a manner of working were established; this is why myths constitute the paradigms for all significant human acts;

(4) that by knowing the myth one knows the "origin" of things and hence can control and manipulate them at will; this is not an "external," "abstract" knowledge but a knowledge that one "experiences" ritualistically, either by ceremonially recounting the myth or by performing the ritual for which it is the justification; (5) that in one way or another one "lives" the myth, in the sense that one is seized by the sacred, exalting power of the events recollected or re-enacted.[25]

In all five definitions Eliade emphasizes the "nature" of myth as that which radically alters perceivable reality from exterior space—the space of the supernaturals. Of course this Eliadean "re-marking" is entirely different from a Žižekian "re-marking" or "short-circuiting," but the notion that some "bolt" cuts across the space of perception is shared—except that one offers "supernaturals," and the other does not.

For Eliade the "phenomenology" of religious experience is governed by these five points defining myth, with the key understanding of a "supernatural" source critical to all experience that one would characterize as "religious." The "crypto-commerce," as I describe it, is then made possible as this "supernatural" exterior forms a conduit to the human mind, a mind that is for Eliade fundamentally structured to "receive" the sacred. The passage from myth to understanding, or from "saying" to "understanding," is authenticated by the "sacred," and it is moreover this sacred that allegedly erases any "gap," "rift," "fissure," or "difference," for that matter, from the "saying"/"understanding" event. While there is a plurality in saying, a univocal understanding is protected by the origin of all communication, the sacred. Of course, Eliade's discussion of religious ideas and his interpretations of various religious phenomena are complex, especially as Eliade weaves together disparate themes and images, but the basic methodological procedure underlying all of his readings relies on what he calls the "supernaturals."

One exemplary study from Eliade's *Images and Symbols: Studies in Religious Symbolism* demonstrates his rhetorically nuanced invocation of these "supernaturals": "Observations of the Symbolism of Shells."[26] In the essay Eliade provides a wide-ranging discussion of the role of seashells in religious practice, ceremony, and custom. His analysis draws from the turn-of-the-century work of a number of ethnographers, but it is Eliade who pulls these "local" studies into a larger symbolic framework. "Oysters, sea-shells,

the snail and the pearl," Eliade writes, "figure constantly in aquatic cosmology as well as in sexual symbolism. They all participate, indeed, in the
sacred powers which are concentrated in the Waters, in the Moon, and in
Woman."[27] The first point is fairly easy to accept: oysters, seashells, and
pearls are found across different religious traditions, especially in cloth-
ing, dietary habits, and narrative contexts. One could view this from an
environmental perspective; that is to say, people living in coastal regions or
near larger bodies of water would make use of objects in their world for religious or cultural practices—this would include aquatic life. Bedouins, for
instance, because of geographical location would not incorporate seashells
into their religious discourse.

"Oysters, sea-shells, the snail, and the pearl," however, represent more
than ready-to-hand objects for Eliade. These objects are thought to have
"symbolic" value: "They are, moreover, emblems of these forces for a variety of reasons—the resemblance between the marine shell and the genital
organs of woman, the relations between oysters, waters and the moon, and,
lastly the gynaecological and embryological symbolism of the pearl formed
within the oyster."[28] Here the crypto-commerce between the mollusk kingdom and sacred reality takes place along the visual and thematic axes.
Shells, according to Eliade, "look like" female genitalia, pearls undergo a
gestation, and bivalves take the shape of embryos. This can be approached
from two different assumptions regarding the "origin" of religious ritual
practice and symbol.

The Eliadean perspective asserts that there are "supernatural" forces
shaping the choice of ritual object. Like a Platonic bifurcated reality, the
eternal symbols of human fertility, male and female genitalia, are repro-
duced in nature, seashells, snails, and oysters. Archaic people, Eliade believed, were able to see this correspondence between eternal symbol and
natural object and thus forge a bond with the sacred. In all aspects of life,
then, sacred reality is assumed to secretly inscribe itself into the natural
world, leaving a path back to its wider horizon. The Eliadean paranoid
"method," if you will, is predicated on this bridgeable division of the sacred
and profane. A historical or material perspective, however, would see all the
instances of crypto-commerce pointed out by Eliade but conclude that it is
collective coincidence or the functioning of the human imagination. In this

light seashells merely look like female genitalia when the imagination does its work of construction.

Two entirely different arguments then emerge from this "similitude" of objects—the sacred order writes itself into the natural world, and the human imagination is highly adept at forging systems of likenesses. Eliade's catalog of seashells in religious ritual across the world's religions is quite impressive but ultimately does nothing more than make the numerical case for "hierophany." In other words, just because we see seashells in pre-Columbian, ancient Chinese, ancient Japanese, Hindu, Greek, predynastic Egyptian, and Christian traditions doesn't mean that this likeness is sacred "homology" or that it is formed in accordance with "sacred models."[29] Human beings all over the world and across time share an anatomy, and it is entirely plausible that these appendages, organs, and whatever else human beings have would "be seen" in the vastness of the natural world—horses and seahorses merely look alike; there is no necessary homology apart from our human ability to determine likeness that draws them together. The final analysis stated here, however, would have been viewed by Eliade as "reductionist" insofar as it rests on an explanatory set of assumptions devoid of sacred reality as an eternal, determining, ultimate state of affairs.

Let us examine briefly Eliade's final "pearl as symbol" example from "Observations on the Symbolism of Shells." While seashells resemble female genitalia and oysters look like embryos, pearls participate more directly in the process of symbolization. Citing an ancient Eastern myth, Eliade develops the idea of the pearl as a symbol of conception: "A tradition of Eastern origin explains the birth of a pearl as the child of lightning penetrating into a mussel; the pearl this being the result of union between Fire and Water. St. Ephrem makes use of this ancient myth to illustrate the Immaculate Conception as well as the spiritual birth of the Christ in the baptism of Fire."[30] The mythical trajectory toward Christianity is continued as Eliade refers to an Iranian symbolization in which the pearl represents the "Saviour." Again Eliade moves closer to the Christian tradition with references to Origen and pseudo-Macarius:

> The Pearl, great, precious and royal, belonging to the royal diadem, is appropriate only to the king. The king alone may wear this pearl. No one else is allowed to wear a pearl like it. Thus, a man who is not born of the royal

and divine spirit, and is not one of the sons of God—of whom it is written that: "as many as received him, to them gave he power to become the sons of God"—cannot wear the precious heavenly pearl, image of the ineffable light which is the Saviour. For he has not become a son of the king. Those who wear and possess the pearl will live and reign with the Christ for all eternity."[31]

Spanning several disparate religious traditions and touching upon themes in Gnostic Christianity, the symbol of the pearl, with its "conception" through Water and Fire, comes not only to mean the Christian Savior but to encapsulate all the Christian narrative.

By invoking the Gnostic text *Acts of Thomas,* Eliade opens the symbolism of the pearl to include a second "Fall," the incarnation, baptism, the human soul, and salvation: "In the famous Gnostic scripture *Acts of Thomas,* the quest of the pearl symbolizes the spiritual drama of the fall of man and his salvation; a Prince from the Orient arrives in Egypt in search of the pearl, which is guarded by monstrous serpents. To obtain it, the Prince has to pass through a number of initiatory trials."[32] The story of the Prince continues with a struggle and the intercession of God the Father after the Prince's sacrifice. From the Gnostic point of view, the pearl resonates with the idea of a divinity within all people, and the "quest" becomes one's journey to salvation, which Eliade sees more fully in Christian terms:

> The pearl signifies the mystery of the transcendent revealed to the senses, the manifestation of God in the Cosmos. Thanks to Gnosticism and to Christian theology, this ancient symbol of Reality and of Life-without-Death acquired new valencies; the immortal soul, the "Saviour saved," the Christ-king. Let us underline once more the *continuity* of the various meanings of the pearl, from the most archaic and elementary to the most complex symbolisms elaborated by Gnostic and orthodox speculation.[33]

Eliade's analysis of the myth of the pearl allows him to create an all-encompassing, hegemonic Reality within which each instantiation of the pearl moves the "object-symbol" ever closer to the "Christ-king."

The key term here, which appears italicized in Eliade's text, is "continuity." This "continuity," or crypto-commerce, is the work of the dialectic that forever moves these various objects closer to their full symbolic meaning, which is for Eliade exclusively Christian. "Exclusively Christian," however, appears as an unacknowledged problem for Eliade insofar as he must venture "outside" the Christian tradition "proper" (to Gnosticism) to authenticate his "Christian" pearl. The pearl, as a symbol, is or would be the Žižekian "hard kernel," the Lacan *l'objet petit a* that cuts across all discourse and experience, leaving in its wake not totality but "gap." The difference within Eliade's understanding of the dialectic, however, comes as the division of opposites is finally reconciled within/as the sacred Reality.

The obvious question at this point is, does the dialectic actually overcome the "gap" between object and symbol? Or does the Hegelian/Žižekian "hard kernel" persist? There are at least two ways of approaching this question. First, Eliade's dialectic or "continuity" of the "symbol" was developed to address what he considered to be a panhistorical, transcultural existential yearning for some greater meaning in human life: the "history of religions" is fundamentally, as David Cave acknowledges in the title of his book, a "new humanism." Second, in developing the dialectic of the "symbol," Eliade was attempting to overcome a "modern" practice of "reduction" or totalization of religious phenomena and experience, for example, rendering all things "religious" as neurosis or as simple elements within an agricultural cycle.

In both instances one can see the greatness in Eliade's scholarship, along with his commitment to confronting something "postmodernists" find so objectionable in "modernism"—the insistence on totality. The problem, if one sees a problem, is that Eliade's dialectic does not curtail "reductionism"; it merely makes it more palatable by associating it with the sacred, which is no different philosophically than denouncing reductionism in the name of the unconscious or the economic. In this sense Eliade never manages to accomplish his "antireductionist" mission insofar as he gathers (reduces) all phenomena under the "continuity" of the sacred, which eventually becomes an "ironic," wholly Christian sacred.

Released from the totality of the Christian sacred, the symbol of the pearl can take on very different meanings. For instance, the pearl could be the Lacanian *l'objet petit a,* or it could be "Life-without-Injustice," as one would find in a Christian atheism. What is significant about Eliade's work is its emphasis on tracking the commerce between allegedly separate spheres—the sacred and the profane. The basic philosophical problem of joining particulars with the universal, which he identifies as a religious concern, is not only a philosophical endeavor of figuring out the rules of a system but a larger theoretical burden of identifying the system of systems that makes any use of the dialectic possible.

Mircea Eliade's "history of religions" was informed by his scholarly work in comparative world religions. He was not an ethnographer, but he relied heavily on the fieldwork of anthropologists, from which he developed many of his cultural facts. His theory of symbols and archetypes shares a great deal with Jungian depth psychology, to which Eliade was more than sympathetic. During his later career many compared his writings with those of the structuralist anthropologist Claude Lévi-Strauss. The comparisons at first are rather easily made. Lévi-Strauss and Eliade shared an interest in the same content area, mythology and non-Western cultures. Both men seemed to relate the particulars of human life to some wider system—the sacred for Eliade and linguistic structure for Lévi-Strauss.

The comparison, however, begins to wane after these generalities. This becomes clearer with a historical footnote. On a rainy night, as reported in Eliade's journal, Lévi-Strauss and Eliade shared a cab ride after a dinner party in Chicago and accidentally ended up switching raincoats. The two never really spoke, and the "exchange" that took place remained at the level of rain apparel, which is fairly close to where the "intellectual" exchange and similarity ends as well. Where Eliade saw the "continuity" of symbols with a sacred Real, Lévi-Strauss saw the logic of structure, primarily a linguistic structure with a similar, yet vastly divergent understanding of the dialectic. Marcel Hénaff describes the differences between Eliade and Lévi-Strauss more assertively when he describes myths as not being situated on the side of "plausibility or reference," which is to say that, according to Lévi-Strauss, myths function according to an "internal unity" and "logical coherency," not some extranarrative historical reality or supernatural reality.[34]

2.3 Lévi-Strauss and Myth-Systems

Mythology confronts the students with a situation which at first sight appears contradictory. On the one hand it would seem that in the course of a myth anything is likely to happen. There is no logic, no continuity. Any characteristic can be attributed to any subject; every conceivable relation can be found. With myth, everything becomes possible. But on the other hand, this apparent arbitrariness is belied by the astounding similarity be-

tween myths collected in widely different regions. Therefore the problem: If the content of a myth is contingent, how are we going to explain the fact that myths throughout the world are so similar?
                                    —Claude Lévi-Strauss, *Structural Anthropology*

As we have seen, Eliade's attempts to bridge the sacred/profane binary lead him to develop a "methodology" in which dialectical reversal allegedly subverts scientific reduction. The initial problem, however, of joining "saying" and "understanding" through symbols and archetypes leaves a number of irresolvable issues, with the question of "sacred reductionism" still pending. Fundamentally, Eliade's dialectic of the sacred requires a blind acceptance of the power of the sacred to overcome difference and fix, finally, all references within itself as symbol. The tension between structuralist anthropologists and "symbolists" (Mircea Eliade and Carl Jung) over the concept of reference, at this juncture, returns us to issues of language.

While Lévi-Strauss and Eliade, at first glance, seem to be involved in the same enterprise, we learn rather quickly that their respective methodologies could not be more opposed. This obvious opposition is further complicated by the addition of hermeneutics to the conversation, which again places the question of methodology and language at the center of the debate. Marcel Hénaff, in *Claude Lévi-Strauss and the Making of Structuralism,* writes that making this distinction between structuralist and symbolist projects is crucial to understanding the stakes of structural anthropology: "These analyses (symbolist, psychological, and sociological) consider myths to be waiting for their conceptual translation. This is the kind of presupposition that Lévi-Strauss wants to set aside from the beginning. For him, myths must be taken as they present themselves, not so that they can be translated into another form of discourse, but to show that these myths say very well, very completely, what they say."[35] Here one can see the influence of Georges Dumézil in Lévi-Strauss's structuralist project. Contrary to the method of classical comparative mythology or, indeed, Eliade's "symbolist" approach, Dumézil perceived the significance of understanding mythic equivalences or homologies in the context of structures, not particulars, as one would find in "onomastics," which informed his early work.[36]

What myths say "very well" is that a text is governed by the logic of its narrative structure—Lévi-Strauss's "Structural Analysis of Myth," in which he examines the Oedipus story, is a classic of this structuralist ex-egesis. The move, for example, from the symbolist approach to the struc-turalist method, to which Oedipus analysis belongs, requires a relocation of meaning into the narrative itself, which is taken to be a complete linguistic "system." The "setting aside," as it were, of "conceptual translation," as Hé-naff states, necessitates a redefinition of narrative as an economy of linguis-tic elements rather than an instantiation of a sacred totality:

> Myths not only provide information about one type of society: they tell us about the very processes of their production. In fact, what Lévi-Strauss pro-poses is a radical change in the method of approaching mythical narratives. The key is to understand the process of formation of such narratives, a pro-cess that essentially follows laws of transformation. It includes operations such as permutations, substitutions, inversions, symmetry, and so on. The narrative is, in a way, a dramatization of these logical operations. Each of them corresponds to a variant or variation. Thus the existence of different versions of a narrative is far from being a difficulty (as was thought by my-thologists who searched for a "correct" or "true" version). To the contrary, it is the system of their transformation that interests mythologists and allows them to reconstitute, or rather to display, the logical operation developed in the narrative. The narrative does not, for all that, lose its referential value (in other words its relation to the social and natural surroundings), but this value can be read differently: in the system of relations and not in isolated content.[37]

By setting aside previous approaches to myth, Lévi-Strauss develops an un-derstanding of narrative based on difference, not on an ontological same-ness or cosmic homology.

While Eliade's "symbolist" or "phenomenological" perspective on myth championed the cause of antireductionism, it nevertheless sought to anchor meaning in or "reduce" meaning to the sacred, stopping the interpretation process by way of cosmology. Furthermore, Eliade's seemingly step-by-step inquiry in which the pearl, for instance, becomes the symbol of Jesus Christ actually works in reverse. In other words, with the Christian cosmology al-ready in place, Eliade's conclusion that the pearl "evolves," over historical time, to represent Jesus Christ is misguided. The "pearl" as Christian sym-bol is not the conclusion; it is in effect the starting point—an unconscious invocation of a preexisting belief. Lévi-Strauss, on the other hand, offers a less self-fulfilling method by understanding that a "system of relations" outweighs "isolated content." At the same time, Hénaff notes, all relation to the social and natural surroundings is not simply cast aside; the "system of relations" provides, according to Lévi-Strauss, a new way of reading such textual references.

Structuralism, in its turn away from transcendental meaning as such, began to emphasize meaning as narrative function, and it is Lévi-Strauss's structural anthropology that radically changes myth studies. Central to this project of "reading differently" is the notion of variation. In Eliade, for instance, differences or variations in myths are rectified by a final governing cosmology—the symbol of the "pearl" evolves into Jesus Christ. Lévi-Strauss, on the other hand, does not view variation as something in need of a remedy; in fact, it is in variation that meaning is possible. This analysis of variation is a critical element in structural analysis beyond anthropology, and it is the work of Lévi-Strauss, especially as it is articulated in his classic study *Structural Anthropology,* that exemplifies this approach.

Like Eliade, Lévi-Strauss views language as a key element in discerning the most fundamental aspects of human action and culture. This is not to say, however, that Eliade and Lévi-Strauss define language in complementary terms or that Eliade abandons the notion of an identifiable empirical reality to which language corresponds, albeit tangentially. The point of association, rather, is that Eliade and Lévi-Strauss relocate the point of correspondence between word and reality to symbol and experience or word and structure. The structural element that informs Lévi-Strauss's analysis, for instance, renders language as a coded system that reveals not only a structural reality by way of linguistic analysis but also an ideational reality that adheres to certain rules that are operationally *collective,* which will be discussed later. Eliade, as we have discussed, similarly identifies "deeper" structures, but by way of a phenomenology that emphasizes the ecstatic experience contained within the linguistic event as symbol. While the two methods move along the same path, the orientation, as Lévi-Strauss describes it, is radically different.

In *Structural Anthropology* Lévi-Strauss refers to Saussure's linguistic insights in order to replace what he sees as a "clever dialectics" that "pretend a meaning has been found."[38] The question of "origins" with which we began leads to an examination of the "similarity" of world myths as a condition for a new science of mythology. Lévi-Strauss, in this context, is careful not to limit "myth" to neurophysiology or some other physical or biological science. The "science" that he is proposing is a general linguistic analysis that stands in contradistinction to approaches that are "too easy" or too narrow in their tendency to index all data to some other plane of discourse. Giving the example of how the retina works, Lévi-Strauss offers "structure" (a relational system) as a means of uniting mind and experience: "This whole problem of experience versus mind seems to have a solution in the structure of the nervous system, not in the structure of the mind and experience, but somewhere between mind and experience in the way our nervous system is built and in the way it mediates between mind and experience."[39]

The antimony between mind and experience noted by Lévi-Strauss relates to an interpretative, grounding process of bringing order to chaos, either transcendent order and chaos or its apparent presence within the discourse of myth. Do myths mean simply anything, an interpretative free-for-all, or do they mean particular things? This is the point at which to begin our discussion. Inquiry begins when a set of circumstances or a situation is moved from an indiscriminate collection of phenomena to something bearing an order or prefiguring an order. In archaeology, for instance, there is a typology of stones in which "natural" stones will have or are presumed to have erratic edges; that is to say, no coherent pattern will be discernible. Stone "tools," on the other hand, will have patterned edges or shapes that are not "naturally" occurring. The problem, of course, is that "patterns" are identified and defined by the viewer, who is invested in a typology organized by a sense of design. Stones with patterns are marked by function, and stones with no pattern—which is to say a pattern without a function or intentionality behind it—are categorized as "not tools." Is a stone an arrowhead, or does it just "look" like an arrowhead?

The identification of myth can be processed through a similar typology or universalization of patterns and the functions they reveal. Lévi-Strauss sees this as an interpretive problem that can be solved by a methodology borrowed from Saussurean linguistics:

[Ancient philosophers] did notice that in a given language certain sequences of sounds were associated with definite meaning, and they earnestly aimed at discovering a reason for the linkage between those *sounds* and that *mean-*

ing. Their attempt, however, was thwarted from the very beginning by the fact that the same sounds were equally present in other languages although the meaning they conveyed was totally different. The contradiction was surmounted only by the discovery that it is the combination of sounds, not the sounds themselves, which provided the significant data.[40]

Lévi-Strauss provides this early description of a phenomenon that would later be of concern for "post-structuralist" figures such as Paul de Man and Jacques Derrida.

Linking *sounds* and *meaning* is the key problem, as we have discussed, in ascertaining the status of oracular speech and the significance of myth. Not only is there an initial problem of identifying a *sound* with a word (a stone with a function), but the attachment of meaning to the actual linkage is the theoretical impasse that drives the inquiry into all matters deemed symbolic. The interesting point of Lévi-Strauss's observation of language follows his attention to the *sound* and *meaning* aporia, which converts anthropology and myth studies into linguistic analysis. The insurmountable element of the contradiction, for Lévi-Strauss, is that the direction for ascertaining *meaning* is divided; that is to say, the *meaning,* such as it is, does not come from the sound but from the "combination of sounds."[41] The historian, for example, settles on the particular "surface" activities in his or her quest for meaning, while the anthropologist sees this "surface" as an invitation to discover a deep structure that explains not only the event but the process that created the event.

With this insight from Saussure, Lévi-Strauss was able to push *meaning* away from the world (referentiality) and into language itself as a differential system of sounds motivated by universal (deep) structures:

> To invite the mythologist to compare his precarious situation with that of a linguist in the prescientific stage is not enough. As a matter of fact we may thus be led only from one difficulty to another. There is a very good reason why myth cannot simply be treated as language if its specific problems are to be solved; myth *is* language: to be known, myth has to be told; it is a part of human speech. In order to preserve its specificity we must be able to show that it is both the same thing as language, and also something different from it. Here, too, the past experience of linguists may help us. For language itself can be analyzed into things which are at the same time similar and yet

different. This is precisely what is expressed in Saussure's distinction between *langue* and *parole,* one being the structural side of language, the other the statistical aspect of it, *langue* belonging to a reversible time, *parole* being non-reversible. If those two levels already exist in language, then a third one can conceivably be isolated.[42]

The statement "myth *is* language" directs us away from a search for meaning within a naive referential paradigm, and it is to be understood, I'll argue, in the same fashion as Jacques Lacan's "the unconscious is structured like a language."

Structural Anthropology then, as a complete work, moves along a purely linguistic axis, with a clear correlation between the differential play of "sounds" and the differential play of "mythemes" in their respective fields. This structuralist approach doesn't serve, for instance, as a propaedeutic for another layer of investigation—it is the investigation. Lévi-Strauss thus provides a revolutionary possibility within myth studies that sets aside the literal reading or *first-order* rendering of the myth as narrative in favor of a "structuralist explanation" that exposes its (the myth's) "deep structure." In this sense the myth narrative doesn't function as a story to be understood as a retelling of an event or a disguised reformulation of a set of thematic principles.

In this instance Lévi-Strauss and Eliade could be said to share an interpretative goal—to move beyond the literal to the "symbolic" in order to recover a "deeper" meaning in the text. The difference, however, is in Lévi-Strauss's concept of the absolute text that can be exhausted by structural analyses. Eliade, of course, invests in a phenomenology that places understanding against structuralist explanation. While the two methodologies differ, one can find in both a decisive stepping-away from the surface of the text, although the later Eliade, informed by Jung, sees the deeper structure tied to the literal narrative and the speaking subject. Lévi-Strauss, on the other hand, treats the surface of the narrative as an obstacle to be overcome; moreover, the surface of narrative may in fact present itself as altogether unintelligible and only meaningful as an articulation of synchronic elements: "I therefore claim to show, not how men think in myths, but how myths operate in men's minds without their being aware of the fact. . . . And, as I have already suggested, it would perhaps be better to go still further and, disregarding the thinking subject completely, proceed as if the thinking process were taking place in the myths, in their reflection upon themselves and their interrelation."[43]

The "structuralist" idea of myth operating in Lévi-Strauss is predicated on differential narrative elements, which are separate from the reflective, conscious intent of an individual author. Additionally, these differential elements become significant in their "interrelation" and not in their reference to some empirical reality. This division of word and world appears similar to Eliade's sacred/profane realities, with the sacred as the ultimate reality. Lévi-Strauss, however, is not indexing narrative to some other plane of reality by way of division. The bracketing of empirical reality is not proposed in order to glimpse a so-called higher reality; the bracketing of the empirical is part of a process that allows function to emerge as fundamental to narrative. Men don't "think" in myths, according to Lévi-Strauss; myths "operate" in "men's minds."

This does not mean that myths are simply neuro-effects or that myths merely mirror brain function, although Wendy Doniger, in her introduction to Lévi-Strauss's *Myth and Meaning: Cracking the Code of Culture,* strongly makes this association: "Underneath language lies the binary nature of the brain itself. Right and left, good and evil, life and death—these are inevitable dichotomies produced by the brain that has two lobes and controls two eyes, two hands."[44] There is no question about Lévi-Strauss's interest in "cerebral structures," but these structures are knowable only through relational structures or, finally, through themselves as functions within a system. Ultimately, nature's codes or any phenomena become intelligible within the aggregate laws of symbolic function: "The unconscious ceases to be the ultimate haven of individual peculiarities—the repository of a unique history which makes each of us an irreplaceable being. It is reducible to function—the symbolic function, which no doubt is specifically human, and which is carried out according to the same laws among all men and actually corresponds to the aggregate of these laws."[45]

The various divisions separating one level of existence from another (e.g., archaic from modern) are, for Lévi-Strauss, rectified in these structural laws that govern not only societies but myths as well. Just as Eliade utilized an all-powerful sacred to smooth over difference and fix references, Lévi-Strauss relies on the equally omnipresent and knowable "structure" that forms the basis of all human acts. While the resolutions offered by

Eliade and Lévi-Strauss could not be more different, their problem is oddly very similar—overcoming the rift between "saying" and "understanding." As deceptively simple as Eliade's phenomenology is, it also points clearly to a more pervasive theoretical obstacle of reconciling two different or opposing fields of experience or discourse. Lévi-Strauss, similarly, identifies the same task of reconciliation in a much more complex way, devising a structural methodology that not only eclipses Eliade's "symbolist" approach but further complicates the concept of difference inherent in the framing of the initial problem. Rather than follow the established practice of ethnographic data collection, Lévi-Strauss, as Richard Kearney writes, "demonstrate[s] how the *pensée sauvage* of myth and symbol unfolds according to a 'logic of analogy' which permits the mind to hold together disparate orders of meaning—e.g. human, divine, animal, vegetal—in a 'reciprocity of perspectives.'"[46]

Lévi-Strauss's examination of "disparate orders of meaning" prepares the way for a reoriented field of anthropology and much more linguistically sensitive social sciences and humanities in general. Unlike Eliade's crypto-commerce, Lévi-Strauss's "reciprocity of perspectives" eliminates a transcendental plane in favor of a more analytical system of mythemes that can be tied to narrative structures, social practices, and, for better or worse, universal cerebral structures. Additionally, the method of structural anthropology and its focus on systems of difference moved the contest over meaning away from traditional religious binaries (sacred/profane), person-centered discourses (psychology), and empirical investigation (ethnography). Language, as the space within which "disparate orders" become meaningful, is sufficiently "re-marked" by Lévi-Strauss, and it is this reinvestment in "structural laws" that opened, at the time, new possibilities for addressing the rift between "saying" and "understanding."

2.4 Ricoeur and the Hermeneutics of Myth

To what does speculation refer us? To living experience? Not yet. Behind speculation, and beneath gnosis and anti-gnostic constructions, we find *myths.* Myth will here be taken to mean what the history of religions now finds in it: not a false explanation by means of images and fables, but a traditional narration which relates to events that happened at the beginning of time and which has the purpose of providing grounds for the ritual actions of men of today and, in a general manner, establishing all the forms of action and thought by which man understands himself in his world.

—Paul Ricoeur, *The Symbolism of Evil*

Paul Ricoeur's hermeneutics in many ways stands in sharp contrast to the structuralist methodology developed by Lévi-Strauss, especially in its most fundamental understanding of language and the human subject, which Ricoeur sees as retaining a focal importance in the process of interpretation. It is not enough to say, however, that Ricoeur's hermeneutics is simply opposed to Lévi-Strauss's structuralism; his concepts of the "symbol" and the "subject," critical to both Eliade and Lévi-Strauss, are oriented toward an entirely different problematic than that of his structuralist contemporary. In fact, Ricoeur's understanding of the "symbol," as sympathetic as Ricoeur is toward Eliade's approach, derives in part from a distancing from Eliade's "symbolist" understanding; it is important to keep in mind the intellectual context of Ricoeur's strong affiliations with an Eliadean "new humanism" as a means of preserving person-centered hermeneutics—very much contrary to Lévi-Strauss's formal, nonpersonal "system of differences."[47] The human subject, however, begins for Ricoeur not in an abstract formulation of structural differences nor in a transcendental realm; the human subject develops in and through others, history, culture, and finally texts.

This emphasis on the subject is critical to the development of symbol and myth beyond the analyses offered by Eliade and Lévi-Strauss. Ricoeur views myth as a necessary "other" through which the subject passes in his or her quest for identity. In this sense myth is much more than simple narrative; it is part of the symbolic expression of becoming human. Richard Kearney, in *On Paul Ricoeur: The Owl of Minerva,* summarizes this commitment to continuing a humanistic tradition via hermeneutics: "Philosophy is hermeneutical to the extent that it reads hidden meanings in the text of apparent meaning. And the task of hermeneutics is to show how existence arrives at expression, and later again at reflection, through perpetual exploration of the significations that emerge in the symbolic works culture. More particularly, human existence only becomes a self by retrieving meanings which first reside 'outside' of itself in the social institutions and cultural monuments in which the life of the spirit is objectified."[48]

If we consider as points of contrast Eliade's sacred/profane binary along-side Lévi-Strauss's structural homologies, we find a common problem involving a rift between "saying" and "understanding." This rift, for Ricoeur, is not an obstacle to be overcome; it is, more precisely, the condition of being human. While "symbolist" and "structuralist," as different as they are, both seek to uncover determinate meaning, thus overcoming the rift, the rift in hermeneutics allows the subject to enter into the process of interpretation and self-discovery, without determinate or final meaning. To summarize, Eliade covers this "rift" by means of a crypto-commerce in which the power of the sacred solidifies symbols across time and culture—for example, the "pearl." The "rift" for Lévi-Strauss, on the other hand, demands a considerable reorientation of the problem—one in which the traditionally configured two planes of reality (sacred and profane) give way to a new theoretical framework in which language forms the infrastructure of universal "aggregate laws"; in other words, structural "totality" mediates linguistic spaces. In either instance the "rift" purportedly vanishes, leaving in its wake a dialectical synthesis of sacred and profane or a complete system of differences that can be read according to the logic of structure or symbol.

The question now is, to what extent does Paul Ricoeur's hermeneutics—given all Ricoeur's sympathies with an Eliadean intuitive "symbolist" approach and antagonisms toward Lévi-Strauss's nonreflective, nonhuman structures—provide a possible third way of addressing the "rift"? And if Ricoeur's hermeneutics prevails or fails against the rift, what does this teach us about the nature of this fundamental problem of "saying" and "understanding"?

A comprehensive study of Ricoeur's life work would be impractical in this context; however, a selective analysis of his understanding of subject, symbol, and the nature of the sacred will extend this study of the "rift," with which the inquiry began. To return to this issue of the rift, it is useful to examine the critical instance of the interpreting subject—the cornerstone of Ricoeur's philosophical enterprise and the point of radical divergence among the three figures.

The subject within Eliadean intuitive "symbolism"—or, if one prefers, phenomenology—is "self-present": the subject is aware of awareness and its limits. Additionally, through the power of the sacred and the immediacy of the symbol, the subject comes to full consciousness, especially as he or she abandons the reductive nature of modern thinking. This in part explains Eliade's contempt for Freudian psychoanalysis, which, in alignment with all modern reductionisms, according to Eliade, places "sacred" existence, thought, and awareness out of reach. David Cave, in *Mircea Eliade's Vision for a New Humanism,* concisely describes Eliade's feeling: "For humanness is not something discovered but something re-discovered, since the essential human condition, for Eliade, precedes the actual human condition. The essential human condition is more 'consciously' one with being, the real. It is where the human is one with the fullness of existence and where there is no conscious awareness of the self; one fully is and acts with full spontaneity of action."[49] Cave continues this description of Eliade's concept of the human with a reference to Eliade's autobiographical reflections, in which he recounts being lost in the time of his memories—being lost in the sacred.[50] The "I" of modern sensibility, if one follows Eliade, is a limited instantiation of the "real," which is, to no one's surprise, very much consistent with the Hindu concept of Ătman.

Lévi-Strauss, on the other hand, views the subject as contained within biological and cultural limits, with no appeal to a transcendent reality. Like the Italian Marxist Antonio Gramsci, whose famous dictum proposes that the subject is an "ensemble of social relations," Lévi-Strauss posits that the subject is comprised of a mind (universal capacities) and of wider cultural, "unconscious" structures of which the "subject" is not fully aware and over which he or she has no control. Marcel Hénaff explains the conflict: "[It is] not a question of denying the individual aspect of . . . the existence of the brain and central nervous system as the unavoidable medium of all rational activity and even simply of all human activity. However, this medium functions only in a collective system that we have already encountered under the name of 'symbolic system' and that is simultaneously the framework of language, institutions . . . activities. . . and systems of representation (logical classifications, myths)."[51] Simply put, the subject, given the two possibilities presented, either dances to the cosmic rhythm of the one eternal "real consciousness" (Eliade) or functions in accordance with the algorithms of symbolic systems within the limitations of its cerebral, linguistic capacities. In the end the subject finds some determinate, fixed measure of meaning and reality in the universe—either transcendent or structural.

As previously discussed, hermeneutics moves in a different direction when it comes to determinacy. The process of interpretation or the possibilities for meaning continue into an endless linguistic, historical, political, and existential horizon, with any finality preempted by the wide horizon of new understanding. While this is true of hermeneutics by definition, it is especially true of Paul Ricoeur's hermeneutics, with its emphasis on "otherness" and "creativity," a creativity that is markedly different from previous humanist configurations. With the possibility of interpretive impossibility foreclosed, creativity opens onto not only more interpretation but greater understanding, positing the human subject as an eternal "work in progress." "Ricoeur," Richard Kearney writes, "explodes the pretensions of the *cogito* to be self-founding and self-knowing."[52]

This "exploding" of the Cartesian subject is, more importantly for Ricoeur, a rejection of self-generation and all that it implies. If the subject were self-founding, then everything "outside" the subject would be secondary. This stable, unified "self," for Ricoeur, completely contradicts the most fundamental aspect of human existence. John D. Caputo, for instance, in *Radical Hermeneutics: Repetition, Deconstruction, and the Hermeneutic Project,* goes so far as to say, in affirmation, that the self is not placid but "much more a place of disruption, irruption, solicitation."[53] Not only do we find in hermeneutics generally and Ricoeur specifically a rejection of a Cartesian cogito, but we also see a rejection of the solipsism of an early Husserl. The subject comes into existence, Ricoeur's hermeneutics will demonstrate, through the detour through the "other." This hermeneutic self, quite apart from the Cartesian and Husserlian subject, articulates a much more dynamic formation of subjectivity; as Richard Kearney writes, "human being, for Ricoeur, is always, a *being-interpreted*."[54]

At this juncture we leave behind the limits of Mircea Eliade's and Claude Lévi-Strauss's theories. In part Ricoeur's hermeneutics, with its emphasis on viewing the "rift" as a condition of human subjectivity rather than as an obstacle to "understanding," allows a new understanding of self, symbol, and myth as that which marks the rise of the human subject in history. This "new understanding," as I describe it, makes the study of myth more than a search for narrative meaning. Interpretation, following Ricouer, extends beyond the correlation of "saying" and "understanding" to some third term that mediates all difference. Ricoeurean hermeneutics, then, redefines both the subject and the myth as that which is "being-interpreted" in relation to each other.

Myth, for Ricoeur, is the site of "being-interpreted," as we have discussed it, and it is also at the center of what he refers to as the "grounds for ritual action," where humankind finds value and meaning in the world. Finding meaning in the "world," as I have argued, is contingent upon finding meaning in the "word," and this is where we can see the important separation among Eliadean "symbolist" phenomenology, Lévi-Straussian structuralism, and Ricoeurean hermeneutics within the study of myth. The relevance of myth, within these approaches and as it relates to the function of linking "saying" and "understanding," has been the topic of numerous interdisciplinary inquiries in this area and has, as we shall see, far-reaching implications for religion and literature.

A key element of this "function of linking" and myth is temporality. Ricoeur identifies myth as critical to a community's understanding of itself, and the "saying"/"understanding" rift speaks to a question of origins, which Ricoeur will eventually distinguish from beginnings. The Eliadean and Lévi-Straussian approaches to myth tend toward determinate interpretation—the "what does the myth ultimately mean?" Ricoeur, obviously, is aware of the need to place myths in history; however, myth, within hermeneutics, also speaks to another end of temporality: the future. With this futurity comes myth's political significance, which falls within the parameters of critique. For Ricoeur myth, then, occupies multiple planes of relevance—origin, beginning, future, and alternative (future) possibilities. These multiple planes, as Ricoeur understands them, make myth much more than "coded history," "sacred intent," or "structural form." Myth speaks additionally to creative aspects of a knowable, forthcoming world. Richard Kearney explains this Ricoeurean turn on myth as the site of "hermeneutic disclosure":

> Hermeneutic understanding . . . discriminates between positive and negative symbols. And so myth, as a narrative of symbolic events, can be salvaged as a constructive mediation between tradition and history, maintaining both elements in a relationship of creative tension. So salvaged, myth may legitimately [fulfill] its dual potential of creation and critique: the hermeneutic disclosure of possible worlds which are suppressed in our present reality and whose very otherness provides alternatives to the established order. By projecting ulterior modes of understanding, albeit on an imaginary plane, myth can function as a salutary indictment of the status quo.[55]

"Hermeneutic disclosure," as a departure from the search for determinate meaning, prepares the way for several layers of myth analysis. First, the symbol (that which has double meaning) is open to a plurality of interpretive possibilities—much different from Eliade's "pearl," which finds ultimate relevance in relation to Jesus Christ. The plural symbol not only exceeds determinate meaning but has, as Kearney describes, multiple creative and critical potentialities. Second, narrative "symbolic" events in the form of myth mediate between these apparently disparate layers of analysis. Third—a point that I'll argue approaches the postmodern Lyotardian sense of narrative—myth has undisclosed potentialities that are not possible in the present, leaving open the prospect of alternatives to a political or ideological status quo. It is the political and philosophical implications of this heretofore undisclosed "future possibility" that correlate to and further complicate the question of myth in Ricoeur's hermeneutics, Lyotardian postmodernism, Derridean deconstruction, and Žižekian "re-marking."

Unlike the Eliadean or Lévi-Straussian approaches, Ricoeurean hermeneutics does not "pathologize" the rift between "saying" and "understanding." In fact, Ricoeur's departure from the limits of "symbolist" phenomenology and structuralism, I would argue, does much more than "salvage" myth, as Kearney describes it; it allows a new methodology to develop around myth and narrative studies. This is described concisely by Ricoeur in "Philosophy and Religious Language": "It is this referential dimension that is absolutely original with fictional and poetic works that, for me, poses the most fundamental hermeneutical problem. If we can no longer define hermeneutics as the search for another person and psychological intentions that hide behind the text, and if we do not want to reduce interpretation to the identification of structures, what remains to be interpreted? My response is that to interpret is to explicate the sort of being-in-the-world unfolded in front of the text."[56]

Ricoeur clarifies his proposition by developing a reading practice from Heidegger in which "understanding" (Verstehen) occurs as one engages with one's world, dialectically. In this sense interpretation is not simply an act of historical or structural recovery or designation; it is an embracing of the "rift" between "saying" and "understanding" or, in this precise instance, text and reader. While myth traditionally has been the test site for this dialectical "unfolding," Ricoeur, following Heidegger, is willing to extend hermeneutic disclosure to nonmythical narrative as well. What is ultimately "disclosed," according to Ricoeur, is not a static textual meaning; it is actually a world that is disclosed: "In effect, what is to be interpreted in a text is a proposed world, a world that I might inhabit and wherein I might project my ownmost possibilities. This is what I call the world of the text, the world probably belonging to this unique text."[57]

The "rift" between "saying" and "understanding" appears, within Ricoeurean hermeneutics, as a passage or detour by which one engages the other, for example, the person, history, or text. The final interpretive "outcome" is that there is no total interpretive outcome; the "other" continuously renews itself in the world. In further contrasting Ricouer's hermeneutics with structuralism, Kearney shows the significance of "existence" in interpretation: "Ricoeur's hermeneutic model renounces the structuralist hypostasis of language—the cult of the text as an end in itself. . . . Language itself, as a signifying milieu . . . must be referred to existence."[58] With this Ricoeur, in the hermeneutic tradition, has seemingly resolved the age-old anxiety regarding the quest for meaning, definitive meaning. Meaning, in its totality, corresponds to existence, but it can never be made fully present, which reflects the modernist aesthetic in which one gains the assurance of plurality without the full disclosure of truth—one only can be reassured that it exists.

In a 1978 interview Ricoeur refers to this as a "mythical nucleus" of a culture—a determining center that does not yield to discourse. This "nucleus" would function as a "primary site" only insofar as it perpetually presents an opportunity for an infinitely interpretable "new world":

> The mythical nucleus of a society is only *indirectly* recognizable. But it is indirectly recognizable not only by what is said (discourse), but also by what and how one lives (*praxis*), and third, as I suggested, by the distribution between different functional levels of a society. We cannot, for example, say that in all countries the economic layer is determining. This is true of our Western society. But, as Lévi-Strauss has shown in his analysis of many primitive societies, this is not universally true. In several cultures the significance of economic and historical consideration would seem to be minor. In our culture the economic factor is indeed determining; but that does not mean that the predominance of economics is itself explicable purely in terms of economic science. This predominance is perhaps more correctly

understood as but one constituent of the overall evaluation of what is primary and what is secondary. And it is only by analysis of the hierarchical structuring and evaluation of the different constituents of a society (that is, the role of politics, nature, art, religion and so on) that we may penetrate to its hidden *mytho-poetic nucleus*.[59]

While this interview, appropriately entitled "Myth as the Bearer of Possible Worlds," took place at a time when structuralism and post-structuralism dominated the intellectual landscape of the humanities, it is nevertheless significant for its strong restatement of the founding principles of hermeneutics, namely the concept of "indirectness" of approach and a concern for the human situation. Ricoeur's hermeneutics takes the "mythical nucleus" to be unreachable by any measure of discourse; one is able only to approach it "indirectly," since its true relevance ultimately is contingent upon historical context; that is to say, time provides the final obstacle to revealing anything in its totality—a concept elaborated in detail with *Memory, History, Forgetting*.[60] As Ricoeur states, while the economic, for example, may in one context be determinate or "determining," this is not exclusively the case across all cultural and historical contexts.

The reminder that totalizing narratives are not totalizing is important for Ricoeur in ways that differ from more recent postmodernist critiques of phenomena. In particular, the concept of nontotalizeable nuclei shows that Ricoeur is eager to preserve the "self" along with "meaning"; this is true in the 1978 interview and again in *Memory, History, Forgetting*. The "mythopoetic nucleus," for Ricoeur, must be tempered by ethics and a general concern for the well-being of human beings: "Only those myths are genuine which can be interpreted in terms of *liberation*."[61] In this sense there is an identifiable boundary around myth or texts that guides one toward an endless (not meaningless) interpretive horizon.

This, one could argue, separates Ricoeur from postmodernism or deconstructionism insofar as his ethics remains linked to human beings, while postmodern, Lyotardian ethics tends to view the ethical in terms of available and unavailable "phrasings." I would contend that possible "phrasings" and possible "worlds" are two very different things, with very different consequences. Here Ricoeur is not talking about "pure" possibility; he is addressing political, if not existential, possibility, which one could argue resonates with the precepts of Romanticism. Nevertheless, "meaning" in myth is not something that is recoverable as a cognitive "thing." Meaning, as it presses against temporality, is not fully revealed—only indirectly revealed as an encouragement toward "liberation." The "veil" that stands between the subject and Reality, then, is the possibility for "liberation" within Ricoeur's hermeneutics: "Poetry and myth are not just nostalgia for some forgotten world. They constitute a disclosure of unprecedented worlds, an opening on to other *possible* worlds which transcend the established limits of our *actual* world."[62]

The limits of our "actual" world, I would argue, reinscribe a division between an "actual" world and a "virtual" world, or a world not-yet formed. In this sense Ricoeur, like Eliade and Lévi-Strauss, never breaks free of hegemony's "gravitational" pull. The "actual" world or the "Real" world can exist either as a "sacred" space, which invites us to participate in its fullness of symbol; a structuralist space, which organizes difference into system for us; or, following Ricoeur, a "hermeneutic" space, which, as incomplete as it is, continually unfolds for us, never fully disclosing itself in our presence. All three, it is clear, depend upon a hegemonic, phantasmic "Real source" that either mediates itself or is mediated by something else.

2.5 Žižekian Comedic Epilogue

If we return to the section epigraphs, we see a consistent concern across differing theoretical frames with myth's ability to make visible a gap between "saying" and "understanding." This gap, as we have discussed it, extends beyond the act of communication, involving the metaphysics of text and language. The rift separating the two "planes," whether it is the ontological difference between "sacred" and "profane," "structural" differences, "mythical nuclei," or "parallax gaps," also appears according to and within the limits of a discursive framework, with each remedy or affirmation of the "rift" configuring myth differently. This ongoing "configuration of myth" requires that each discursive frame must, in effect, occupy a space "outside" of myth, forming a point of view that stands in excess of myth itself.

It is this move to the "outside" that comprises the transgressive turn in all the figures we have examined—Žižek, Eliade, Lévi-Strauss, and Ricoeur. In each instance myth comes to represent a decisive means by which the limits of religion, secularism, and transcendentalism are exceeded. For Ricoeur this recognition of a boundary is viewed as a "liberation" from narrative limit, an opportunity to see myth as a "bearer of possible worlds." Eliade and Lévi-Strauss easily could be viewed as advocating for a similar transgressive narrative moment, although, as we have discussed, their respective projects are oriented toward a much different problematic. Whether it is the overturning of "reductionism," weak "speculation," "totalization," or generic limit, myth is presumed to offer a way above and beyond the status quo, which, as I have argued, is the persistent, interesting problem of myth—its inability, it would seem, to escape hegemony.

It is worthwhile to examine, finally, Žižek's "comedy of Christianity" as an illustration of "mythic" boundary transgression. As we noted in the previous section, Žižek reads the move from myth to agape as a decisive reconfiguration of the failed Hegelian dialectic, a material synthesis rather than a spiritual synthesis. His Cartesian subject, filtered through Lacan, mirrors this failure of synthetic unity, which makes Žižek's Cartesian subject a "ticklish" subject in the history of philosophy. If Christianity is a myth, then Christianity exceeds tragedy, according to Žižek, by expressing itself through comedy or the dialectic of comedy, in which the "coming together" of the Christian narrative is made meaningful by the fact that it falls apart—Christ dies.

Already it is clear that unlike our previous figures, Žižek is not limited by an eternal "Real source." His dialectic between "saying" and "understanding" or "figure" and "ground" presupposes failure, disjunction, and disunity. Jesus, in a manner of speaking, succeeds by failing. Following Žižek and not St. Paul, then, one becomes a "Christian" by identifying with Jesus's atheism on the cross—His failure to reconcile difference. Therefore, to truly be a Christian, within this reversal, one must be an atheist, which means that one, as Žižek states, is closest to God when one denies Him, as He denied Himself—a comic inversion.

Oddly, this is similar, if opposed, to the logic behind framing "despair" as the most serious of sins; in despair one believes that there is no hope, which means that one believes one is beyond the redemptive power of God—a sinful conclusion. What could be more hopeless than that? While despair is a serious condition, it is possible to declare that it is only in this place of abject hopelessness that God genuinely saves by His grace (e.g., Faust).[63] Or one could say that "salvation" comes as a person realizes that there is no "big Other" poised on the other side of our world, no "big Other" ready to rectify suffering.

In typical Žižekian fashion we are confronted with an entire set of comic reversals when it comes to mythic narrative beginnings, as Žižek notes regarding Søren Kierkegaard:

> In "The Ancient Tragical Motif as Reflected in the Modern" . . . Kierkegaard sketches out his fantasy of what a modern Antigone would be like. The conflict is now entirely internalized: there is no longer a need for Creon. While Antigone admires and loves her father Oedipus, the public hero and savior of Thebes, she knows the truth about him (murderer of the father, incestuous marriage). Her deadlock is that she is prevented from sharing this accursed knowledge (like Abraham, who also could not communicate to others the divine injunction to sacrifice his son): she cannot complain, share her pain and sorrow with others. In contrast to Sophocles' Antigone, who acts . . . she is unable to act, condemned forever to impassive suffering.[64]

In this solitude of "impassive suffering," Kierkegaard denies one of the most fundamental aspects of tragedy—Hegel's "eternal justice." Whether it is Greek or Senecan or Shakespearean tragedy, the high are brought low, and some prevailing justice is instantiated, even if it seems disproportionate to the reader; King Lear, of course, stands as an example of this feature. Pure suffering, as in the case of the modernist Antigone, suspends justice and, by implication, the ethical, making suffering exclusively "aesthetic." Žižek adds a "Stalinist twist" to Kierkegaard's modernist Antigone and imagines her publicly "denouncing" her father and his sins, which leaves her more isolated or socially ostracized.

The modern Kierkegaardian Antigone falls on the side of aesthetics, which is pure suffering. The "postmodernist" Antigone is on the other side of the "either/or," the ethical, which is pure renunciation. The common point between the two is the "parallax gap." The modernist Antigone cannot overcome the rift separating her from those who could potentially alleviate her suffering. The postmodernist Antigone, with a "Stalinist twist," is equally isolated insofar as no one, with the exception of Oedipus (were he alive), would understand her renunciation as something other than an unforgivable betrayal.[65] The "aesthetic" and the "ethical" determine very different outcomes, although they share a vision of Antigone in complete isolation. The possible mediating "third" term from Kierkegaard would be in this instance the "religious," which theoretically could supersede both the aesthetic and the ethical.

However, as Žižek points out, the "religious" is not inherently stabilizing, which redirects the question of the "parallax gap" in the narrative, Sophoclean or Christian, to comedy: "Kierkegaard gives no clear priority to the Ethical, he merely confronts the two choices, that of Aesthetics and of Ethics, in a purely parallax way, emphasizing the 'jump' that separates them, the lack of any mediation between them. The religious is by no means the mediating 'synthesis' of the two, but, on the contrary, the radical assertion of the parallax gap."[66]

The "religious" as the "radical assertion" of the parallax is the critical moment in which one can distinguish the differences across the fields of phenomenology, structuralism, and hermeneutics, as they have been discussed thus far. With two discursive systems (aesthetic and ethical) operating in differing and, sometimes, opposing relation, it is philosophically consistent to think that "mediation" is possible. After all, following Hegel, shouldn't all difference yield to some exterior synthesis? Eliade, as one may recall, offers the "sacred" as the ultimate reconciling factor; Lévi-Strauss provides a total system of differences; and Paul Ricoeur presents the "mythic nucleus" that over and over again opens itself to interpretation.

In Žižek, however, the "rift" or "gap" is described as being "parallax," the space between two incommensurate symbolic systems that is itself represented by both, albeit differently. The paradox of the "lack of common measure" creates an "insurmountable abyss between the Finite and the Infinite," Žižek argues.[67] In addition to incommensurability, the parallax gap or "split" in the "religious," unlike the other mediating factors proposed by Eliade, Lévi-Strauss, and Ricoeur, appears "caught up" in a parallax too: "We are never safely within the Religious, doubt forever remains, the same act can be seen as religious or as aesthetic, in a parallax split which can never be abolished, since 'minimal difference' which transubstantiates (what appears to be) an aesthetic act into a religious one can never be specified, located in a determinate property."[68] The resilience or incorrigibility of the "religious" as it comes to terms with "determinate property" gives rise to a particular instance of the "rift" or "gap." Between myth and language, or philosophy and literature, the "religious" intervenes with some putative explanatory power. However, rather than viewing the "religious" as the crucial synthesizing discourse, it is, as Žižek notes, the significant space of "minimal difference," which is the space of incommensurability.

In order to illustrate Žižek's "Christian comedy," it is necessary to examine the way in which Žižek "re-marks" Christian identity through atheism. This process begins with a continuation of his analysis of Kierkegaard's imaginative reworking of Antigone. The idea of reversal of highest and lowest, which links traditional tragedy (high brought low) and comedy (high/low comedy of manners or social misplacement), takes shape around the presentation of Jesus: "Is there anything more comical than Incarnation, this ridiculous overlapping of the Highest and the Lowest, the coincidence of God, creator of the universe, and a miserable man? Take the elementary comical scene from a film: after the trumpets announce the King's entrance to the royal hall, the surprised public sees a miserable crippled clown who enters staggering. . . . This is the logic of Incarnation."[69] Žižek adds that "the point is that the gap that separates God from man in Christ is purely one of parallax: Christ is not a person with two substances, immortal and mortal."[70] As Žižek clarifies, Jesus does not "represent" the divine; nor is he a "symbol" of the divine. In these instances Jesus would only be the object of a phenomenological or hermeneutical or structuralist explication—something to be "totally" reconciled to an ultimate framework: "As this miserable human, Christ directly *is* God. Christ is not *also* human, apart from being God; he is a man precisely *insofar as he is God*."[71]

With Christ "re-marked" as pure "parallax," Žižek has set aside the necessity of "commerce" between dialectical opposed realms, sacred/profane, mytheme/mythos, or text/horizon of meaning. Following a reimagined, failed Hegelian dialectic, Žižek gives an account of a new paradoxical unity with God as "parallax":

> This is how Hegelian "reconciliation" works: not as an immediate synthesis or reconciliation of opposites, but as the redoubling of the gap or antagonism—the two opposed moments are "reconciled" when the gap that separates them is posited as inherent to one of the terms. In Christianity, the gap that separates God from man is not directly "sublated" in the figure of Christ as God-man; it is rather that, in the most tense moment of crucifix-

ion, when Christ himself despairs ("Father, why have you forsaken me?"), the gap that separates God from man is transposed into God himself, as the gap that separates Christ from God-Father; the properly dialectical trick here is that the very feature which appeared to separate me from God turns out to unite me with God.[72]

The Christian theological tradition—across denominations, one could argue—understands Christ to be not only the one who reconciles a fallen humankind with the divine but also the one who brings an end to all symbolic difference—for example, Eliade's "pearl." With Christ the "rift" or gap vanishes, if we "properly" follow through onto-theologically.

A "re-marked" Christianity, however, preserves the "rift" or gap—not as the insurmountable "Otherness" of negative theology but as "redoubled." As Žižek writes, the gap that "separate[s] me from God turns out to unite me with God." This "redoubling" of the interval suspends the need for synthesis and instead ironically positions the "gap" as the ineluctable condition for unity with God. In other words, when one sees the gap between humankind and the divine as the antagonism that makes "reconciliation" possible, one can have "a faith." Here one could offer the following as a creed: "I believe in the God that abandoned himself." Whatever affirmation one chooses, it must reject a "big Other" and underscore the persistence of an impossible unity predicated on separation. This philosophical "re-marking" of Jesus's death is offered as an instance of an incomplete Hegelian dialectic in which the "Universal" and the "Singular" overlap: "While observing Napoleon on a horse in the streets of Jena after the battle of 1807, Hegel remarked that it was as if he saw there the World Spirit riding a horse. The Christological implications of this remark are obvious: what happened in the case of Christ is that God himself, the creator of our entire universe, was walking out there as a common individual."[73]

Žižek earlier comments that if one follows this linking of the Universal and the Singular, the "real" is not revealed as much as the "problem" of the real is made visible in the instance of appearance: "How does appearance itself emerge from the interplay of the Real? The thesis that the Real is just the cut or gap of inconsistency, between two appearances has thus to be supplemented by its opposite: appearance is the cut, the gap, between the two Reals, or more precisely, something that emerges in the gap that separates the Real from itself."[74] The journey through myth, over the gap, to the Real is suspended by Žižek, and the so-called gap or rift is not placed between "saying" and "understanding," or the "sacred" and the "profane"; rather, the gap is, as Žižek notes, within the Real "itself," as a condition of its own possibility. This repositioning of the gap is further clarified when Žižek includes the concept of "Kantian spontaneity" in the discussion: "At the phenomenal level, we are mechanisms, parts of the chain of causes and effects; at the noumenal level, we are again puppets, lifeless mechanisms."[75] Žižek understands that the "gap" between the two levels is the "only place of freedom," the site of appearance.[76] Like Napoleon riding on horseback or, one could imagine, God incarnate on an ass, the Universal and the Singular, within a synthesizing dialectic, are joined, eliminating the "gap." Re-marked, however, the appearance does not form an end to the "rift" but is itself, according to Žižek, the Real-of-the-rift/gap.

The final "re-marking" that occurs in Žižek's analysis of the Christ story again takes up the question of the Real by way of comedy. While tragedy, according to Žižek, "veils" the truth, comedy's work is to "unveil" it. His two illustrative instances are Groucho Marx and Lucille Ball; I'll make my concluding point with just the former. The process of unveiling appears in a Marx Brothers' comedy when, one assumes, Groucho says, "This man looks like an idiot and acts like an idiot; but this should not deceive you—he is an idiot."[77] What truth is revealing, in Žižek's terms, is the fact that the "hidden terrifying secret" is the same—whether it is in front of the veil or behind it.[78] This is much more than a naive, realist pursuit of truth—seeing is believing. The critical insight here is that the "rift" or "gap" is not situated between two planes of existence but within Reality itself: "This very lack of difference between the two elements confronts us with 'pure' difference that separates an element from itself." From this observation Žižek offers a definition of God that, in rejecting prior models predicated on uniting two discrete planes, makes God the instance of the "gap," radical self-same-difference: "And is this not the ultimate definition of the divinity—God, too, has to wear a mask himself? Perhaps 'God' is the name for this supreme split between the Absolute as the noumenal Thing and the Absolute as the appearance of itself, for the fact that the two are the same, that the difference between the two is purely formal."[79] This "formal difference," then, permits one to, as Žižek argues in "From the Myth to Agape," become fully Christian in atheism, with Jesus not God and not man, but the "supreme split."

The emphasis on the "rift" or "gap" allows theoretical inquiry to cover two methodological concerns: the difference "between" things and the difference "within" things. Žižek's retelling of the Christian narrative in which Jesus appears as the "supreme split" finds not another interpretive/theological conclusion but a separate methodological problem: that of posing the problem of difference within identity or difference within origin. This instantiation of difference "within" is the undiscovered void that Eliade, Lévi-Strauss, and, I would argue, Paul Ricoeur overlook. From this perspective one does not simply work formalistically on texts; the problem *of* texts becomes a central intellectual concern. If myth, as we have discussed, can be shown to harbor differences *within* origin, then we have more than a plurality of interpretations. Žižek's "parallax gap" drives at the metaphysics of texts or, as he pursues in *On Belief,* the belief that makes belief possible in understanding myths—something that is both apparent and hidden in, for example, Eliade's "Christian" dialectic of the sacred and the profane. The "rift" between "saying" and "understanding" not only requires a formal arrangement of texts according to their implicit limits but demands a form of thinking that makes the "ground" of texts themselves part of the inquiry.

IIII

Literary Conditions

3.1 Literary Intervals

On the surface, there is no history of thought that cannot be traced, and thus the dialectic of enlightenment is obviously the "natural" structure of the process of civilization. But the *history* of thought (in the sense of *what* makes thought historical) is precisely whatever links thought to daily life, to what is immediate and mortal, to what is inevitable and ephemeral—to what is *untraceable* precisely because it is immediately drawn upon, like water that runs to the root of a tree. What makes thought historical is that it disappears into the pathways of life, that it is absorbed in the ultimately untraceable process by which life demonstrates (its) mortality.

—Stathis Gourgouris, *Does Literature Think?*

Thinking in a text—which is here to be understood as a "text, in the infrastructural sense that we now give to that word," that is, as a system of references which could be neither a text in the usual sense of, for example, a philosophical text, or a public discourse, or even the text of the situation of our time—owes its birth to the recognition that thinking, philosophical thinking, for example, is always necessarily "held within" [*prise*] and "overtaken" [*surprise*] by a language and a logic constituting a system that cannot be dominated by thinking: this system has always "sufficiently *surprising* resources" to which discourse, whatever is said, is always otherwise than what is intended. The wonder that causes thinking would thus be nothing less than an awareness of being overtaken by the resources of that in which one is caught.

—Rodolphe Gasché, *The Honor of Thinking*

If myth fails in "thinking," fails in not overcoming its own desire to make totality representable, then what is the state of literature in the so-called antimythical era? In *Does Literature Think? Literature as Theory for an An-*

timythical Era, Stathis Gourgouris, invoking Pierre Macherey's landmark volume entitled *A quoi pense la literature* (*The Object of Literature*), attempts to account for literature's unique "mode of knowledge," its mythical or antimythical legacy, for the specific purpose of restoring a perceived lost confidence in narrative's historical role in providing an autonomous site for intellectual, if not political, inquiry.[1] Challenging the instrumentalist limits placed on "thinking" since the Enlightenment, as his introduction suggests, Gourgouris repositions literature as a critical, "thinking" space for a renewed engagement with knowledge—knowledge that previously has been derived primarily from mythical discourses. Is it possible, Gourgouris asks, to conceive of a literary mode of thinking that has the "capacity to theorize intrinsically, without external tutelage"?[2] At first glance this question seems to suggest that *Does Literature Think?* is yet another anti-Enlightenment valorization of unfettered expression and the autonomy of art.

While one can see the faint shadow of this anti-Enlightenment perspective, especially Benjamin's "Baroque" philosophy, in and around the volume's chapters, the larger theoretical point of Gourgouris's work is free of the reactionary implications of a neomythicalism as a renewal of "old" myth that ironically would make today's literary texts nothing more than the "new" myths of our so-called antimythical era, as Gourgouris has described it. Contrary to any defense of intuitionism, expressionism, or existential creative fidelity, Gourgouris tends toward a demythologizing practice, a long-standing method of interpretation in religious studies, with myth practically understood as narrative that provides social cohesion or has collective importance within a civic space: "This inquiry," Gourgouris writes, "presupposes that myth is a particular mode of social thought, and, indeed, that mythic thought produces a particular mode of knowledge."[3] The question is, what are the contours and ends of this "particular mode of knowledge"? Is "thinking," then, only "social"? Traceable to a historical moment in which "thinking" coalesces into discernible "thought"?

Demythologized myth, then, begins in this study to look very much like modern literature, and this particular literature "thinking," one could suggest, implies at least two possibilities: the first is the conventional point of view in which literature, aided and epistemologically underwritten by some other discipline such as religion, renders useful examples for further reflections on the world—a world that it knows only through mimesis; the second, which takes shape around the concept of "theory," as Gasché identifies it, situates "thinking" in literature within the theoretical, a heterogeneous space in which sociological reference, mimetic limit, and the "traceable" ontic are not determinate. With some qualification it is in between these possibilities that we find Gourgouris's study: "The question is not simply whether literature thinks but whether literature thinks theoretically—whether it has the capacity to theorize the condition of the world from which it emerges and to which it addresses itself."[4]

Having a strictly "untraceable" capacity to theorize the "condition of the world," if this were the case, would place literature into, or at least dangerously near, a category of discourse that is usually reserved for history's great hegemonic narratives—those discursive structures that not only account for the world but also situate their own generation within that world. Of course, this comprehensive metaphysical power to account for all origins is one defining characteristic of myth in general, with its strong emphasis on accounting for the "Real" reality. The troubling question to ask is, is this unveiling of the "really real" the remnant of myth that inheres in literature today? Does freeing literature from its historically imposed "tutelage," and thus allowing it to "think," simply reinscribe the autotelic problem of myth?

The challenge here will be in distinguishing "literature thinking" from a historical myth function in which narrative, as it provides an account of the real, eventually unfolds the purpose of its own telling, which is in effect a disguising of its (myth's) phantasmic, autotelic status. In this ontological situation each instance of a "literature thinking," as it develops as something other than myth, must construct some point of "wonder" or "untraceable" space of excess that the narrative cannot contain. If this instance of narrative excess, in particular, is allowed to preempt a mythic-hegemonic closure around thinking, while preserving the "surprise" of the "untraceable," then literature will successfully cast off myth's totalizing function and approach its capacity to think, as described by Gourgouris.

This is what potentially happens in postmodern films such as *Pulp Fiction,* in which the "real object" is never revealed and the text is exceeded by its own "world." Herman Melville's *Moby Dick,* if one prefers a literary example, produces a similar "untraceable" return to the initial, excessive creative moment—the eyewitness narrator/protagonist, Ishmael, who is both inside and outside (in excess of) the narrative. His "problem" with the great whale, if one will recall, is its plural "whiteness." In this regard, and distinct from myth, "literature thinking" must stipulate to its being "caught" in an untotalizeable, total system of reference, with no traceable recourse to an origin.

As we discussed in previous sections, modern uses of myth—complementing upper-case "Theory," as it is understood in the context of nineteenth-century Romanticism—are conditioned by these two excesses—one external and the other internal. The external, of course, involves the superimposition of other discourses over the sense-making process of interpretation, for example, the divine's dominance of myth and literature. In this instance sacred myth or "Myth" allows multiplicity to be subsumed by univocity, which, recalling Gasché's formulation of "Theory" in Romanticism, leads to a moment of uniformity. The internal excess or "internal transgression," however, which would be closer to lower-case "theory" as a privileging of heterogeneity and difference over uniformity, potentially plays itself out as a superabundance or incommensurability produced within or across the structure or logic of narrative. This excess, as we have discussed it, appears through "re-marking," and it is "re-marking" this internal rift or gap as excessive that allows not just another interpretative possibility but a way to radically resituate an entire signifying "network" through any and all determinations as the generically "possible"—Žižek's "comedy of Christianity," for instance.

The first question one encounters with "literature thinking," then, centers on the problem of reference. Is literature able to identify, locate, and then "think" alongside "excess"? The answer to this question perhaps lies in the tenuous relationship between literature and everything that it has been subordinated to, with religion and theology here representing the most totalizing of discourses.

3.2 Literature Thinking Religion

> The best ideal is the true
> And other truth is none.
> All glory be ascribed to
> The holy Three in One.
>
> —Gerard Manley Hopkins, "Summa"

> First follow Nature, and your Judgment frame
> By her Standard, which is still the same;
> *Unerring Nature,* still divinely bright,
> *One* clear, *unchang'd,* and *Universal Light,*
> Life, Force, and Beauty, must to all impart,
> At once the *Source,* and *End,* and *Test* of Art
>
> —Alexander Pope, *An Essay on Criticism*

The study of literature and religion traditionally has existed within a familiar hierarchy in which "divinity" and "word" form a duality that, ultimately and mysteriously, relates and "marries" the two within a transcendent order, the order, in this instance, of the "One." This resulting unity, as we have seen, is said to come directly through the divine, which takes the multiple or the many and subverts or perhaps elevates it into a singular "ideal truth." Hopkins's "Summa" poetically expresses this mysterious process by which truth and unity not only exclude the many but subsume it within the highest order of divine oneness. If literature is not a simple substitute for myth, imitating its historical function of providing social unity, then how are we to understand the basic function of the literary as a mode of thinking that provides us with, as Hopkins implies, a heterogeneity circumscribed by oneness? In other words, how does literature, "thinking" specifically, give us "the best ideal," as Hopkins, for instance, has affirmed it?

As a representative of a "traditionalist" position, Walter Kaufman, in *The Theological Imagination,* refers to this construction of oneness through the integration of the many as a reconciliation of a "cosmological dualism," a "dualism that he then views as integral to the working of the human imagination—the condition for the literary turn.[5] In fact, one could go so far as to argue that there would be no need for imagination or, subsequently, literature were it not for this ancient duality—a duality in which religion, or in Kaufman's specific case theology, "thinks for" literature, lifting the literary many to the theological One. In giving up this "cosmological dualism," Kaufman writes, there are "several alternative ways of dealing with the tension between the mythic and the metaphysical dimensions in the concept of God [that] seem to open."[6] The first, he notes, is the simplest, with one or the other completely given up and the "duality" reduced to a monolithic mythology or metaphysics: "One may . . . develop a largely mythic notion and make no real attempt to explain how this relates to the rest of our experience and knowledge. . . . Or [second] one may confine oneself to conceptions that are metaphysically plausible but that have little or no religious power."[7]

Kaufman's third possibility, as one could predict, splits the difference and posits a "tension-reduced" duality as a final outcome—one with a supposedly equal emphasis on each side of the divide, viewing the "concept of God" as something, but a something lacking particular attributes. God, following Kaufman's description, has a "name" and a metaphysical absoluteness and reality—neither, however, is fully present to knowing because both exist beyond the human. The remainder between the two, where one would expect to find the human creative act, according to Kaufman leaves the "overwhelming" tension "somewhat reduced":

> I have attempted to hold together the mythic and the metaphysical dimensions in the concept of God and to show how they are related to each other. By identifying God with the mundane cosmic, vital, and historical powers which have given rise to our humanity and which undergird all our efforts to achieve a fully humane society, I have attempted to provide a metaphysically plausible referent for a religiously significant symbol. With this move the tension between the mythic and the metaphysical is somewhat reduced by qualifying both God's "absoluteness" and God's "humaneness." God's absoluteness is qualified by identifying the referent of "God" with those cosmic forces that undergird our distinctively human forms of being; God's humaneness is qualified by interpreting God as a symbol for humanizing and vital powers instead of as "a personal being." By compromising each of these motifs a bit, they are pulled together into a symbol/concept which can claim both metaphysical plausibility and some religious power.[8]

This compromising "somewhat reduced tension" described by Kaufman becomes, within the traditional study of religion and the literary, a universal auxiliary space, which could include literature, film, and the arts—anything that oscillates between the mythic and the metaphysical. The specific goal of Kaufman's analysis is, ultimately, theological oneness—showing the determining force of the divine in mythic and, by implication, literary texts. The metaphysical "absolute," not unlike Eliade's ground of the symbol, serves to bring together two planes divided against each other, with the literary or mythic held in place by "some religious power" that allows literature, in this particular instance, to think.

From this perspective the oppositional force creating a duality is lessened or muted by the metaphorical link that is "God," as symbol/concept. Rather than choosing between the mythical and the metaphysical, or the literary and the religious/theological, Kaufman settles for a less robust tension, which results in taking a little of each. Of course, this contraction of opposites results in a mere description of a relationship—one that ends simply less polarized than it begins. The muted tension between two opposing planes does not, however, address how "Oneness" comes from many. In fact, Hopkins's "Summa" remains, after Kaufman's description of religious "power," just an expression of a mystical, phantasmic happening, with heterogeneity mysteriously erased by a sacred hegemony. The issue that persists after Kaufman's attempt to address the opposition of the mythical and the metaphysical can be further developed as a problem of thinking, especially "literature" thinking. By making the religious/theological dominant, even if "God" becomes in the process a mere "symbol/concept," Kaufman, no matter how one finally understands his argument, leaves the mythical or the literary on a second tier of lesser value. The metaphysical, redefined as the religious/theological, comes first, and literature's relationship to the "real" remains largely mimetic, not creative. This formulation, then, preempts literature's capacity to "think theoretically." On a second tier of lesser value, with a limited mimetic function, literature is not only prohibited from questioning a reality but also, more significantly, barred from creating a reality.

Thinking literature, on the other hand, as Gourgouris argues, "thinking theoretically," questions not just the world as it is but the creation of that world and literature's place in it. If this formulation works, could literature, through theory, "overthrow" Kaufman's mythic/metaphysical dialectic? Even overthrow religious/theological dominance!? A reinvigorated "literature" or poetry, in this instance, would, or at least could, upset the dynamic in which the dangerous supplement of the literary, its capacity to "think theoretically," could emerge as a useful revolutionary force—contrary to the unbridled, much disparaged force of poetic passion that Plato fears would ruin his scrupulous republic. One could question, then, the place of literature's revolutionary importance beyond its realist tendencies to incite action through the mimetic depiction of social struggle. Here, as has been noted before, the power of literature would not reside simply in its capacity to represent a new world or a more just social order, but in its very nature to actually "think" possibility or virtuality into the world.

For Žižek, who returns to this idea of thinking as "re-marking," the spacing of significance—the one of revolutionary potential—that prepares the way for theory is not *between* the mythic and the metaphysical, as Kaufman's analysis suggests; instead the revolutionary force of literature may in fact exist in excess of the world it creates. In other words, and it is worth repeating, literature's power to effect change does not come only from the "new" world it renders but from the very possibility of rendering a world in the first place, a world (existing as Deleuzean "virtuality") unhinged from social referents or an ideological framework.

The revolutionary "rift," "gap," or "fissure" coming from "re-marking" that deserves critical attention, therefore, is *within* the world, as extimacy, as either the mythic or the metaphysical. Split from *within,* or "internally transgressive," these so-called exterior frames of reference cannot sustain their hegemonic force or superimpose their respective organizing logic over literary thinking—the internal "gap" *within* a "myth and metaphysics" problem, as Kaufman describes the polarity, prohibits totalization, and any revolutionary potential that may result exists apart from the reinscription of a specific dominant order. In other words, literature's radicality comes from its possibility for possibilities. Literature "thinking," or literature confronting its condition of being in the world, potentially leads to a degree of political or ideological indeterminacy, an indeterminacy that guards the literary against a dominant external discourse, mythological, metaphysical, or theological. Literature, in this sense, gains its power to "think" from extimacy—its ability to produce a "possibility" for a world—not simply reflect it.

3.3 Returning to the Thinking in Theory

Poetic discourse *takes root* in a wound.
—Jacques Derrida, *Writing and Difference*

The limiting admonition affirming that literature, as it ventures into thinking, needs a disciplinary attendant, as we have seen, appears most dramati-
cally when the study of literature, in a manner of speaking, becomes "theoretical." In the mid-twentieth century, specifically in light of René Wellek
and Austin Warren's 1949 publication of *Theory of Literature,* the question of
methodology was confined to questions of epistemology, which, as James
Comas notes in *Between Politics and Ethics,* only partially address the issue
of literary autonomy. The pressing issue, for Wellek, could be characterized
as one of epistemology, insofar as literature, as it moved between aesthetics
and history, required an "antipositivist" ground, a ground that would do
more than simply provide a causal account of the text: "The problem of the
extrinsic approach is its causal mode of explanation, a mode that is adopted
from the physical sciences and that is believed to be inappropriate not only
for literary studies but also, as the Heidelberg philosophers argued, for the
study of all aspects of human behavior. Thus the role of literary theory for
Wellek and Warren is not to secure autonomous disciplinary knowledge
but to establish an antipositivist epistemological grounding for both criticism and literary history."[9] "Antipositivism," as a "literary" epistemological theory, is synonymous with "thinking," a thinking that qualifies as a
mode of engagement in which literary studies would do more than simply
account for the existence of texts.

In the mid-1960s, when the issue of literary "autonomy" was a central
concern, it was the "comparativist" (not the theorist) René Wellek who
comprehensively addressed the problem of the undue influence of history
and philosophy on the study of literature by proposing a Malrauxian-style
scholarship—one without "walls." Liberating literature, as he viewed it after the New Criticism, from the tutorial domination of other disciplines
required the development of an odd paradox in which "the only way out is a
carefully defined and refined absolutism, a recognition that 'the Absolute is
in the relative, though not finally and fully in it.'"[10] Wellek, before the great
theory wars, advocated for an "unprincipled" thinking, a way forward, al-

beit paradoxical, between literary history, literary criticism, and literary theory, that eventually related, rather than joined, the three in scholarly praxis.

Unlike Kaufman, however, Wellek defined the problem of "tutelage" in a way that made the study of literature, religion, history, and philosophy a much more precarious task, with a final "subdued" tension—the remedy offered by Kaufman—either seemingly out of reach or insufficient. The question arising from Wellek's perspective then is, when one claims a relative autonomy for literature, does that automatically mean that one is advocating for formalism or textualism as a primary essence of reading? In other words, does literature, by its nature, require the intervention of another discipline before interpretation and thinking begin? One could argue that this question is never fully answered by Wellek, insofar as he insists upon a "Baroque" arrangement of history, criticism, literature, and theory. While his methodological preferences may be varied, his understanding of the goal of "reading" remains fairly clear—finding the abundance of meaning in literary texts. Unlike his colleagues J. Hillis Miller and Paul de Man, Wellek, in his understanding of theory, is unwilling to jettison "reading's" grand metaphysical assumption—that literature is grounded in a reality. In this sense Wellek welcomes what Kaufman would wish to seriously tamp down: "cosmological dualism."

This emphasis on irreconcilable antagonisms further explains Wellek's reference to Malraux and his concept of a "wall-less" architecture of interpretation, with the resulting thinking forever wavering in and across a fertile landscape of metaphysically and epistemologically rooted meaning. It also sheds light on Wellek's strong condemnation of deconstruction, which he viewed as a process of stripping this meaning from literature. Given his appreciation of irreconcilable antagonisms and literature's metaphysical and epistemological ground, Wellek, while he enjoyed speculations about the "theory of literature," finally came to view theory's ending of literary metaphysics as a "new nihilism":

> Literary studies would become a specialty, a new anti-aesthetic ivory tower that would deprive literature of its human and social meaning as a representation of reality, as stimulation, admonition and simply enjoyment. It would scare off students who could not possibly see why they should devote their lives to such a negative and finally futile pursuit of dismantling, de-

constructing. One can only hope that deconstruction is a passing fashion and that literary studies will continue to explore the riches of literature in the spirit of tolerance and positive appreciation. In recent decades the great variety of new, and not so new, methodologies has contributed to a deeper understanding of literature: psychoanalytical critics, students of sociology, Marxists, structuralists, semioticians, reader-response critics, feminist critics, comparatists, and others have in their different ways widened our horizons. Only deconstructionism is entirely negative.[11]

It may be unfair to emphasize this late essay by Wellek, with its obvious vitriolic assessment of deconstruction. One could argue that Wellek's differences with his Yale colleagues may not have been his differences with "theory." In any case, his concluding negative view of "deconstruction" seems at odds with many of his own ideas regarding the significance of theory. The "entirely" negative results of deconstruction, as Wellek viewed them, made literary studies in Wellek's mind futile, which is different from making "literature" futile.

This is an important distinction to make, insofar as Wellek's criticisms of "theory" point more explicitly toward "theoretical thinking" than toward methodology; that is to say, for Wellek deconstruction, at least in this later essay, becomes a call to nonthinking, which was, for him, unthinkable. Deconstructionists, I'll argue, and more specifically Derrida, de Man, and Miller, would hardly disagree if by "thinking" Wellek meant making literature an object of cognition, by either "intrinsic" or "extrinsic" means.

"Widening" the horizon of literature, as Wellek describes it, of course does not immediately translate into more thinking, especially the kind of thinking that has been discussed. For literature to "think" from a more traditional point of view it must, in a sense, call out to some metaphysical terrain, some order or origin that vouches for its limited sovereignty. In this instance, recalling Hopkins, theory, from Wellek's position, performs its allegedly subtractive function, diminishing the range and value of the literary by supplanting it with meaningless contradiction. From a theoretical perspective deconstruction, by contrast, would add to the literary, inverting a hierarchy organized by the one horizon of meaningfulness; that is, literature "thinking," theoretically, would result in an antimetaphysics, a departure from the metaphor of horizonality itself. So in the absence of the hegemony of horizontal oneness, which Wellek would seem to prefer, it is not necessarily the case that literature simply would cease to think and tumble down the black hole of nihilism. It is, rather, that literature, as literature, would come to think in terms of *creating* an excess—not only something exterior but an excessive something that is interior, an *internal excess.*

In "The Critic as Host" J. Hillis Miller states that the presumed forgone "wider horizon" of reading that occurs in deconstruction reappears as a complex "equivocal richness" in which "there is no conceptual expression without figure, and no intertwining of concept and figure without an implied story, narrative, or myth."[12] The tension between Miller's "univocal" and "equivocal" approaches to reading literature takes shape around an idea of excess and, more specifically, "creating" an excess, with the latter the end of literature "thinking." In other words, if literature were completely self-contained, univocal by either formal qualities or external contingencies, it wouldn't be literature; it would be . . . mathesis.[13] This conclusion by Miller leaves the discipline to debate the importance of the guiding metaphor—whether reading literature occurs below a "wide" horizon or with an equivocal complexity. "Thinking" literature, of course, demands the latter.

If the problem, at least as it has been discussed, can be identified as the difficulty of capturing literature in the act of "thinking," the instance in which it expresses its *internal* excess or its resistance to external and/or formal determination, then Jean-Michel Rabaté's *The Future of Theory* provides a novel way toward a solution, a way directly through "theory": "Theory *is* literature, if you want, but literature raised to the power of speculation, literature when the term includes the 'question of literature' or 'the thinking of literature.'"[14] In the "Wellekian" or "Bloomian" late 1970s and into the mid-1980s, the early obstacle to "theory," especially "literary theory," was its presupposed displacement of something original, authentic, or primary in literature. Theory, posited as "Theory," was assumed to have the power to remove something from literature, for example, the author, intentionality, history. A "Theory" of everything, many believed—including Wellek, it would seem—meant that any inherent value of an art object or literary work would be entirely dislocated from the fields of historical and aesthetic appreciation and subsequently dropped, more or less, into some larger nihilistic, linguistic problematic. "Theory," during this early era, was synonymous with redaction, and the response to it was, as Rabaté recalls, largely hysterical.[15]

This hysteria-inspiring discourse is, as history has shown, Gasché's "Theory" with a capital *T,* a formulation existing under the burden of a purported universalism. Theory, more generally in the humanities, unfortunately came to be associated with theory in the sciences, which was construed, wrongly, as the "theory of everything." Jean-François Lyotard's *The Postmodern Condition: A Report on Knowledge* offered, quite powerfully, postmodern theory's rebuttal of "Theory," especially as "Theory" served the interests of metanarratives. As Gasché informs us, however, English professors in North America, Frederic Jameson for one, did much to propagate a continued misunderstanding of the postmodern condition by associating "theory" or "postmodernism" with late capitalism and, through an overly literal application of Derridean deconstruction, by performing exclusionary "readings" of texts based on a limited set of propositions gleaned from highly complex philosophical texts. Deconstruction, for instance, was at the time simply understood by many to be the universal practice of "reading the major in terms of the minor," and Foucauldian historicism was rendered, also rather simplistically, as a search for small history with a big political twist.

The annals of "literary theory" are filled with moments in which one side accuses the other of pushing some totalizing claim, which, I would argue, speaks to the fact that "theory" was (is) fundamentally misunderstood and that, oddly, its true, serious threat to a traditional "literary" mode of inquiry was overlooked and ultimately averted through a pure, generic, comprehensive, and "hysterical" gesture of rejection. The antitheory narrative, I will argue, would have us believe that "theory" preempted literature's ability to think, which, as Gasché and Rabaté explain, is not only false but is itself, as a contention, guilty of creating the conditions for the very offense it seems to rail against.

Rabaté's account of theory, which is much more parsimonious, is essential at this point for a variety of reasons. First, Rabaté sees the discussion regarding "theory" as an ongoing debate about theory, not its postmortem. Second, with "theory" very much debatable and alive, the question and future of "theory" remain open, which is to say that "theory" has unfinished business in academia. To follow these comments, I'd like to add that any discussion of literature's creative possibility and possibilities can only take place within a theoretical framework—a self-disclosing mode of analysis.

This means that "theory," contrary to its earlier detractors, does not remove an essential something from literature; theory, as I will argue, is "literature thinking," literature raised to the level of "speculation," as Rabaté states. Without theory, even a new critical theory, how could one even broach the question of literature's relationship to art, to the world, to religion, to philosophy, or to anything?

If literature, then, is more than the space of an "example" or an object in the world, like a stone, how and why does it think? What and how does it create? Does it, in other words, produce knowledge, or does it simply offer a place for religious, philosophical, or any other disciplinary knowing to be exhibited? Rabaté astutely poses this concern:

> If there is always a knowledge conveyed by literature, where does it reside? Is it simply that a good novelist somehow sums up a period whose objects, characters, and attitudes it embalms forever? Or that literature functions as a repository for a culture's material world and a particular tradition's more ethereal values? Secondly, what kind of knowledge is needed to decipher the knowledge at work in literature? Should one trust mimesis and look to literature for a simple reflection of reality, following the old image of a mirror dragged along the way, so as to reconstruct nineteenth-century Paris . . . or should one stress the relative autonomy of the work of art and concentrate on its formal properties? Can the two wishes be reconciled or is the alternative radical?[16]

Knowledge, as it appears in discussions of literature, eventually or by custom, is "conveyed" or, more to the point, "exhibited" through a mimetic or aesthetic act. As we have seen in these instances, theologians such as Walter Kaufman offer "reconciliation" as a way toward "literary knowledge," a knowledge ultimately qualified by a "religious power" residing outside the text. Literary critics, urging the adoption of aesthetic criteria, argue for understanding literature as a "verbal icon," an art object with inherent value and totally free from an extrinsic criteria.

The alternative to these, an alternative that would be radical, as Rabaté invites us to consider, involves a resituating of literature and theory, with the latter posited not as a metadiscourse, forcing a submission of the text to another set of relations, but as an interval that preserves an opportunity for literature thinking.

Here it is worth noting a word of caution on the issue of literature's act of thinking: didactic literature is not what is being proposed. Literary works with a pronounced sociological theme, recalling Proust, are like gifts with the price tag still attached. In other words, as Rabaté writes, the Proustian version of "literature thinking" does not begin with a "program" or hard rule that is designed to govern the movement of text but issues from an awareness that resembles a "religious visitation":

> Proust opposes here aesthetic theories to the "truths" or "laws" one discovers by chance, alone, in the simplest sensations that, ordered together, become like religious visitations. This is of course connected with the concept of involuntary memory, these "resurrections" which force us to discover truth in a fundamental passivity: the book we need to write is the book written in us by reality without our knowledge, in countless material traces left by the impact of sensations. This excludes by definition any literary program, any decision to choose "themes" that will be shared by all, since it is only by descending deep into oneself that one can excavate these buried privileged moments.[17]

Literature's Proustian "resurrections" lead to a way of thinking that is not driven by a prefigured organizing theme, a program that determines, as we have noted, what is to be written; on the other hand, "resurrections" cannot simply be magical events—happenings in which meaning spontaneously appears "within" a literary condition once the pen completes its movement.

Following Proust, "literature thinking" begins in sensation, which *In Search of Lost Time* attests. Rather than reinscribing a Proustian/Bergsonian metaphysics of experience in the space of "literature thinking," one could offer another account of "resurrection"—resurrection not of something lost and regained but of something entirely new, something that finds its way to articulation through literature's capacity to be theoretical, to create a condition of "re-marking." Macherey unenthusiastically describes literature's creative force as another "pathetic and magnificent throw of the dice." This particular metaphor, however, may unfairly limit literature to the finite possibilities contained within the dice.

The point to observe and think past here is that literature certainly has the power to offer new characters or new versions of the world. What must not be overlooked, however, is literature's power to produce new conditions, new territories where thinking can occur. *Creative* or *theoretical* literature, therefore, is more than innovation; it is invention. Where Macherey offers pathetic "chance" circumscribed by the limits of dice, Derrida allows literature to occupy the *new,* a space uncircumscribed: "The law of literature tends, in principle, to defy or lift the law. It therefore allows one to think the essence of the law in the experience of this 'everything to say.' It is an institution which tends to overflow the institution."[18] The "overflow," in this instance, can be attributed to the work of literature as theory, which reveals, as Derrida writes, the power of literature "to say everything, to break free of rules, to displace them, and thereby to institute, to invent and even to suspect the traditional differences between nature and institution, nature and conventional law, nature and history."[19]

3.4 Literature Overflowing the Sacred

> So choose, how do you want us to think of you—as a *man* who does wrong, or as someone *divine?*
> —Plato, *Ion*

When literature "thinks," what happens? For Derrida, as we have discussed, literature "thinking" produces an "overflow," an excess that moves the literary in the direction of pure possibility. This emphasis on excess is also an issue for others, non-deconstructionists such as Žižek, who, borrowing from Gasché, who originally borrows from Derrida, reflects on the action of "re-marking" and the form of knowledge literature yields. This is not to say that Derrida, Gasché, and Žižek come to a complete agreement on the nature of excess, although the effect of excess from "re-marking," a Derridean concept, is central to all concerned.

If, as Žižek argues in *The Parallax View,* the "religious," because of its "mediating" nature, more definitively brings to light the significance of the "rift" or "gap," then it is necessary to see where this religious spacing in literature occurs. As we discussed in the previous section, myth is the "first" expression of the religious, which ties into the ineluctable requirement for unalterable origins. The "second," but in no sense lesser, expression of the religious is "literature" or, better, literary texts. Unlike myth, with its "scriptural" connotations, literature or literary texts traditionally occupy a secondary tier lower than "scripture" and higher than, let's say, rhetoric. Just as myth is subject to the divine, literature or literary texts hold some aspect of a so-called greater reality. It is within this horizon that myth and literature, then, share a status as the register of higher meaning. It is also against this very traditional configuration of literature as an effect of the divine that the possibility opens of viewing the "literary" as that which "re-marks" limits of the religious.

Maurice Blanchot, for instance, in *The Space of Literature*, turns to Hölderlin's *The Poet's Vocation* to explore the limits of religion and literature. "Man must, then," Blanchot writes, explaining Hölderlin, "turn back. He must turn away from the realm of the gods, Christ, who has disappeared and calls upon us to disappear."[20] Following this emphasis on turning away, Blanchot implicitly offers two possible ends of literature; it can, as we have seen, strive beyond its disciplinary confines for the divine, that is, approach the standing of scripture. Or it can "turn" its back on this configuration of the divine and seek something else. The first turn, as it is described, represents the traditional relationship between the religious or divine text and literature—one that is asymmetrically arranged, with the latter always at least one level below the former and struggling unsuccessfully to close the distance between the two. This process of turning to close the interval of separation also serves as a key element in "paleo" literary aesthetics, which offers the divine as a critical measure of literary value, a value predicated on literature "not" thinking.

Socrates, for instance, with his characteristically unkind and wounding appraisal of the rhapsodes in *Ion,* addresses this issue directly when he distinguishes between those "with" and those "without" their respective intellects: "You see, it's not mastery that enables them to speak those verses, but a divine power, since if they knew how to speak beautifully on one type of poetry by mastering the subject, they could do so for all the others also."[21] The point being made by Socrates is simple and, if one reads it with its full implications in mind, devastating. The rhapsode is an instrument of the god, a servant without intellect: "The god takes their intellect away from them when he uses them as his servants, as he does prophets and godly diviners, so that we who hear should know that *they* are not the ones who speak those verses that are of such high value, for their intellect is not in them."[22] This conclusion sheds light on the opening line of the dialogue, in which Socrates expresses his contempt for the "contest" that brings Ion into conversation with him: "Don't tell me the Epidaurians hold a contest for *rhapsodes* in honor of the god?"[23] One can also read in this contemptuous remark a more generic criticism of poetry (literature). The poem, if it is beautiful, is not from the speaker, which makes any act of appraisal meaningless since the literary object in question comes from the god. More precisely, if poetry is good, then it is not by "man."

The value of a literary object, as Socrates notes, simply is contingent upon locating its origin, which, as we see in *Ion,* is the divine. The measure of any literary object must take this issue of origin into account. This, of course, is not limited to the ancient world. One of the greatest proponents of divine-source verse is Alexander Pope. His "Muse"-inspired aesthetic, as it is presented in the epigraph, reiterates the secondariness of the literary object by imposing upon it an outside "Nature" that tests the "Life, Force, and Beauty" of the art. The divine element within the poetic object removes it from literary-aesthetic appraisal or "contest" and allows it to supersede the confines of "proud Man's pretending Wit."[24] Just as the rhapsode must decide between being "divine" and being "wrong," so too must the critic, who must acknowledge the presence of the Muse and the continuity of the divine and the poetic.

3.5 Literature's Turning Away

> The Universe is God's sanctuary.
> —Paul Tillich, *Theology of Culture*

Blanchot's reading of Hölderlin's "turn away" from the "realm of the gods," with its Romantic nuances, presents a possibility for poetry or literature that defies or represents a "re-marking" of the traditional "divine/word" relationship. Expressed initially as a "reversal" or "revolt," Hölderlin's insights appear to Blanchot as a moment of liberation:

> But how is this reversal possible? Is it an entirely human revolt? Is man urged to stand up against the superior forces which are hostile to him because they would turn away from his terrestrial task? No, and it is here that Hölderlin's thought, though already veiled by madness, appears more reflective, less

facile than that of humanism. If Western men are to bring about this decisive turning point, they must do so in the wake of the gods who themselves accomplished what Hölderlin calls "the categorical reversal."[25]

If the aspirant discipline of literature, historically, has been religion, as we have seen in Plato, Pope, and countless others, then there is no "turn to" the religious, only a "climb"—perhaps eventually even a "turning away." This misalignment of the two, however, does not exist free of contestation, as with Paul Tillich's all-encompassing existential theology, in which the "Universe is God's sanctuary."

This expansion of Hölderlin's "turning away" prefigures Paul Tillich's observation regarding a god that, in a sense, turns away from the divine. Tillich's expanded godly sanctuary, with its radical subversion of the sacred/secular opposition, opens new possibilities for the study of art, culture, and literature.

To say that only good poetry contains the divine is to eliminate the divine from the universe; in other words, with the "universe as God's sanctuary," there is no "test" of art that would result in a separation of poetry and the divine. Tillich's formulation in "Aspects of a Religious Analysis of Culture" places the work of culture, including poetry, within the existential domain of human life—not in an exclusive reserve of the sacred: "Every work day is a day of the Lord, every supper a Lord's supper, every work the fulfillment of a divine task, every joy a joy in God. In all preliminary concerns, ultimate concern is present, consecrating them. Essentially the religious and the secular are not separated realms. Rather they are within each other."[26]

While the primary focus of Tillich's comments is on the church/culture divide, it is worth noting that the collapse of the secular and the sacred makes possible the concept of a "turning" toward rather than a "climbing" to, which he associates with idolatry. By "turning" theology loose from the exclusivity of the divine, Tillich dismantles the asymmetrical divide between church and culture, as well as theology and literature. A key element in Tillich's proto-deconstruction of this divide is language, particularly theological language, which he views as ultimately pliable and diverse in nature:

There is no sacred language which has fallen from a supernatural heaven and been put between the covers of a book. But there is human language, based on man's encounter with reality, changing through the millennia, used for the needs of daily life, for expression and communication, for literature and poetry, and used also for the expression and communication of our ultimate concern. In each of these cases the language is different. Religious language is ordinary language, changed under the power of what it expresses, the ultimate of being and meaning. The expression of it can be narrative (mythological, legendary, historical), or it can be prophetic, poetic, liturgical. It becomes holy for those to whom it expresses their ultimate concern from generation to generation. But there is no holy language in itself, as translations and revisions show.[27]

Writing theology and writing literature involve the same "human language." This, for Tillich, is a revolutionary concept and one in which language undergoes change not by the power of the "god" but by the existential power of that which it expresses, "the ultimate of being and meaning." "No sacred language," as the "turning-away" condition of possibility for Tillich's existential theology, frees theology and literature from their previous inequitable contract. Much more, of course, can be said here of the status of literature as a product of human language. This would include the prophetic function of literature and the genius of the author, which weigh heavily on the critical tradition.

Keeping in mind all the subtleties that various theories of literature contain, it is necessary to make one fundamental, historical distinction between theological and literary texts as they are traditionally construed: only one, the theological text, inherently makes manifest a divine message. Literary texts, in contrast, can only approximate this function—they are not Scripture. Tillich's existential linguistic theory defies this arrangement and subverts the concept of sacred speech, providing for a so-called new theology of the "word" that is indexed to human rather than divine expression. To return to Plato for contrast, one is not faced with merely two possibilities that are conditioned by only one ultimate reality, being "wrong" or being "divine." Tillich's emphasis on the fact that there is "no holy language" expands, not diminishes, the possibilities for theological expression.

In this construction literary language does not aspire to sacred speech as much as it diversifies, cuts against, and enriches expression of an ultimate concern, a concern that is fundamentally human. Theology's "turn" toward literature, as noted by Tillich, is significant insofar as it leaves us with a universe and a God that are much larger than the ones with which we began. This "Tillichian existential/linguistic turn" has greater implications still for the study of theology and literature.

Postmodern theologians working from Tillich's insights, for instance, surpassed his existential theology and began viewing theology as a "semantic" activity representing a turn not toward the divine or toward experience, but toward theology's own processes of signification. Charles E. Winquist, in *Epiphanies of Darkness,* carries this observation to its extreme when he defines theology as "writing" (*écriture*):

> Theology must stop and look around at its own semantic achievement when experience can no longer sustain the literal connection between theology's words and the world's it represents. Theology is not a mirror. It is writing, and writing is a substitution and a repression. Theology represents a world, but the connection is not literal. As in other disciplines of the imagination, its scene of origination is metaphorical. Perhaps theology always knew it was metaphorical as it led readers through the labyrinth of a dark night of the soul, or up the sides of magical mountains, or into the complexities of an inner verbum. Maybe it always disguised its second order of reflection in the first order display of the world it claimed to represent or even present. Now, after inflicting wounds on itself, it must take account of the semantic achievement that is its construction.[28]

Winquist's "theology is writing" turns on (against) Tillich's earlier "turn," with radical consequences.[29] The existential dimension to which Tillich appeals for a subversion of the sacred/secular divide is further displaced by Winquist's invocation of deconstructive discourse, a discourse that he finds in a "strong" reading of Tillich. Not only is language strictly human; it is nonreferential or not contingent upon a divine order, with all the Derridean complications.

In his later work, *Desiring Theology,* Winquist makes the following Deleuze-inspired extended argument concerning the nature of writing and theology:

Since we are always already within specific discursive practices, singularities will occur within these practices, although their status is of a nature that does not always fit the prevailing practice. That is, an event occurs that can no longer be thought of as singular in the sense that it resists explanation in the current interpretive practice. A new thinking, a new speaking, a new writing flows from the singularity. This new thinking can be within the framework of current interpretive practice, but singular events also can be indexed on multiple registers that are not contained within the frame of prevailing interpretive practices. They are always "other," but these alterities can be empiricities that escape interpretation, heterodoxies that conflict with interpretation, or multiplicities that extend beyond the range of interpretation.[30]

The alleged power of language to disclose a divine or eschatological reality is further interrupted as "semantic activity" shows that even human speech is disconnected from the world it purportedly represents or "presents." The transparency or existentially expressive power of human speech gives way, under Winquist's "theology is writing," to a fully metaphorical or literary "sacred" that results in a "hermeneutics of expansion" in which meaning is unmoored from any transcendent plane of origin.[31]

"Theology is writing" provides that "every text can be lifted into a more complex pattern of meaning or recollected under a larger horizon."[32] The "concept of God," as Winquist writes, "is the teleological fulfillment of the metaphorical potential in discourse."[33] "Theology is writing" is a concept of "thinking" as self-wounding, an opening of the closed body of the text to ever-increasing possibilities for meaning, meanings that paradoxically resist absolute meaningfulness and transgress the "limits of intelligibility."[34]

Theology's "thinking," its literary wound, as a transgression by the new, has tremendous significance for literature, especially if, as Derrida claims, "poetic discourse *takes root* in a wound." The specific reference, of course, is to Edmond Jabès and the "question" of the book. For Derrida, Jabès exposes a deeply rooted problem of the origin, the origin of writing. Rather than the asymmetrical relation between theology and literature with which we began, Derrida reads in Jabès another asymmetry. This one is more sustainable for literature in the end: "God separated himself from himself in order to let us speak, in order to astonish and interrogate us. He did so not by speaking but by keeping still, by letting silence interrupt his voice and his signs, by letting the Tables be broken."[35]

With this assessment we are confronted with a theology that has "no sacred language," a theology predicated on silence and stillness. If we were to resuscitate our former dynamic, with literature aspiring to theology, then we would be left with a literature in pursuit of silence and stillness, a literature of interrogation. Here we would have "literature's theological wound," not an opening between the sacred and profane or the divine and existential, but a tear across the fabric of life. "If," as Derrida observes, "writing is not a tearing of the self toward the other within a confession of infinite separation, if it is a delectation of itself, the pleasure of writing for its own sake, the satisfaction of the artist, then it destroys itself."[36] This "infinite separation" can be construed as a transposition of the earlier equation—"writing is theology," with writing (literature) now occupying the place of perpetual interrogation.

The proliferation of God or the divine into semantic activity erases the traditional theology/literature coupling and, in a more radical way than Tillich realized, makes theology an expression of the poetic, along with everything else, which oddly validates the proposition that "the Universe is God's sanctuary." It is also important to note that both the "Universe" and "God"—beyond Tillich's definition, not Derrida's—participate in the most radical form of semantic expansion, an expansion that permits the theological and the literary to cross, leaving each one's trace within the other. It is only through exchanging these traces as wounds that theology and literature's conditions of possibility can be transgressed and continually resituated within more complex patterns of signification.

Complex patterns of "signification," however, should not imply some ultimate pattern, a determining design within which all shapes exist. More specifically, complexity is not limited to style or genre within any cultural era. Winquist writes: "Theology [as a complex pattern] inhabits the edges and cracks of the dominant culture. It is a nomad discipline wandering, wondering, and erring."[37] Wandering, wondering, and erring, for Winquist, are Deleuzean folds of excess in theological and literary discourse, limits to our ability to know an object or make present an object or fully mourn its loss.[38] In this sense Winquist's thinking is a thinking that disappoints, accepts the failure of representation, accepts the "internal transgression" or "ingression" of all discourse. As untraceable surfaces, then, the theology of literature and the literature of theology remain held together through a mutual limitlessness, an unclosable interval in which the nomadic quality of each flows across distinct "incommensurabilities."

This tension between theological and literary discourse that one finds in Winquist's writings corresponds directly with Deleuze's language on God, a language of difference. For Winquist difference is the condition of desire, an ironic desire that desperately reaches for simplicity and complexity:

> Desire is an ambiguous gift. The capacity to formulate and think a *term* of the ontological argument secures an affirmation of the existence of such a capacity to think. It marks or re-marks a desire for ultimacy. It is a formal achievement of thinking. It does not secure a content for thinking. There is a distinction between the formal and the material infrastructure of thinking. Thinking the concept of "that than which nothing greater can be thought" does not provide an image. It is, as Tillich understood, a non-symbolic concept. To have an ultimate concern says much about what it means to be consciously human. But, it does not in-itself provide an object or tell us about the object of the ultimate concern. Desire is an ambiguous gift because it is an unfinished reality. Desire cannot guarantee its satisfaction.[39]

With desire one finds mourning and an "unfinished reality" that is, for Winquist, "God."

The anticipated return of the ultimate object, or the attempted restoration of narrative plenitude through desire, is undercut by mourning, the ineluctable failure of satisfaction. Desire does not "guarantee" the escape from the unsatisfying, the recovery of an object, or the reconciliation of difference; instead desire begets mourning, creating not a space of fullness but one of loss: "But the image is more profound because it frees itself from its object in order to become a process itself, that is, an event as a 'possible' that no longer even needs to be realized in a body or an object, somewhat like the smile without a cat in Lewis Carroll."[40] In loss, desire and mourning are, as Winquist states, "ambiguous gifts." Each, paradoxically, begins before the other, yielding a condition of possibility that was, is, or shall be nothing more or less than a "fold," a "movement," a "cut," a "passage," or a "cloud."[41]

If theology is a "folding" practice, then so too is literature or the literary, with one moving across the other, expressing the other's limits.[42] Does literature free theological and religious discourse from the burden of superiority? Does a weakened theology or a weak religious discourse create a possibility for literature, a possibility that only can exist, as Deleuze observes, as a "smile without a cat"? Perhaps a turn to literature is now required, with Tolstoy "rethinking" Christianity, the exhibition *The City of K.* "rethinking" Kafka, and Christoph Ransmayr "rethinking" Ovid's *Metamorphosis*.

3.6 Tolstoy's "Re-Marking" the Gospel

> I know that the explanation of all things, like the origin of all things, must remain hidden in infinity. But I do want to understand in order that I might be brought to the inevitably incomprehensible.
>
> —Leo Tolstoy, *Confession*

"The reader must not forget," Leo Tolstoy writes in *The Gospel in Brief,* "that it is the teaching of Christ which may be sacred, but in no way can a certain measure of verses and syllables be so; and that certain verses, from here to here, say, cannot be sacred merely because men say they are so."[43] These remarks suggest that Tolstoy was attempting to separate, if not free, theology from the confines of dogmatism and the mythological. While Tolstoy's endeavor to render the Gospel in brief arises from his profound personal existential despair over a lack of meaning in his life, as a writer he attempted, albeit incompletely, to satisfy his desire to make the sacred universally available, in excess of the theological and the religious. The attempt to find or unfold "essential" meaning in the depths of his depression, to represent an undiscovered social meaning to a Christian community, came at a high personal price for Tolstoy. While Tolstoy's excommunication from and later return to the Church meant personal sacrifice and anguish, it was his desire to make religion larger, more expansive, by removing from it a supernatural God that deserves attention here.

Rather than rehearse the biographical circumstances leading to the writing of *The Gospel in Brief,* let us attend to the "thinking" that makes the work possible. In moving to free himself from despair, Tolstoy had to free himself from God, a supernatural God. To do this, Tolstoy had to abandon the literary as a pure theological surface; displace the seeming metaphysics of literary language with "objective" language; and establish a condensed, "re-marked" theoretical language of "light." As a writer of an abbreviated "Gospel," he was obliged, therefore, to cast off or free theology from both theological metaphysics and literary mimesis.

Tolstoy's theological aesthetics requires a diminishing of "measure of verses and syllables" in order to bring about a depth of understanding, based on a fact that he believes is exterior to yet graspable by language: "I knew not the light, and I thought there was no sure truth in life; but when I perceived that only light enables men to live, I sought to find the sources of the light. And I found them in the Gospels, despite the false commentaries of the Churches."[44] Tolstoy directs the reader to a social-spiritual understanding of the Gospel that becomes, potentially, a "re-marked" theology—an atheistic theology ironically made possible through the rethinking or deconstruction of "sacred" language.

The Gospel in Brief achieves its brevity for Tolstoy, its accuracy, through a synoptic mode of linguistic practice, a move later heralded by Ludwig Wittgenstein, who praised Tolstoy's achievement.[45] The desupernaturalization of the story of Jesus, for Tolstoy, is designed to return religious "belief" as the lost object of theology through linguistic clarity. This Gospel, written in brief and from "light," according to Tolstoy, results in a condensed literalness, a literalness that eradicates a supernatural excess in order to reaffirm a social-spiritual excess. The desire for clarity and the elimination of supernatural excess in this instance begin with the literary attempt to exclusively bind "light" to word, when the literary and the theological can do nothing more than fold "light" over word and drift across excessive, ironic, and synoptic forms.

Tolstoy's desire for an enlightened theology, for a language of "light," necessitates a mourning of literature as art, a mourning that forces Tolstoy to reluctantly reinvest in the servitude of the literary to the theological. Unlike other texts—literary or single-authored texts that would be "art" for Tolstoy—the "Gospels are the work of thousands of brains and hands of men."[46] The problem with sacred writings is that they are, according to Tolstoy, multiple, poorly composed, and complicated by mythological discourse that stands in the way of theological understanding. In this instance the reader, according to Tolstoy, must persist in reading, excuse the "many hands of men," and remember that an element of the sacred remains in the Gospels—no matter how submerged: "The reader must not forget that, far from it being blamable to disencumber the Gospels of useless passages, and to illuminate passages the one by the other, it is on the contrary, unreasonable not to do this, and hold a certain number of verses and syllables as sacred."[47] From this conflict one can see that Tolstoy's aim is to "disencumber" theological, biblical discourse, rendering in the clearest possible terms its purported true meaning.

The Gospel in Brief is, then, a "re-marked" text, a linguistic compromise between a Word that is beyond language and a word that is too easily adapted to the machinery of doctrine. More than a pursuit of accuracy, "scientific" and theological, Tolstoy's vision is uneasily committed to the objective use of language to reveal the "light" or message of religion, more precisely Christianity. By merging the four Gospels together into a single narrative, free from the complications of "many hands," Tolstoy's metasynoptic mode allows the literariness of theology to resist mythology and return to original "light," with abbreviation functioning as a linguistic prism to focus the message of Christianity.

In its condensed form *The Gospel in Brief* maintains the order of the four Gospels, with changes made to emphasize "the real sense of the teaching."[48] However, the "real sense" of the teaching folds back against Tolstoy's condensing practice, as he discovers to his astonishment that "the Lord's Prayer is nothing less than Christ's whole teaching, stated in most concise form."[49] Thus, chapters of *The Gospel in Brief* appear under twelve headings corresponding to the Lord's Prayer:

1. Our Father / Man is the son of the Father.
2. Which art in heaven / God is the infinite spiritual source of life.
3. Hallowed be Thy name / May the Source of Life be held holy.
4. Thy kingdom come / May His powers be established over all men.
5. They will be done, as in heaven / May His will be fulfilled, as it is in Himself.
6. So also on earth / So also in the bodily life.
7. Give us our daily bread / The temporal life is the food of the true life.

8. This day / The true life is in the present.

9. And forgive us our debts as we forgive our debtors / May the faults and errors of the past not hide this true life from us.

10. And lead us not into temptation / And may they not lead us into delusion.

11. But deliver us from evil / So that no evil may come to us.

12. For Thine is the kingdom, the power and the glory / And there shall be order, and strength, and reason.[50]

The selection process, as Tolstoy explains, is remarkably simple, insofar as "the Gospel according to the four Evangelists is presented in full."[51]

However, the fullness of presentation is qualified by a statement concerning omission: "But in the rendering now given, all passages are omitted which treat the following matters, namely,—John the Baptist's conception and birth, his imprisonment and death; Christ's birth, and his genealogy; his mother's flight with him to Egypt; his miracles at Cana and Capernaum; the casting out of devils; the walking on the sea; the cursing of the fig-tree; the healing of sick, and raising of dead people; the resurrection of Christ Himself."[52] Tolstoy's Gospel gestures at removing the mythological or fantastical from scripture, leaving for the reader a message that is free of "passages . . . containing nothing of the teaching, and [that describe] only events which passed before, during, or after the period in which Jesus taught, they complicate the exposition."[53] The metasynoptic narrative form yields a series of intensities as theology becomes antimythology and the literary becomes "pure" message. With the omission of Christ's resurrection from *The Gospel in Brief*, Tolstoy formulates Christianity as a behavioral paradigm, free from the "complication" of a metaphysical or mythological source—much like the effect of Wittgenstein's *Tractatus*, which outlined the proper use of language in philosophy.

The abbreviated message of *The Gospel in Brief*, however, cannot sustain its unity or perform its "pure teachings of Jesus" without in some respects investing in a process of desire and mourning. That is, *The Gospel in Brief* attempts to recover the lost object of theology, the pure message, and in doing so, as an act of mourning, must desacralize or demythologize the Gospels. In negating the divinity of Jesus and the mythological elements of the Gospels, Tolstoy believes that he has provided the "source of light," separating, as he says, the "pure, life-giving water" from the "mire and slime unrightfully mingled therewith."[54] This division, initiated under the notions of "purity" and "contamination," works to rid, according to Tolstoy, the superadded elements from Christianity, namely the miracles. Excising the supernatural/mythological, Tolstoy composes a Gospel that purportedly is more pure in its rendering of events, more faithful to the "source light" that inspired him—in other words, more literary.

This a/theistic gospel, however, in reducing message to precise, nonmythological literary language based on accuracy, places "light" not in a concrete "reality," as Tolstoy believes, but in the "reality" of language, which is, from a deconstructive position, a series a differences, deferrals, or games. From this one could argue that Tolstoy's attempted "re-marking" of Christianity simply exchanges one metaphysical plane for another, perhaps one that is, as a matter of taste, less supernatural.

The desire, which comes from Tolstoy, for the lost object of theology, the message, necessitates a mourning for that reality that is believed to be obscured by the alleged improper use of language. The condensed gospel in brief moves to strip language of its multiplicity and metaphoricity, leaving it bare, disclosed, and purely functional. In mourning, as it gestures to retrieve in a "new" language that which is designated by desire, the awareness occurs that such a recovery is impossible. Tolstoy's Lord's Prayer illustrates this incommensurability of languages:

> Our Father, without beginning and without end, like heaven!
> May Thy being only be holy.
> May power be only Thine, so that Thy will be done, without
> Beginning and without end, on earth.
> Give me food for life in the present.
> Smooth out my former mistakes, and wipe them away; even as I so do with
> all the mistakes of my brothers, that I may not fall into temptation,
> and may be saved from evil.[55]

"May Thy being only be holy" redirects sacrality away from a metaphysical reality, "like heaven," toward "being" that is presented in a "new" language of precision.

Removed from the supernatural, the Lord's Prayer, and the Gospel in total, must now participate in a "foreign" language, the objective linguistic order, an order that is no more available than the transcendent order of walking on water, casting out devils, or raising others and oneself from the dead. Where Tolstoy, and for that matter Wittgenstein, saw a clarity or purity in the condensation of language, correlated to a objective reality, one finds here a much more dynamic series of events, of which both Jesus and the message become "moveable" limits. Ironically, the desire to restore the object of Christianity, the message, to a Christian community amplifies a sense of mourning, leaving a religious discourse that was once indexed to a supernatural reality fatally bound to the process of language—*The Gospel in Brief,* after the revision to the Lord's Prayer, is, in Deleuzean terms, "a smile without a cat."

The revised prayer, while remaining in/as language, expresses a performative element, even as it deemphasizes the supernatural reality of "heaven." This prayer as performance appears in *The Gospel in Brief* under a prohibition, however. Jesus, in Tolstoy, as in the Gospel of Matthew, preempts the performance by saying, "When you pray, do not chatter with your tongue."[56] The speech-act is interrupted by the "event" of prayer, culminating in Jesus's statement that "your Father knows what you want before you open your lips."[57] In this disarticulated prayer Tolstoy attempts to do more than make language more theologically accurate as to the "message" of Jesus, which is his purpose. He introduces a tension between performance and event, revealing the incommensurability of theology and literature, with prayer as theological performance and literature as interruption.

To pray, then, is not to speak or perform, but to become an event in which the supplicant enters into a foreignness that is and is not his/her own—much like Alice in Carroll's *Through the Looking Glass,* who "becomes larger" than she was and "smaller" than she is.[58] Becoming larger but being smaller is prayer as event, requiring that Tolstoy return to the literary that he has attempted to leave behind. The condensed Lord's Prayer renders God not as a transcendent being but as a being only "like heaven." Tolstoy's Lord's Prayer, much to his consternation, one could imagine, leads to a linguistic God that is implicated in a series of differences and repetitions "like heaven" without beginning or end, a process.

Tolstoy's *Gospel in Brief,* though condensed and seemingly objective in language, permits Christianity (proper) to end with the death of Jesus. The so-called objective language, or language uncontaminated with "slime," reaches its limit as it approaches this death, which also becomes language's death, since objective discourse remains silent once Jesus lets his head fall and gives up "the ghost."[59] The silence, however, is not simply the inaccessibility of a supernatural reality, a reality dismissed by Tolstoy, but the folding of language. Tolstoy's objective language must recognize its desire, purity of message, and through mourning open a surface for thinking that begins with a possibility of the impossibility of either bringing the desired object to presence or properly mourning its loss.

The "Jesus event" creates an aporia in condensed language, with the ghost that is "given" up functioning as a figure of speech, a figure without ground. It is, however, the figure in the figure of speech that points to an incommensurability between the word of objective reality and the Word of the supernatural. The word of objective reality, just like the Word of the supernatural, is a referential sign, a mark that points to something beyond itself. The death of objective language occurs when the sign has nothing more to point to, other than death, and, in pointing, folds into death. Theological or theographical inquiry addresses the limit of the "Jesus event" and similar limits, presenting a collision of incommensurable surfaces.[60]

The question to ask is not what is this theological or theographical inquiry, but *where* is it? For Gilles Deleuze the collision or folding of surfaces means that language is not limited to referral or deferral of meaning; rather, language is "about" what event gives rise to meaning, even a nonmeaning. "It is still a question of the possible," Deleuze writes, "but in a new fashion: the Others are *possible worlds,* on which the voices confer a reality that is always variable, depending on the force they have, and revocable, depending on the silences they create."[61] The silence created by objective language in *The Gospel in Brief* is death; however, in silence something is created, an incommensurability directing us to exist in relation to a new world, a new surface on which possibilities for thinking are present. As one turns from the presence of God (metaphysics) or word (objectivity), one finds a silence of possibility, structures to be created in search of "foreign" languages to follow the so-called internal trace of the other. Desire and mourning are preparations for thinking, moveable limits that allow the recontouring of ultimacy not in reference to or in light of something else, but as a becoming something other. Literature moves across theology, and theology moves across literature, colliding at times to form aporias, events, folds, as calls to thinking. If we begin with theology as nomadic, resistant to hegemony, then theology places us under an obligation to seek other conceptual worlds and other languages for writing, thinking, and forming ourselves along a series of possibility.

3.7 Kafka's Re-Marking K.

"So the doorkeeper cheated the man," said K. immediately, who had been captivated by the story. "Don't be too quick," said the priest, "don't take somebody else's opinion without checking it. I told you the story exactly as it was written. There's nothing in there about cheating." "But it's quite clear," said K., "and your first interpretation of it was quite correct."
—Franz Kafka, *The Trial*

Esteemed Director:
I am writing this letter in bed. I wanted to return to Prague on the 19th of this month, but I am afraid that it won't be possible. For several months I have been almost free of fever, but on Sunday I woke with a fever which climbed to over 38 degrees and still continues today. It's probably not the result of a cold, but one of those chance things common to lung disease which one cannot avoid. The doctor who examined me and found my lungs to be in good condition except for a stubborn remnant considers this acute fever to have little significance.
—Franz Kafka, letter, 17 August 1921

Franz Kafka, K., and "Franz Kafka" are territories, surfaces upon which hegemonic phantasms are recorded and "re-marked." In other words, these three manifestations of the writer present us with missed opportunities to think. This fluid, erring Kafkan recordability is noted in Réda Bensmaïa's foreword to Deleuze and Guattari's *Kafka: Toward a Minor Literature*. Bensmaïa, referring to Walter Benjamin's observation that Kafka's works are missed in two ways, "naturally" and "supernaturally," amplifies this notion of "missing" by arguing that "one misses the mark in Kafka either by putting him in the nursery—by oedipalizing and relating him to mother-father narratives—or by trying to limit him to theological-metaphysical speculations to the detriment of all the political, ethical, and ideological dimensions that run through his work and give it a special status in the history of literature."[62] In each act of "missing" Kafka becomes the recorded, "un-re-marked" figure that is reduced to its ground(s), a figure seemingly fixed and free from allegory and gap.

If putting Kafka in a "nursery" entails missing something, according to Benjamin, what can be said, then, of putting him in a museum? "Exhibiting" or archiving him? The dangers of "exhibiting" and "archiving," in general, return us to the issue of figure and ground. If the exhibition or archive works to bring figure and ground together, seamlessly, then Benjamin's concern that something is "missed," especially in Kafka, is justified. Such a collapse of figure and ground would result in an "archive fever," a condition in which an incomplete totality would artificially become hegemony. What if, however, the exhibition or archive maintains an internal point of transgression? That is, what if the exhibition or archive refuses hegemony? The benefit of this transgressing exhibition space could be stated in the following way: Kafka, in his works, is attentive to *becoming,* and insofar as the museum is potentially a new territory for "re-marking," it is important to register this "becoming" and other possibilities for *deterritorialization* and *reterritorialization.*

The interest in displaying Kafka as "territories" is a departure from the limits of traditional biographical scholarship, which attempts to contextualize, fix, or record the person or his/her works. In 2002–3, the Centre de Cultural Contemporània de Barcelona (CCCB), under the direction of Juan Insua, undertook a "postmodern" project that focused on Kafka's resistance to "recordability." This exhibition, first at the Jewish Museum in New York and now on permanent display at the Kafka Museum in Prague, in many ways accepts the "territoriality" of Kafka, leaving spaces between the figure of Kafka and the grounds of history, culture, and biography. In other words, *The City of K.: Franz Kafka and Prague* exhibits "Kafka" as a problem of re-marking, a problem of resisting totality.

In *The City of K.,* an ambitious and sometimes unsettling exhibition including original documents, facsimiles, and materials relating to Franz Kafka's literary works, life, and cultural surroundings, these "territories" are carefully presented in a series of thematically organized "districts": "The Primal Scene," "A Little 'Ravachol,'" "Life in a Circle," "The Civil Servant and the Artist," "The Theater of Purity," "The Constantly Postponed Marriages," "The God of Suffocation," "The Burrow," "The Endless Office,"

"The Castle," "In the Penal Colony," and "The Threshold." The alignment of such diverse items as photographs, audiovisual installations, letters, and music allows the exhibition space to disrupt Kafka's or K.'s existential space by extending an opposition between figure and ground into the various aspects of the author's literary works and Jewish cultural life in early twentieth-century Prague. Key passages from Kafka's diaries, novels, and short stories, written in white block letters on dark, "muddy" walls, wooden pallets, and an ascending staircase leading nowhere, interrupt the eye as one passes from one exhibit to the next. Within and between installations the problem of "linkage" becomes increasingly apparent. Early on photographs of the Old Town rest submerged on a rock bed against a wall-length, portrait-filled genealogy of the Kafka family. Of the several excerpts inaugurating the exhibit, a line from the "Third Octavo Notebook" seems best to capture the spatial and existential tensions presented throughout the exhibition: "A cage went in search of a bird."

The City of K. presents turn-of-the-century Prague as a geographical and psychological enclosure, an endless and seemingly inescapable complex of literary, cultural, familial, and employment circles. For the exhibit's "Kafka" Prague becomes a "cage," a "fissure," a "vortex," a "crone" that will not yield. The city space, with its discrete parts, becomes an elusive territory, occupying both a literal and a figurative place throughout the exhibit:

> This is not a city. It is a fissure in the ocean bed of time, covered with stony rubble of burned-out dreams and passions, through which we—as if in a diving bell—take a walk. It is interesting, but after a time one loses one's breath.[63]

> Prague doesn't let go. Of either of us. This old crone has claws. One has to yield, or else. We would have to set fire to it on two sides, at the Vyšehrad and at the Hradčany; then it would be possible for us to get away.[64]

The two primary surfaces of the exhibition, "Kafka in Prague: Existential Space" and "Prague in Kafka: Imaginary Topography," represent an attempt to partially reconcile or perhaps amplify the plurality of Kafka's creative works with the circumstances of his life.

This "psycho-historical" approach, of course, is not new to Kafka scholarship. The City of K., one observes, is clearly influenced by and in some ways critical of such landmark Kafka studies as Ernst Pawell's The Night-

mare of Reason: The Life of Franz Kafka; Stanley Corngold's *Franz Kafka: The Necessity of Form;* Gilles Deleuze and Félix Guattari's *Kafka: Toward a Minor Literature;* Mark M. Anderson's *Kafka's Clothes;* and Sander L. Gilman's *Franz Kafka: The Jewish Patient,* one of the most detailed and insightful examinations of Kafka published in the last two decades. The intriguing aspect of *The City of K.* is its "submerged" awareness of these and other recent scholarly writings and its self-conscious avoidance of reducing "Franz Kafka" to a literary or historical style, a psychobiography, or a political and theological allegory. In this respect *The City of K.* is much more than an elaborate author profile or a celebration of an artistic life. With its emphasis on producing an existential and intellectual "experience" of the subtle complexities of "Franz Kafka," the exhibition succeeds where the academy often has failed.

For instance, "Life in a Circle" features an audiovisual installation, *Verkehr* (Traffic), in which the score of Tema K. and distorted documentary footage of life in Prague provide a contrast to displays of documents from Kafka's university days, along with copies of assorted influential magazines and books of the era: *Die Neue Rundschau, Der Kunstwart,* and G. W. F. Hegel's *Phenomenology of Spirit.* While these displays fill in informational details, the installation, with its mutating cityscape transforming into partially recognizable architectural shapes, illuminates the darkened room, causing a grid work or map of shadows to form on the floor beneath the circular display cases. Books, magazines, and portraits, in a shadow space, form circular maps. These distorted, re-marked images on screen, encased historical documents, and shadow circles and grids prompt an awareness of figure and ground in connection with the mutability of experience that is so much a part of Kafka's legacy.

The traditional, "introduction to literature"–style themes of person versus society, him/herself, nature, institutions, and machine run like bait along the surface of "The Civil Servant and the Artist" and "The Endless Office." Oversized, perhaps "coroner-sized" file cabinets and a makeshift desk containing facsimiles of Kafka's correspondence with his "superiors" point to the idea of Kafka as a critic of modern life—an understanding of Kafka that would be most recognizable to the casual museumgoer. The installation leaves the impression that Kafka has just walked away from his desk, which, I would argue, challenges the notion of historical access—the phantasmic idea that the museum space could deliver Kafka to the viewer. A copy of a report written by Kafka entitled "Measures for the Prevention of Accidents with Mechanical Planes," for instance, represents his encounter with a bureaucratic sensibility, with its detachment from unsettling instances of workplace amputation. This suggests the "amputation" of Kafka from the sociocritical commentary that often accompanies his work.

In addition, sketches of a languishing office worker also suggest an existential slicing-away of collective humanity in the age of bureaucracies. Again the exhibit draws attention to a complicated relationship between figure and ground. Resisting the temptation to overstate the observation that Kafka was first and foremost a "critic of modernity," "The Civil Servant and the Artist" advances a less tidy conflict between the artist Kafka and his administrative career: "Writing and office cannot be reconciled, since writing has its center of gravity in depth, whereas the office is on the surface of life. So it goes up and down, and one is bound to be torn asunder in the process."[65] "The Civil Servant and the Artist" portrays Kafka as a "double agent," serving two irreconcilable logics, business and literature. Were it simply the case of a conflict seeking resolution, Kafka would be just another writer in search of a few uninterrupted hours of work. Instead the contrast between figure and ground allows for a more profound insight into Kafka's "process," a perpetuation of a steady and anxious tension in which one side of the contrast will be torn asunder by the other. From this perspective writing and literature, as well as business, fully participate in a risk of annihilation.

"The Theater of Purity," "The Constantly Postponed Marriages," and "The God of Suffocation" all focus on the issue of identity in Kafka's life and writings. His interest in Yiddish theater is revealed through a well-chronicled friendship with the actor Jizchak Löwry, which is shown to have been critical in his reexamination of Jewish life.[66] Through theater programs, diary entries, and copies of influential readings such as M. Pines's *Histoire de la Littérature Judéo-Allemande,* H. Graetz's *Volkstümliche Geschichte der Juden,* and, interestingly, Martin Buber's *Hundert Chassidische Geschichten,* "The Theater of Purity" establishes, fragmentarily, the biographical and intellectual context for Kafka's category of "minor literature," adopted and made famous by French theorists Gilles Deleuze and Félix Guattari in the subtitle of their short theoretical study of Kafka.

The displacements and margins reserved for Yiddish theater and minor literature are echoed in the subsequent exhibits on Kafka's failed romantic life. Occupying the transition from theater to romance is a "vortex" screen featuring floating images of Kafka's love interests. The spiral path through the vortex is completed by a series of letters and photographs documenting Kafka's struggle with his love of writing, self-hatred, and desire for romantic connection: "Without forebears, without marriage, without heirs, with a fierce longing for forebears, marriage, and heirs. They all of them stretch out their hands to me: forebears, marriage, and heirs, but too far away for me. There is an artificial, miserable substitute for everything, for forebears, marriage, and heirs. Feverishly you contrive these substitutes, and if the fever has not already destroyed you, the hopelessness of the substitute will."[67]

The "fever" as desire and the fever of disease (tuberculosis) unite in "The God of Suffocation," lending to the first part of the exhibit's overarching atmosphere of despair, before one enters the second division, entitled "Prague in Kafka: Imaginary Topography." Inside Kafka one finds the symptoms of organic and societal disease, with the silence brought on by laryngeal tuberculosis smothering Kafka's words and life. The theological issue—God as one who suffocates—especially as it relates to identity and death, appears as a fold in the exhibit, giving the installations devised around Kafka's later works an important religious dimension.

"The Burrow," "The Endless Office," "The Castle," "In the Penal Colony," and "The Threshold" engage more directly with the theology of Kafka's works. Again, "The Burrow" and "The Endless Office" simulate the bureaucratic themes in Kafka's novels and short stories: loss of humanity through modernization. "The Castle" and "In the Penal Colony," however, transcend these earlier themes and the various acts of simulation by offering highly abstract "interpretations," perhaps critiques, of the corresponding later works. In particular, "The Castle," with its audiovideo montage, mirrored walls, white carpet, and white cubes, offers a view of the land surveyor K. making his way across a landscape. The overwhelming whiteness, mixed with the reflections of museum visitors sitting attentively on white cubes, brings together the familiar and the unfamiliar: "You're not from the Castle, you're not from the village, you are nothing. Unfortunately, though, you are something, a stranger."[68] A stranger to whom? Others? Oneself?

God? The ethereal space of "The Castle" proceeds to more abstract designs, such as the multisurfaced panels of "In the Penal Colony" in which passages from the novella appear below each portion of the apparatus, leather straps, cotton, needles (harrows), and "flesh."

In the ambient light of the museum's foyer, the exhibition ends on a practical note, with many examples of Kafka's works in translation, illustrating the worldwide significance of his literary contribution. More importantly, however, the final portion of *The City of K.* suggests that "The City of K." is much larger than one may have originally thought, perhaps larger than one would like to admit. "Prague," "The Castle," "The Burrow," "The Office," and "In the Penal Colony" are omnipresent, just one step away from where *you* are. This is the central point of the exhibition, as I see it. The collected works of Kafka have a connection to a particular time and place, but they also rupture, supersede, and exceed that time and place in a multiplicity of ways. The epigraph above, for instance, reveals Kafka as an ironic reader of his own symptomology, however falsely optimistic. To this extent Kafka is a reader of his own complexity, engaged in the same acts of deciphering performed by museum visitors in the space of the exhibition. Encircling Kafka, or confining Kafka to a "city," is an impossibility. And the exhibition in a variety of ways acknowledges Kafka's "escape" from circumscription. This leads to a final observation: *The City of K.* is not a place but an evitable process, a logic in which the familiar is always, already strange and the surface is always, already paradoxically deep.

"Re-marking" Kafka occurs as a uniquely "literary," if not theoretical, moment, a moment in which a "gap" is chronically opened between figure and ground, word and person, and text and context. "I have no interest in literature," Kafka writes, "what happens is that I am made of literature, I am nothing else and cannot be anything else."[69] On one level this could be understood as a writer professing his love of the literary craft, but in Kafka's case it is, obviously, much more. Being made of literature means accepting literature's power of "re-marking," its refusal to be joined to anything completely. Whether it is a human being "re-marked" as an insect, an animal "re-marked" as a human being, a voice "re-marked" as sound, or some other entity that breaks free from its "ontological" or phantasmic moorings to become something else, it is always literature for Kafka.

"Re-marking" the literary appears in Žižek's *Parallax View* as a problem of "unlearning" reference or the temptation of reducing a figure to some ground:

> Reading Kafka demands a great effort of abstraction—not of learning more (the proper interpretive horizon of understanding his work), but of *unlearning* the standard interpretive references, so that we become able to open up to the raw force of Kafka's writing. There are three such interpretive frames: theological (the anxious search for the absent God); socio-critical (Kafka's staging of the nightmarish world of modern alienated bureaucracy); psycho-analytic (Kafka's "unresolved Oedipus complex," which prevented him from engaging in a "normal" sexual relationship). All this has to be erased; a kind of childish naivety has to be regained in order for the reader to be able to feel the raw force of Kafka's universe.[70]

The "raw" force of Kafka's universe is precisely this notion of being "made" of literature, becoming "unhinged" or free from origin and absolute reference.

The particular Kafkan figure cited by Žižek in this instance is "Odradek," an "object" whose name seems to be without origin. The opening lines of "The Cares of a Family Man" state that, "Some say the word Odradek is of Slavonic origin, and try to account for it on that basis. Others again believe it to be of German origin, only influenced by Slavonic. The uncertainty of both interpretations allows one to assume with justice that neither is accurate, especially as neither of them provides an intelligent meaning of the word."[71] The "uncertainty" of interpretation is predicated on the lack of origin, which, as we learn, results in a moment of unintelligibility—not from ambiguity, however, but from the lack of reference, a uniting of figure and ground. This emphasis on the interval between figure and ground also appears in Kafka's *The Metamorphosis,* in which Gregor changes into a "giant bug," a bug that, as Kafka remarked to the illustrator Ottomar Starke, "must not be included in the illustrations. It must not make even the remotest appearance."[72]

For Žižek it is "Odradek" that embodies "bodiliness," an amorphous, "unillustratable" state in which as an object "Odradek" is "transgenerational, immortal, outside finitude, outside time, displaying no goal-oriented activity, no purpose, no utility."[73] This status, however, exists as a paradox, with, as Žižek notes, "Odradek" as the transcendent object or the ridiculous object. "Odradek" is *jouissance*, "that which we can never reach, attain, *and* that which we can never get rid of."[74]

"Odradek" serves as the "Kafkan Thing" that is made of literature. This power, embodied in the disembodied object named "Odradek," to address, rend, and renegotiate foundation belongs to a thinking, as Kafka's work offers and Gilles Deleuze's theory affirms, "which engenders thought within thought, for thought thinks only by means of difference, around this point of ungrounding."[75] In saying that he is "made" of literature, Kafka presents a thinking that does not move toward ground; instead, being "made" of literature is "ungrounding," separating or keeping open the space between figure and ground—thinking, as Deleuze writes, "without an image." In this instance it seems that literature, after Kafka, is uniquely situated to perforate hegemony and bring difference to order, reestablishing the "gap" that always has existed between figure and ground.

3.8 Ransmayr's Re-Marking Ovid

My purpose is to tell of bodies which have been transformed into shapes of a different kind.

—Ovid, *Metamorphoses*

This was Naso's path. Banned from Rome, from the realm of necessity and reason, the poet had finished telling his *Metamorphoses* beside the Black Sea, transforming this barren craggy coast, where he froze and ached with homesickness, into *his* coast, transforming these barbarians, who harassed and drove him to the forsaken world of Trachila, into *his* characters. And telling *every* story to its conclusion, Naso had freed his world of human beings, of their rules and regulations. And then no doubt he had himself entered the landscape devoid of humans—an indestructible pebble rolling down the slopes, a cormorant sweeping above the foam-crested breakers, a swatch of triumphant purple moss perched atop the last crumbling wall of a town.

—Christoph Ransmayr, *The Last World*

James I of Aragon (1213–76), in fulfilling his monarchial duties, opened an assembly of religious leaders with a provocative line of "Scripture": "Nor is it less a talent to protect what you have than to find it."[76] The line, of course, is not from "Scripture" but from Ovid's *Ars Amatoria*. It is interesting to note that while the line is not Scripture, it could have been, or at least was perceived by those in attendance to be theological in character. This, one could argue, is the challenge of all poetry, to aspire to sacrality, to sound theological.

Given that passages from Ovid's epics and elegies often have been mis-identified over the centuries as originating from sacred texts, it is accurate to say that Ovid met this poetic challenge with tremendous success.[77] One could go so far as to claim that Ovidian verse is, in a manner of speaking, essentially scriptural, especially with opening lines that chronicle the beginning of the Cosmos: "Before there was any earth or sea, before the canopy of heaven stretched overhead . . . nothing had any lasting shape, but everything got in the way of everything else; for, within that one body, cold warred with hot, moist with dry, soft with hard, and light with heavy."[78] This "strife," as Ovid describes it, was brought to an end by "a god," "a natu-ral force of a higher kind, who separated the earth from heaven, and the waters from the earth, and set clear air apart from cloudy atmosphere."[79] While in mythological discourse "strife" ends through the intercession of a God, in philosophical discourse it is ontological phantasm that, in a man-ner of speaking, does the "trick."

At the immanent level Ovid's epic poem recounts the transformation of shapelessness into a hegemonic, "harmonious union."[80] This "unbroken thread of verse, from the earliest beginnings of the world, down to [his] own times," does much more than chronicle the forming of Order from Chaos; it purportedly creates it through the force of poetic language. Ovid's "unbroken thread of verse" provides the universe with *provenance,* revealing the mytho-narrative structures of Ovid's times. The "unbrokenness" of the *Metamorphoses* also suggests a theory of poetry, with verse representing the eternal dialectical inversion of order and chaos, a mimetic aftereffect of a more encompassing process of creation. Ovid's epic, with its discontinuities of style, content, and voice, aligns words and things, revealing a precarious harmony that is simultaneously linguistic, cosmological, and theological.

The *Metamorphoses,* as it attempts to give structure to 250 interconnect-ing myths, legends, and stories within stories, is fundamentally an exten-sion of creation, a bringing forth, as both creative process and product, of the categorization of a "shapeless uncoordinated mass" that preexisted the earth, sea, and heaven. Shaping shapelessness as a theological endeavor that forms an analytics of order in the form of poetry, for Ovid, is underwritten by a subtle dialectical inversion of separated similarities. When released from the constraints of kinship in "that one body," these become *theographical* in character, allowing for the emergence of a radical difference that is prior to a primal equivalency as a condition of meaning. This primal equivalency of logos and cosmos, however, undergoes an initial transformation in the *Metamorphoses* as Ovid manipulates the ambiguity of words across shifting contexts. A second, more radical transformation or "re-marking" at the interpretative level occurs within the postmodern moment as words transform into signs escaping ambiguity, with logos and cosmos giving way to signification. Before examining this concept of radical linguistic heterogeneity giving way to signification, however, it is necessary to delineate the poetic imagination's traditional function as a uniting force bringing, as Ovid states, shape to shapelessness.

The nineteenth-century literary critic and essayist Walter Pater (1839–94) noted in his seminal study of Dionysus that religion is an indispensable element of all literature, classical and modern. He wistfully reflects on the classical mind and on "the dainty *Metamorphoses* of Ovid [as] a fossilized form of one morsel here and there, from a whole world of transformation, with which their nimble fancy was perpetually playing."[81] Pater's impulse toward a comparative science of religion is with us today in the form of dialectical literary criticism attempting to bring these "morsels" from here and there together again. The result of this interpretive endeavor is a remarkable repositioning of language-story-theology uniting all three within the spatiality of God. It is through an analysis of this traditional triangulation that a *creative* or "re-marked" literature will emerge.

The language-story-theology interplay within religious and literary studies, as we have seen, attempts to bridge the great divide between figure and ground or the finite and the infinite. Theology becomes story through language, and it is the perceived limits of the latter that becomes the focus of theological inquiry. In *The Dark Interval: Towards a Theology of the Story,* for instance, John Dominic Crossan begins his analysis of theology and narrative form with an extended passage from Rilke's *The Duino Elegies:*

> But because being here is much, and because
> All this

That's here, so fleeting, seems to require us
  And strangely
Concerns us. Us the most fleeting of all.
  Just once,
Everything, only for once. Once and no more.
  And we, too,
once. And never Again. But this
having been once, though only once,
having been once on earth—can it ever be cancelled?[82]

Crossan's explication emphasizes the elegy's theme of finality (finitude) expressed through the repetition of "once," leaving the reader to ponder the unsettling thoughts of a fleeting "life-toward-death."

While death is indeed a limit, it is not the "fundamental limit" that Crossan sees as most significant in Rilke's elegy. "Death," "Crossan writes, "may be only a sign and a reminder of this more fundamental limit"—a fundamental limit "which is language itself."[83] Quoting Wittgenstein's aphorism that "man has the urge to thrust against the limits of language . . . but the tendency, the thrust, points to something," Crossan offers a theory of language that is fundamentally allegorical.[84] That is, Crossan, à la a "foundationalist" Wittgenstein, sees language pointing toward something beyond itself, referring to a primal identity that is "deeply" theological. Rilke's elegy then, while turning on the theme of human finitude, also becomes a crypto-poetic exercise in which language initially fails then succeeds in revealing a depth of human experience. Poetic language, in Crossan's study, as a foundational language that provides access to "depth," rests on a notion of direct referentiality. Whether words point back toward a thing in the world, a mental picture, or a use in context, the results are the same, a linguistic allegory in which language functions referentially, revealing a depth to the world (ontology), humankind (anthropology), society (sociology), or God (theology).

The "thrust" that motions toward something—a depth, as Crossan suggests—leads to a false "language limit" to the extent that language is forced to operate under an extralinguistic demand that may be characterized as theological insofar as the "other" of language is determined to be God. The structure of narratives or stories within this conceptual model, argued by Crossan, necessarily directs language toward a foundation of meaning (God) that is, as Crossan states, "found only at the edge of language and the limit of the story." Further, "the only way to find that excitement is to test those edges and those limits."[85]

The interesting issue here is not the deferred invocation of God one finds throughout Crossan's text, but the use of spatial metaphors to express (repress) a supposed inevitable transcendent readerly experience. "Edge" quietly invokes an inestimable "center" upon which the narrative or story must rest. One easily can substitute "surface" for "edge" and "depth" for "center" to arrive at a more precise binary opposition that informs Crossan's theo-literary critical approach to God as an extralinguistic presence in/outside narrative.

A story or narrative's meaning, Crossan argues, generates from a tension between "edge" and "center" or "surface" and "depth." Within this traditional approach language is poised against its "other" (God), an other that is accessible only through reflective experience: the greater the depth, the greater the meaning, the greater the experience. Theo-literary approaches to narratives, as we have seen, require that the "concept" of depth be articulated as a temporal (Rilke) or spatial exigency, rectifying the *mysterium* of poetic language.

A postmodern theology, as a secular theology, forms at the conceptual limit of this crypto-poetics with a notion of "depth," as Winquist observes in *Desiring Theology,* configured as "a complex inscription on the recording surface of experience."[86] Winquist's argument for a postmodern secular theology begins with an analysis of a cultural despondency over the lack of meaning and value in everyday life that does not force discourse toward an inestimable center or unfathomable depth. This lack of "depth," as Winquist sees it, incites a desire for theology as a longing for connectedness that "begin[s] [as] an interrogation of life."[87] This imperative to interrogate life allows Winquist to turn to the existential (secular) theology of Paul Tillich in such a way as to open an inquiry into the nature of theology itself—a move Crossan resists. Contrary to the crypto-poetic aesthetic honoring spatial "depth" that is advanced within a traditional theo-literary perspective, Winquist comes to revalue "surface" as an occasion for thinking theologically and poetically.

The crisis identified by Crossan in Rilke's elegy, as his explication would suggest, may be construed as a recasting of an age-old bipartition of world in which language (phenomena) must continually yield to God (noumena), reinscribing meaningfulness as a product of transcendence. Theology and literature, within this perspective, are symbiotic, revealing depth through (extralinguistic) symbols. The exigency of theology and literature for Winquist, however, necessitates a thinking in extremis that reformulates spatial relations into discursive relations:

> Conceiving of theology as a minor literature is a tactical implementation of the multiple strategies of acoluthetic reason, erring, deconstructive and hermeneutical tropologies, bricolage, radical criticism, parabolic and paradoxical narratives in the context of a dominant discourse of commodification. A minor literature is made of texts that are unsafe and are a contagion that makes all texts unsafe. Minor literatures teach us to stammer in our own language.[88]

Crypto-poetics asks, how does one come to know depth through literature? "Re-marking" literature as "minor literature" presents the problem of "knowing depth" as a discursive, hegemonic problem, not a metaphysical problem in which one must prevail in order to reunite words and ideas. That is, language doesn't fail to (re)present "reality"; it deconstructs that reality through a differential sign system that is inextricably woven into the fabric of lived experience. Depth then, for Winquist, is a discursive surface, not a spatial limit.

Winquist's postmodern theology depends upon a thinking in extremis that is linguistic, not epistemological or metaphysical. *Desiring Theology,* or a desire for theology, begins with a concept of "unconditionality" that one finds articulated in Paul Tillich's sermon entitled "The Depth of Existence," in which two epigraphs designate the aim of theological thinking: "But God hath revealed them unto us by his Spirit: For the Spirit searcheth all things, yea, the deep things of God (I Corinthians 2:10)" and "Out of the depth have I cried unto thee, O Lord (Psalm 130:01)." For Winquist depth, as a concept, retains "a secular mandate for theology even in the context of transitoriness, contingency, and dissimulation of postmodern thinking."[89] In this regard spatiality undergoes a deconstruction in Tillich's sermon,

with the words "deep" and "depth," as Tillich notes, being "used in our daily life, in poetry and philosophy, in the Bible, and in many other religious
documents, to indicate a spiritual attitude, although the words themselves
are taken from spatial experience. Depth is a dimension of space; yet at the
same time it is a symbol for a spiritual quality."[90]

How should one define this "spiritual quality" to which Tillich refers?
First, we must consider the meaning of depth and its apparent opposite,
surface. Tillich views the tension between "surface" and "depth," like Crossan, as a spatial representation of humankind's quest for absolute meaning
and value, in much the same way as Ovid offers verse as a reconciliation of
chaos to order. This spatial limit is breached, however, by the introduction
of a spiritual "quality," in which the "surface" of experience is argued to be
mutable, inauthentic; it is, Tillich writes, "that side of things which first appears to us."[91] And it is this first appearance that is, finally, disappointing.
Depth, on the other hand, is presumed to be that side of things that only appears to us through theological reflection beyond the limit of language. The
"quality" of depth, for Tillich, is more than the supposed inauthenticity of
appearance; it is an apprehension of a profound, sublime, "spiritual quality," a truth that does not "disappoint."[92] How could one come to a theology
that does not disappoint without returning to Crossan transcendental poetics? Find a truth that in the end is not deep but is nevertheless meaningful?
Find a way of thinking about God as a surface?

Postmodern theology, as a way of thinking theology's relationship to
literature and the arts, begins with a turn away from words toward signs,
abandoning, as Carl A. Raschke observes in *The End of Theology*, the "western epoch of metaphysics."[93] While theology in the postmodern moment
is characterized by an abandonment of metaphysical discourse, questions
concerning meaning and value in lived experience endure. Along with these
questions comes the significance of the sign of God, not as a metaphysical
entity but as a linguistic construct offering a logic of heterogeneity and a
"disjunctive diversity" resulting in text production, the "unconditionality"
of artistic creation.[94] The sign of God is not the "name of God," the inadequate linguistic expression of an all-powerful being, but a condition of the
possibility of signification. The sign of God is an economy of concepts that
takes "shape" as grammatological arrangements. God, freed from a spatial
limit, no longer is language's "other"; nor is God philosophy's first princi-

ple—God is a sign-network. And in this regard it is important to remember that, as Winquist writes, a theology that can only "simulate" its first principles "need not be a cause of despair."[95]

The loss of modes of transcendence, opportunities for realities more real than language allows, permits a revaluation of the limit—a limit that is not an "edge" but an illimitable surface for recording signs, a network. Theology's "unconditionality," then, is found in Tillich's reformulation of depth as a "quality," signaling, as Winquist writes, a forthcoming problem in which "the experience of originality without origins and serious thinking without foundations keeps us bound to surfaces that are the space and theater of meaning."[96] If, in the absence of originality with origins, thinking with foundations, we are forced to return to the theater of meaning as a space for staging the Ovidian impulse to give shape to shapelessness through poetic expression, to re-mark surfaces, this is no simple return to creative activity; it is a reversal of that initial creative act articulated by Ovid: "My purpose is to tell of bodies which have been transformed into shapes of a different kind." Postmodern theology, as an artistic endeavor, becomes "literary" and transforms shape into shapelessness, with shape refigured as a becoming "disbecoming."

The brief history of postmodern theology, following Raschke's and Winquist's analyses, takes shape around the concept of "shapelessness" and disbecoming. As we have seen, Winquist advances a desiring theology precipitated by a longing to "interrogate life" as an extended surface of experimental constructions, epistemological as well as ethical. Raschke, in a similar context, has argued for a theology emancipated from metaphysical discourse: "Metaphysical thinking has always been based on difference, which is at the same time a dissemblance, a sheer taking off and putting on of comparative disguises."[97] Metaphysical thinking's "disguise" is its "depth," a concealing of signification with spatiality. This metaphysical (de)masking returns us to Winquist's "theater of meaning," in which theology becomes theography, the (un)writing of God, an anti-*Metamorphoses.*

As Ovid's *Metamorphoses* attempts to remedy shaplessness with shape, Christoph Ransmayr's *The Last World: A Novel with an Ovidian Repertory* (*Die letzte Welt*) deconstructs Ovid's poetic achievement insofar as Ovid presents the "harmonious union" of word and world transforming into signification.[98] The novel's protagonist, Cotta, sets sail on the *Trivia* in search of the exiled poet Naso (Ovid). The novel brings the Roman Empire into the present through an anachronistic presentation of Ovid's life and final work. The characters that populate the island of Tomi, to which Cotta ventures, are re-creations from the *Metamorphoses,* each one "disbecoming" into his or her corresponding mythological character at the end of the novel. Cotta's journey becomes an antijourney in which language, reality, and representation ultimately fail, leaving Cotta bereft of meaning beyond the infinite distribution of signs into the world. Ransmayr's tragic hero is a man seeking "depth," hoping to find the great Naso, who will reveal to him the transcendent meaning of his works.

His investigation leads nowhere, insane figures supplying him with bits and pieces of useless information until he comes upon fifteen inscribed stone columns on the outskirts of town:

Cotta unriddled and whispered the words like someone learning to read, tearing a blanket of slugs away with his bare hands wherever he suspected new words. He patched together what was revealed, checked it for sense and syntax, discarded it once, twice, began anew elsewhere, until at last it seemed to him that he had exhausted all the possibilities for combining and connecting fragments into a single message:

I HAVE COMPLETED A WORK
THAT WILL WITHSTAND FIRE
AND IRON
EVEN THE WRATH OF GOD AND
ALL-CONSUMING TIME

WHENEVER IT WILL LET DEATH NOW COME
HAVING ONLY MY BODY
WITHIN ITS POWER
AND END MY LIFE

BUT THROUGH THIS WORK
I WILL LIVE ON AND
LIFT MYSELF HIGH ABOVE THE STARS
AND MY NAME
WILL BE INDESTRUCTIBLE[99]

Cotta solves the riddle and is energized by his findings, and even though he knows only one man who could have created the column, he calls into "the darkness" to Naso's insane servant, Pythagoras, "Who wrote this?"

The quest for Naso and the secrets he may reveal leads Cotta through his own metamorphosis. He sees the people of the island transform into birds and beasts, causing him to look more intensely for the great poet and his book. In his exhaustion Cotta comes to realize that "reality, once discovered, no longer needed recording."[100] Naso, the book, and the promise of transcendence are gone, leaving one final inscription to discover: "He would find it on a banner buried in the silvery luster of the Trachila or on the boulder-strewn flanks of the new mountain. He was sure it would be a small banner—after all, it carried only two syllables. When he stopped to catch his breath, standing there so tiny under the overhanging rocks, Cotta sometimes flung those syllables against the stone, and answered, *Here!* as the echo of his shout came back to him. For what reverberated from the walls—broken and familiar—was his own name."[101]

Ransmayr's *The Last World* is more than a protracted allusion to Ovid; it is a richly diverse text that disallows symbolic correspondences between surface and depth, edge and center, figure and ground, refraining from placing the *Metamorphoses* in the role of the ur-narrative. In fact, Ransmayr's novel returns us to Winquist's "theater of meaning," as the repertory elements suggested by the novel's subtitle interrupt the possibility of *a* story. In this sense *The Last World* enacts a theographical logic by resisting the metaphysical reflex, allowing the "broken and familiar" nature of signs to reverberate back to Cotta, to us. While Ransmayr leaves Cotta distributed and "re-marked" across the sign-universe, answering his own call, "*Here!*," he reaffirms Naso's (Ovid's) immortality by making him responsible for the transformation of the island and its people into "*his* characters." Ironically, by the novel's end Naso achieves the opposite of what literary history has given him credit for, creating disorder. Ransmayr's "Great Poet" transforms shape into shapelessness that is beyond the laws of Rome and the gods.

Theography, or signs of God, begins with an identification of a theo-literary tradition that synthesizes diverse conceptual elements into a unity, a spatial depth. Ovid, the poet of ages, stands within this tradition as the exemplar of this poetic activity of bringing "shape" to "shapelessness."

Through a deconstructive analysis of the spatial metaphors and presuppositions regarding the primacy of identity in language, the Derridean metaphysics of presence, we arrive at a revaluation of "surface," not as the spatial opposite of "depth" but as a separate category of thinking. That is, surface denotes a turning-away from words toward signs, leaving aside a referential schema grounding meaning in theology and literature.

> In this sense of theography "meaning" is distributive across singular economies of signs precariously arranged within narrative forms. These conceptual singular economies are overdetermined and may be viewed as narratives within narratives, referring to Ransmayr's Ovidian repertory.[102] Secular theology, then, is theography, a nonallegorical linguistic "journey" designating "meaning" through differential signifying chains located within irreducible economies of meaning. Cotta's journey, in this regard, becomes an antijourney, a journey without closure, without an endpoint. In the postmodern situation and at the end of spatiality, all texts and all journeys, like those of Ovid and Cotta, may be confused with "Scripture" insofar as all texts simulate their first principles, rehearsing Cotta's own moment of inescapable "re-marking": *Here!*

3.9 "Re-Marking" Thinking

> The question is whether we will strategically and tactically implement desire in what we call and know as thinking. That is, are we willing to say *yes* to desire by experimentally developing strategies and tactics within our discursive and thinking practices to constantly intertwine the given of actuality with the given of possibility?
> —Charles E. Winquist, *The Surface of the Deep*

The feeling of wonder that provokes philosophical thinking is a shock unlike any other shock caused by individual things that can strike us as curious, strange, or surprising. It is a shock that is incomparable to any other commotion. Its violence has no equivalent because it challenges all unreflective faith in its entirety. To hold that philosophy originates in wonder is thus also to assert the uniqueness of this pathos. Only the shock caused by wonder possesses the required violence to initiate a passage from doxa to philosophy—that is, from the relativity of opinions and beliefs to what is shareable by all, hence, universal. However, if this extraordinary, highly unique, and uncommon experience of wonder that unsettles everydayness provokes philosophical reflection, is it not because this experience reveals something that concerns everything and everybody, despite—or rather because of—its exceptional, even pathological, nature? The very extraordinariness of the feeling of wonder must not be understood solely from and in view of the ordinary that this feeling interrupts. When this feeling interrupts ordinary experience, the relativity of everything ordinary comes into view. The feeling of wonder is, therefore, the feeling of awe in the face of and the marvel at something that, in distinction from the world of doxa, is universally binding.

That wonder should lie at the origin of philosophy—and should indeed constitute its sole origin—has been so well established that it has become self-evident, ever since, Plato in his Theaetetus, and Aristotle in his Metaphysics recognized in this pathos the power to break with doxa. Not that this is any longer surprising. However, when philosophers have spoken of wonder, they have not always meant the same thing—attributing wonder, for example, to different sources in a range of different subjective experiences. Even though Plato, for example, does not explicitly state what causes wonder, it is generally acknowledged that it is a question for Plato of the perception of, and even an admiration for, the invisible whole—the non-phenomenal totality, or the world in its entirety—that is manifested in the retrait of particular phenomena.

—Rodolphe Gasché, The Honor of Thinking

Tolstoy, Kafka, and Ransmayr, as distinct and as separable as they are in terms of history, aesthetics, and perhaps, artistic vision, share a desire for thinking, a thinking that attempts to undo, "re-mark," "shock," or perforate hegemonic discourse with the "given of possibility," as Winquist describes it. In the case of Tolstoy, for instance, the hegemony of Christian dogmatism feels some resistance from a literature aspiring to achieve a "demythologized" narrative clarity, a clarity that, finally and ironically, imposes its own orthodox limit on thinking. Franz Kafka, on the other hand, is so adept at perforating, shocking hegemony and "deterritorializing" narrative orthodoxy that it is his readers who must supply the necessary interpretive limit to his writings: Kafka the "theologian," the "anti-bureaucrat," the "prophet," the "consumptive"—all of these limits, including even those from the writer Franz Kafka, cannot contain the "Kafkan Thing," the "Odradek," for example, that becomes a literary figure that betrays literature, literature understood as that which diminishes possibility and reconciles thinking to a world. This irreconcilable interval between thinking and world becomes Christoph Ransmayr's creation of an "uncreated" world, an attempt to "think" the genesis of order, an order that, as Cotta learns, was never anything more than phantasm, a myth.

The difficulty in the end, however, is that there is no "literature" that "thinks" or affirms something that would find the limit to the "given of possibility," no paradigmatic example of literature thinking that could be the template for all theoretical-literary endeavors. Literature, like thinking, always disappoints, as it should. This disappointment, more generally, is the burden placed on any, if not all, discourse by and of thinking, a non-teleological, shocking thinking or thinking extricated from that which is or can be thought at a given moment. Thinking here is a troubling, strange act, a "sense," for Deleuze, in which the content of thought is made vulnerable and inadequate by the very condition of thinking, the "deracinating" power of thinking itself.

The question therefore is not, does literature think? It is, rather, does literature ever not think? Does it always and precisely not end with closure? Does it not resist adhering to an "image of thought"? Interpretation may and does impose a limit, but literature, literarity, as we have discussed it, never relinquishes its power to resist, to create the possibility of the "given of possibility" alongside the "given of actuality." Paradoxically, this not-thinking, in the traditional sense, is a "desire to think," a thinking that betrays the presentation of an object and intertwines "the given of actuality with the given of possibility," with no end.

In Franz Kafka's "The Great Wall and the Tower of Babel" ("Die Chinesische Mauer Und Der Trumbau Von Babel"), the narrator tells the story of a scholar in search of the exact, empirical reasons for the Tower of Babel's failure: "First, then, it must be said that in those days things were achieved scarcely inferior during the early days of building to the construction of the Tower of Babel, although as regards divine approval, at least according to human reckoning, strongly at variance with that work. I say this because a scholar wrote a book in which he drew the comparison in the most exhaustive way."[103] Kafka's "scholar" appears as an ancient, obsessed structural

engineer, a seeker of the truth in architectural design—-perhaps remi-
niscent of Proust's Swann. As the story continues, the narrator recounts
that this scholar sought to prove that the Tower failed to reach its goal "not
because of the reasons universally advanced, or at least that among those
recognized reasons the most important of all was not to be found."[104] The
primary reason for the Tower's failure, according to the scholar, was the
"weakness of the foundation."[105] With the architectural puzzle supposedly
solved, the scholar champions a new idea: "the Great Wall [of China] alone
would provide for the first time in the history of mankind a secure foundation for a new Tower of Babel."[106]

The outlandish, literal-minded prospect of rebuilding the Tower, from
the narrator's position, is a real possibility that is in retrospect hampered by
the inclusion of the metaphorical: "His book was in everybody's hands at
the time, but I admit that even today I cannot quite make out how he conceived this tower. How could the wall, which did not form even a circle, but
only a sort of quarter or half-circle, provide the foundation of the tower?
That could obviously be meant only in the spiritual sense."[107] The narrator becomes further perplexed when he or she considers the purpose of the
actual wall and tower. Why, the narrator asks, are there "somewhat nebulous planes" and "proposals" for "mobilizing the people's energies for the
stupendous new work"?

These questions, in their specificity, are left unanswered, except for one
speculative idea, the "single aim":

> There were many wild ideas in people's heads at the time—this scholar's
> book is only one example—perhaps simply because so many were trying to
> join forces as far as they could for the achievement of a single aim. Human
> nature, essentially changeable, unstable as the dust, can endure no restraint;
> if it binds itself it soon begins to tear madly at its bonds, until it rends every-
> thing asunder, the wall, the bonds and its very self.[108]

The "single aim" in this instance could simply be the coming together of a
collective will, something that occupies or distracts humanity from its condition or gives humanity a rhetorical "absolute origin" upon which to build
not just a tower but the Tower of Babel.

It is, however, not that simple, and the German text provides a space for
"re-marking" this conclusion:

Das menschliche Wesen, leichtfertig in seinem Grund, von der Natur des auffliegenden Staubes, verträgt keine Fesselung; fesselt es sich selbst, wird es bald wahnsinning an den Fesslen zu rütteln anfangen und Mauer, Kette und sich selbst in all Himmelsrichtungen zerreißen.[109]

The "single aim" originally was or becomes, in "auf einen Zweck hin zu semmeln schucten," a "collective purpose" toward grounding discourse. It is from this grounding discourse then that "essentially changeable" or, perhaps better, "lightly grounded" ("leichtenfertig in seinem Grund") human nature ultimately flees.

   With this in mind, the nearly nonsensical "unstable as dust" rendition of "von der Nature des auffliegenden Staubes" becomes "a human nature that flies away like dust from the ground." The emphasis then is not only on the "single aim" but on the space or gap (occupied by the Tower and, metaphorically, literature) between ground and sky or air. The scholar's "book," which prompts the narrator's inquiry, contains design plans, albeit "somewhat nebulous," for the Tower, and it is this structure, we learn, that purportedly will close the gap between ground and sky. Human nature then, according to the narrator, caught in this prospective closure and under restraining conditions, "tears itself apart in all directions" ("fesselt es sich selbst, wird es bald wahnsinning an den Fesseln zu rütteln anfangen und Mauer, Kette und sich selbst in all Himmelsrictungen zerreißen"). It seems that the Tower and human nature and literature are antithetical variables in the narrative; the Tower, any tower, aims toward the sky—it ascends from a foundation, filling a gap. Human nature and literature, from Kafka's perspective, are nonvertical, filling nothing. Human nature and literature in this instance are dust, and "dust" does not ascend uniformly like some Tower—it scatters, swirling not in one "single" direction but in all directions (*Himmelsrichtungen*), not heavenward nor skyward (*Himmelwärts gerichtet*).

   The Great Wall, as foundation, however ill-formed, serves as the origin that stands against thinking, against the "given of possibility." The prospective new Tower, and its "quarter-circle" or "half-circle" new foundation, define the problem of hegemonic phantasm—the putative whole structure that appears as a totality, a totality that, too soon, forms the "restraints," the "bonds" against which thinking must tear madly in all directions.

To return to Kafka one last time, then, not only is human nature like the dust that flies away from the ground in all directions, but so too is literature—swirling in all directions from the ground, above the ground, and against ground.

NOTES

I. Vanishing Origins

1. Charles E. Winquist, *Desiring Theology* (Chicago: University of Chicago Press, 1995), 31.

2. Martin Heidegger, "What Is Metaphysics?" in *Martin Heidegger: The Basic Writings*, ed. David Farrell Krell (San Francisco: Harper, 1977), 111.

3. Reiner Schürmann, *Broken Hegemonies*, trans. Reginald Lily (Bloomington: Indiana University Press, 2003), 8.

4. Rodolphe Gasché, *The Honor of Thinking: Critique, Theory, Philosophy* (Stanford: Stanford University Press, 2007), 360–61.

5. Ibid., 361.

6. Ibid., 362.

7. Ibid.

8. Michel Foucault, "Nietzsche, Genealogy, History," in *Language, Counter-Memory, Practice: Selected Essays and Interviews*, ed. Donald F. Bouchard, trans. Sherry Simon (Ithaca: Cornell University Press, 1977), 139.

9. Schürmann's *Broken Hegemonies* begins with a reassessment of Parmenides and the question of Being's relationship to being. From this Schürmann posits that each age (Ancient, Medieval, and Modern) offers a hegemonic solution to the problem of linking Being to being, nature, Christian God, cogito.

10. Franz Kafka, "The Problem of Our Laws," in *The Complete Stories*, ed. Nahum Glatzer (New York: Schocken Books, 1971), 437.

11. Schürmann, *Broken Hegemonies*, 9.

12. Ibid., 10.

13. Robert Frost, "Stars," in *A Boy's Will* (Whitefish, MT: Kessinger Publishers, 2004), 3.

14. John D. Caputo, "The Experience of God and the Axiology of the Impossible," in *Religion after Metaphysics*, ed. Mark A. Wrathall (Cambridge: Cambridge University Press, 2003), 124.

15. Martin Heidegger, "Letter on Humanism," in *Basic Writings*, 262.

16. Ibid., 124.

17. Ibid., 258.

18. Ibid., 449.

19. Caputo, "Experience of God," 125.

20. Mark C. Taylor, *Altarity* (Chicago: University of Chicago Press, 1987), xxix.

21. Slavoj Žižek, *The Sublime Object of Ideology* (New York: Verso, 1989). The concept of "re-marking" here comes from two sources. The first is Derrida, and the second is Slavoj Žižek by way of Rodolphe Gasché's *The Tain of the Mirror: Derrida and the Philosophy of Reflection* (Cambridge: Harvard University Press, 1986).

22. Mark C. Taylor, *Altarity*, 93.

23. Ibid., 94.

24. Ibid., 93.

25. J. Hillis Miller, *The Linguistic Moment: From Wordsworth to Stevens* (Princeton: Princeton University Press, 1983), 77–78.

26. Žižek, in *The Sublime Object of Ideology*, describes this "external intimacy" as a "radical effacement" of the symbolic order: "The symbolic order is striving for homeostatic balance, but there is in its kernel, at its very center, some strange, traumatic element which cannot be symbolized, integrated into the symbolic order—the Thing. Lacan coined a neologism for it: *L'extimité*—external intimacy . . . Exactly the opposite of the symbolic order: the possibility of the 'second death,' the radical annihilation of the symbolic texture through which the so-called reality is constituted. The very existence of the symbolic order implies a possibility of its radical effacement, of 'symbolic death'—not death of the so-called 'real object' in its symbol, but the obliteration of the signifying network itself" (132).

27. Žižek, *Sublime Object of Ideology*, 132.

28. Jacques-Alain Miller, "Extimité," in *Lacanian Theory of Discourse: Subject, Structure and Society*, ed. M. Bracher (New York: New York University Press, 1994), 76–77.

29. Victor E. Taylor, *Para/Inquiry: Postmodern Religion and Culture* (New York and London: Routledge, 2000).

30. J. Hillis Miller, "The Critic as Host," *Critical Inquiry* 3, no. 3 (1977): 441.

31. Mladen Dolar, "I Shall Be with You on Your Wedding Night: Lacan and the Uncanny," *October* 58 (1991): 6.

32. Malcolm Bowie, *Freud, Proust and Lacan: Theory as Fiction* (London: Cambridge University Press, 1987), 19.

33. Roger Shattuck, *Proust's Way: A Field Guide to* In Search of Lost Time (New York: W. W. Norton & Co., 2000), 214.

34. Ibid.

35. Ibid., 215.

36. Bowie, *Freud, Proust and Lacan*, 68.

37. Ibid., 58.

38. Stanley Cavell, *Disowning Knowledge in Six Plays of Shakespeare* (Cambridge: Cambridge University Press, 1987), 126.

39. Marcel Proust, *In Search of Lost Time*, vol. 1, trans. C. K. Scott Moncrieff and Terence Kilmartin (New York: Random House, 2003), 386.

40. Ibid.

41. Ibid.

42. Ibid., 387.

43. Cavell, *Disowning Knowledge*, 127.

44. Proust, *In Search of Lost Time*, 387.

45. Ibid., 388.

46. Ibid., 390.

47. Ibid., 390–91.

48. Slavoj Žižek, *The Parallax View* (Cambridge: MIT Press, 2006), 147.

49. Ibid., 162.

50. Slavoj Žižek, *Enjoy Your Symptom! Jacques Lacan in Hollywood and Out* (New York/London: Routledge, 1992), 102.

51. Slavoj Žižek, *Tarrying with the Negative: Kant, Hegel, and the Critique of Ideology* (Durham: Duke University Press, 1993), 189.

52. Ibid.

53. See Slavoj Žižek, *For They Know Not What They Do: Enjoyment as a Political Factor* (London: Verso, 1991), 182–97.

54. Žižek, *Sublime Object of Ideology*, 6.

55. Slavoj Žižek, *The Ticklish Subject: The Absent Centre of Political Ontology* (London/New York: Verso, 1999), 352.

56. Žižek, *For They Know Not What They Do*, 75.

57. Ibid., 76.

58. See Žižek, *Parallax View*.

59. Mark C. Taylor, *The Picture in Question: Mark Tansey and the Ends of Representation* (Chicago: University of Chicago Press, 1999), 55–56.

60. Gasché, *Tain of the Mirror*, 222.

61. Gilles Deleuze, *Essays Critical and Clinical*, trans. Daniel W. Smith and Michael A. Greco (Minneapolis: University of Minnesota Press, 1997), 3.

62. Ibid., 4.

63. Ibid.

64. Peter Hallward, *Out of This World: Deleuze and the Philosophy of Creation* (London/New York: Verso, 2006), 104.

65. Ibid.

66. Martin Heidegger, "Language," in *Poetry, Language, Thought*, trans. Albert Hofstadter (New York: Harper Collins, 1971), 189.

67. Giorgio Agamben, *The End of the Poem: Studies in Poetics*, trans. Daniel Heller-Roazen (Stanford: Stanford University Press, 1999), 66.

68. Plato, *Ion*, in *Plato: The Collected Dialogues*, ed. Edith Hamilton and Huntington Cairns (Princeton: Princeton University Press, 1961), 219–20.

69. The "literary" beginning to which I am referring is informed by Philippe Lacoue-Labarthe's and Jean-Luc Nancy's reading of Derrida, especially as it is de-

veloped in Lacoue-Labarthes's *The Subject of Philosophy,* ed. Thomas Trezise, trans. Thomas Tresize et al. (Minneapolis: University of Minnesota Press, 1993).

70. Rodolphe Gasché, in *The Wild Card of Reading: On Paul de Man* (Cambridge: Harvard University Press, 1998), points to a key difference between Derrida's hermeneutic horizon and de Man's "dissymmetries": "While the Derridean reading also questions understanding to the extent that it shows understanding to depend for its possibility on the medium of undecideability of writing, or the *pharmakon,* de Man's theory of reading is considerably more radical. Its concern is not with the limits of understanding—limits being also that within which, or from which, something becomes possible—but the possibility of understanding altogether. Reading, indeed, is out to prove that any effort to understand is vain, illusory, self-defeating" (9).

71. Alexander Pope, "An Essay on Man," in *The Norton Anthology of Western Literature,* vol. 1, ed. Sarah Lawall (New York: W. W. Norton & Co., 2006), 374.

72. Richard Kearney, *On Stories* (London/New York: Routledge, 2001).

73. Paul Ricoeur, "The Model of the Text: Meaningful Action Considered as a Text," in *Hermeneutics and the Human Sciences: Essays on Language, Action, and Interpretation* (Cambridge: Cambridge University Press, 1981), 197.

74. Heidegger, "Letter on Humanism," 210.

75. Jacques Derrida and Manrizio Ferraris, *A Taste for the Secret* (Cambridge: Polity Press, 2001), 15–16.

76. John D. Caputo, *The Prayers and Tears of Jacques Derrida: Religion without Religion* (Bloomington: Indiana University Press, 1997), 101.

77. Ibid.

78. Ibid., 102.

79. Ibid.

80. Ernst Cassirer, *Language and Myth,* trans. Susanne K. Langer (New York: Dover Publications, 1946), 1.

81. Ibid.

82. Ibid., 2.

83. Ibid.

84. Qtd. in Michael Wood, *The Road to Delphi: The Life and Afterlife of Oracles* (New York: Farrar, Straus and Giroux, 2003), 43.

85. Aristotle, in his *Poetics,* describes this element of reversal: "Reversal of the Situation is a change by which the action veers round to its opposite, subject always to our rule of probability or necessity. Thus in the Oedipus, the messenger comes to cheer Oedipus and free him from his alarms about his mother, but by revealing who he is, he produces the opposite effect. Again in the Lynceus, Lynceus is being led away to his death, and Danaus goes with him, meaning to slay him; but the outcome of the preceding incidents is that Danaus is killed and Lynceus saved" (Aristotle, *Poetics* [New York: Penguin Classics, 1997], 54).

86. Mladen Dolar, *A Voice and Nothing More* (Cambridge: MIT Press, 2006), 14.

87. Ibid., 15.

88. Ibid.

89. Frost, "Mowing," in *Boy's Will*, 10.

90. Žižek, *Ticklish Subject*, 54.

91. Wood, *Road to Delphi*, 17.

92. William Shakespeare. *The Tragedy of Macbeth*, in *The Norton Shakespeare*, ed. Stephen Greenblatt (New York: W. W. Norton & Co., 1997), 2600.

93. Wood, *Road to Delphi*, 42–53.

94. Kearney, *On Stories*, 9.

95. Ibid.

96. Wood, *Road to Delphi*, 45–46.

97. Plato, *Cratylus*, in *Collected Dialogues*, 472–73.

98. Cassirer, *Language and Myth*, 3.

99. Valerie Shepard, *Literature about Language* (New York/London: Routledge, 1993).

100. Kevin Hart, *The Trespass of the Sign: Deconstruction, Theology, and Philosophy* (New York: Fordham University Press, 2000), 7.

101. Geoffrey Galt Harpham, *Language Alone: The Critical Fetish of Modernity* (New York/London: Routledge, 2002), 2.

102. Stanley Cavell, *In Quest of the Ordinary: Lines of Skepticism and Romanticism* (Chicago: University of Chicago Press, 1988), 147–48.

103. Harpham, *Language Alone*, 2.

104. Stanley Cavell, *Must We Mean What We Say?* (Cambridge: Cambridge University Press, 1969), 52.

105. Stanley Cavell, *The Claim of Reason: Wittgenstein, Skepticism, Morality, and Tragedy* (Oxford: Oxford University Press, 1979), 180.

106. Cavell, *Must We Mean What We Say?* 50.

107. Harpham, *Language Alone*, 4.

108. Ibid., 5.

109. By way of Richard Rorty, Harpham identifies two lines of linguistic inquiry within the analytic tradition: "In the first ('Cambridge') turning, philosophy sought to reform language by developing what Rudolf Carnap called 'logical syntax of language,' or 'ideal language theory.' Legitimate philosophy, Carnap argued, was philosophy of language; and philosophy so defined constituted the syntax and even the semantics of the language of science. If only philosophers could process out all the metaphysical pseudo-problems that had obstructed clear vision, then, Carnap prophesied, 'all the questions and theorems of philosophy [would] consequently find their place in the formal structure theory of language'" (*Language Alone*, 9). Divorcing the "formal structure theory of language" from the

world is further advanced by other followers of Frege's thought, Russell and Wittgenstein, whose work "concentrated in a series of arguments worked out in impressive abstraction: first, that the goal of philosophy was the analysis of the formal aspects of thought; second, that thought was to be distinguished from the dynamic and contingent—the merely psychological—business of thinking; third, that the only way to get at thought was by analyzing language, especially language purified of defects and illogicalities that beset natural languages" (9). The second line of inquiry ("Oxford") is viewed as a partial retreat from the high aspirations of the Cambridge perspective. This "linguistic turn," writes Harpham, "settled for trying to understand more about the pragmatics of 'ordinary' or nonideal language. The task here was not one of purifying language, but of understanding it—and even, down the road, of discovering new, more interesting ways of talking" (9).

110. Ibid., 5.

111. Ibid.

112. Walter Benn Michaels, *The Shape of the Signifier: 1967 to the End of History* (Princeton/Oxford: Princeton University Press, 2004), 107.

113. Harpham, *Language Alone*, 18 (my emphasis).

114. François Dosse, in *History of Structuralism: The Rising Sign 1945–1966*, trans. Deborah Glassman (Minneapolis: University of Minnesota Press, 1998)), provides a concise description of Saussure's insight: "The other fundamental aspect of the Saussurean approach was to see language as hermetic. The linguistic sign does not join a thing with its name, but a concept with an acoustic image whose link is arbitrary; reality, or the referent, is therefore placed outside the field of study in order to define the linguist's perspective, which is limited, by definition. The Saussurean sign only concerns the relationship between the signified (the concept) and the signifier (the acoustic image), and excludes the referent. Signs differ from symbols, which retain a natural link in the signified/signifier relationship. 'Language is a system that knows only its own order.' 'Language is form and not substance.' Therefore, the linguistic unit, by virtue of its phonic and semantic character, always points to all the other units in a purely endogenous combinatory activity" (48–49).

115. Harpham, *Language Alone*, 21.

116. Dosse, *History of Structuralism*, 51.

117. Michel Foucault, *The Order of Things: An Archaeology of the Human Sciences*, trans. Donald F. Bouchard and Sherry Simon (New York: Vintage Books, 1973), 387.

118. Michel Foucault, "Nietzsche, Freud, Marx," in *Transforming the Hermeneutic Context: From Nietzsche to Nancy*, ed. Gayle L. Ormiston and Alan D. Schrift (Albany: SUNY Press, 1989), 17.

119. Schürmann, *Broken Hegemonies*, 541.

120. William R. Everdell, *The First Moderns* (Chicago: University of Chicago Press, 1997), 15.

121. Harpham, *Language Alone*, 161.

122. Gasché, *Honor of Thinking*, 147.

123. Ibid., 149–50.

124. Ibid., 150.

125. Ibid.

126. Ibid.

127. Ibid.

128. Ibid., 152.

129. Ibid.

130. Carl A. Raschke, *The End of Theology* (Aurora, CO: Davies Group, 2000), ix–x.

131. Winquist, *Desiring Theology*, 26–27.

132. Daniel Heller-Roazen, *Echolalias: On the Forgetting of Language* (New York: Zone Books, 2005), 221.

133. Jacques Derrida, "Des tours Babel," in *Acts of Religion*, trans. Gil Anidjar (New York/London: Routledge, 2002), 107.

134. Caputo, *Prayers and Tears of Jacques Derrida*, 62.

II. "Re-Marking" Myths and Crypto-Commerce

1. Mircea Eliade, *Myth and Reality*, trans. Willard Trask (New York: Harper & Row Publishers, 1963), 1.

2. Martin Heidegger, *Schelling's Treatise on the Essence of Human Freedom*, trans. Joan Stambaugh (Athens: Ohio University Press, 1985), 146.

3. Slavoj Žižek, *The Puppet and the Dwarf: The Perverse Core of Christianity* (Cambridge: MIT Press, 2003), 86.

4. Slavoj Žižek, "From the Myth to Agape," *Journal of European Psychoanalysis* 8–9 (Fall–Winter 1999): 1.

5. Ibid.

6. Ibid.

7. In *The Ticklish Subject* Žižek makes the point that the history of the Oedipal complex, as read through Jacques Lacan, is a specific crisis within the modern bourgeois society. More to the point Žižek notes that Freud switches myths, moving away from Oedipus to the myth of the "primordial father" who returns after death: "On the level of mythical narrative, Freud felt the compulsion to supplement the Oedipal myth with another mythical narrative, that of the 'primordial father' (in *Totem and Taboo*)—the lesson of this myth is the exact obverse of that of Oedipus; that is to say, here, far from having to deal with the father who intervenes

as the Third, the agent who prevents direct contact with the incestuous object (and so sustains the illusion that his annihilation would give us free access to this object), it is the killing of the Father-Thing (the *realization* of the Oedipal wish) which gives rise to symbolic prohibition (the dead father returns as his Name)" (314–15).

8. Žižek, "From the Myth to Agape," 2.

9. Ibid.

10. Ibid.

11. Ibid., 3.

12. Ibid., 4.

13. Ibid.

14. Ibid., 6.

15. Ibid.

16. Ibid.

17. Ibid., 8.

18. John D. Caputo, *The Weakness of God: A Theology of the Event* (Bloomington: Indiana University Press, 2006), 43.

19. Žižek, "From the Myth to Agape," 8.

20. Žižek, *Puppet and the Dwarf,* 171.

21. David Cave, *Mircea Eliade's Vision for a New Humanism* (Oxford: Oxford University Press, 1993), 4.

22. Victor E. Taylor, *Para/Inquiry: Postmodern Religion and Culture* (New York/London: Routledge, 2000).

23. Thomas J. J. Altizer, *Mircea Eliade and the Dialectic of the Sacred* (Philadelphia: Westminster Press, 1963).

24. Mircea Eliade, *Images and Symbols: Studies in Religious Symbolism,* trans. Philip Mairet (Princeton: Princeton University Press, 1991), 175.

25. Douglas Allen, *Myth and Religion in Mircea Eliade* (New York/London: Routledge, 2002), 189.

26. Eliade, *Images and Symbols,* 125.

27. Ibid.

28. Ibid.

29. Ibid., 141.

30. Ibid., 148.

31. Ibid., 149.

32. Ibid.

33. Ibid.

34. Marcel Hénaff, *Claude Lévi-Strauss and the Making of Structural Anthropology,* trans. Mary Baker (Minneapolis: University of Minnesota Press, 1998), 160.

35. Ibid.

36. In describing his friendship with Eliade, Paul Ricoeur, in *Critique and Conviction: Conversations with François Azouvi and Marc de Launay* (New York: Columbia

University Press, 1998), makes the following points that show his differences with Eliade's "antihistoricism": "I had been struck by the singular nature of his work, appearing under the title of *Traité d'histoire des religions*, whereas it was actually a study of religious *patterns*. As Dumézil's preface points out, this is a tropological, structural analysis. Instead of following a historicist schema in the old perspective of the comparative history of religions—in which religions are classified, from the most primitive to the most developed, from an evolutionist perspective—he restructured his investigations around dominant themes, essentially great cosmic polarities: the sky, the waters, rocks, the wind, and so on, borrowing examples from different bodies of writing, practices, and rites. It was this antihistoricist approach that struck me. But it was as if this structural conception was stifled by an almost ideological obsession: the opposition of the sacred and the profane. As a result, the diversity of the figures of the sacred was crushed by a sort of monotony of preference, regardless of the cultural context, for the notion of the sacred and the polarity of the sacred/profane; what might have been a strength from a methodological point of view in the idea of a diversified symbolism was as if diminished by it" (30).

Ricoeur adds to these differences by explaining his differences with Eliade over the status of the sacred and textuality: "He thought that I overvalued the role of textuality in the production of meaning; for him, the textual level was if not superficial, at least a surface phenomenon in comparison with the depth created by the oral tradition and sentiment. Not without provoking resistance from the specialist, he thought that the religious sphere possessed autonomy and that it was auto-structured by the predominance of the category of the sacred. Eliade held closely to the hypothesis of the immanent comprehension of the religious phenomenon" (*Critique and Conviction*, 32).

37. Hénaff, *Claude Lévi-Strauss*, 160–61.

38. Claude Lévi-Strauss, *Structural Anthropology* (New York: Basic Books, 1963), 207–8.

39. Claude Lévi-Strauss, *Myth and Meaning: Cracking the Code of Culture* (New York: Schocken Books, 1995), 8–9.

40. Lévi-Strauss, *Structural Anthropology*, 208.

41. In "History and Anthropology," the introduction to *Structural Anthropology*, Lévi-Strauss writes: "It would be inaccurate, therefore, to say that on the road toward the understanding of man, which goes from the study of conscious content to that of the unconscious forms, the historian and the anthropologist travel in opposite directions. On the contrary, they have undertaken the same journey on the same road in the same direction; only their orientation is different. The anthropologist goes forward, seeking to attain, through the conscious, of which he is always aware, more and more of the unconscious; whereas the historian advances, so to speak, backward, keeping his eyes fixed on concrete and specific activities

from which he withdraws only to consider them from a more complete and richer perspective. A true two-faced Janus, it is the solidarity of the two disciples that makes it possible to keep the whole road in sight" (24)

42. Lévi-Strauss, *Structural Anthropology*, 209.

43. Claude Lévi-Strauss, *The Raw and the Cooked: Mythologiques* (Chicago: University of Chicago Press, 1983), 12.

44. Wendy Doniger, introduction, *Myth and Meaning*, viii.

45. Lévi-Strauss, *Structural Anthropology*, 202–3.

46. Richard Kearney, *Modern Movements in European Philosophy: Phenomenology, Critical Theory, Structuralism* (Manchester: University of Manchester Press, 1994), 267.

47. Steven M. Wasserstrom, in *Religion after Religion: Gershom Scholem, Mircea Eliade, and Henry Corbin* (Princeton: Princeton University Press, 1999), notes that Ricoeur's *Symbolism of Evil* "explicitly" is indebted to Eliade (92). In fact, while Jung argued that symbols could be translated into symbols, Eliade, followed by Ricoeur, stated that symbols cannot always be translated into "concepts." This positing of the symbol as crucial to the enigma of interpretation forms an important component of Ricoeur's philosophy.

48. Richard Kearney, *On Paul Ricoeur: The Owl of Minerva* (Burlington, VT: Ashgate, 2004), 1–2.

49. Cave, *Mircea Eliade's Vision*, 74.

50. Ibid., 75.

51. Hénaff, *Claude Lévi-Strauss*, 114.

52. Kearney, *On Paul Ricoeur*, 2.

53. John D. Caputo, *Radical Hermeneutics: Repetition, Deconstruction, and the Hermeneutic Project* (Bloomington/Indianapolis: Indiana University Press, 1987), 289.

54. Kearney, *On Paul Ricoeur*, 14.

55. Ibid., 68.

56. Paul Ricoeur, "Philosophy and Religious Language," in *Figuring the Sacred: Religion, Narrative, and Imagination* (Minneapolis: Fortress Press, 1995), 42–43.

57. Ibid., 43.

58. Kearney, *On Paul Ricoeur*, 25.

59. Ibid., 118.

60. "Once again," Ricoeur writes, "it is not principally the phenomenology of lived times or the exercises of popular or scholarly narratives that history confronts here, but an order of thought that ignores the sense of limits. And the categories that come from it have not ceased to construct the temporal 'architecture' of 'our civilization.' In this regard, the time of history proceeds as much by limiting this immense order of what is thinkable as by surpassing the order of lived experience." See Paul Ricouer, *Memory, History, Forgetting*, trans. K. Blamey and D. Pellauer (Chicago: University of Chicago Press, 2004), 156.

61. Kearney, *On Paul Ricoeur*, 120.

62. Ibid., 124.

63. In *The Ticklish Subject* Žižek comments on "grace" as the equivalent of "free choice": "It is fundamentally the choice of 'freely assuming' one's imposed destiny. This paradox, necessary if one is to avoid the vulgar liberal notion of freedom of choice, indicates the theological problem of *predestination* and *Grace:* a true decision/choice (not a choice between a series of objects leaving my subjective position intact, but the fundamental choice by means of which I 'choose myself') presupposes that I assume a passive attitude of 'letting myself be chosen'—in short, *free choice and Grace are strictly equivalent;* or, as Deleuze put it, we really choose only when we are *chosen*" (18).

64. Žižek, *Parallax View*, 105.

65. Ibid., 104.

66. Ibid., 104–5.

67. Ibid., 105.

68. Ibid.

69. Ibid.

70. Ibid.

71. Ibid., 105–6.

72. Ibid., 106.

73. Ibid., 110.

74. Ibid., 106–7.

75. Ibid., 107.

76. In *The Ticklish Subject* Žižek describes this tension between appearance and essence in the following Hegelian terms: "So—back to Hegel: 'the suprasensible is appearance *qua* appearance' does not simply mean that the Suprasensible is not a positive entity *beyond* phenomena, but the inherent power of negativity which makes appearance 'merely as appearance,' that is, something that is not in itself fully actual, but condemned to perish in the process of self-sublation. It also means that the Suprasensible is effective only as redoubled, self-reflected, self-related appearance: the Suprasensible comes into existence in the guise of an appearance of Another Dimension which interrupts the standard normal order of appearance *qua* phenomena" (196–97).

77. Žižek, *Parallax View,* 109.

78. Ibid.

79. Ibid.

III. Literary Conditions

1. Pierre Macherey, *The Object of Literature,* trans. David Macey (Cambridge: Cambridge University Press, 1995). Macherey's "problem," as Michael Sprinker notes in the foreword to *The Object of Literature,* is that he balances between the

exterior and the interior sides of literary studies. On the one hand, Macherey, as Terry Eagleton observes, is too much the formalist. On the other hand, as Sprinker comments, Macherey seems at times too interested in literary "production." This so-called problem, however, is not a confusion on Macherey's part. The tension between the two approaches is, one could argue, the "object" of literature: "The problematical thought which runs through all literary texts is rather like the philosophical consciousness of a historical period. The role of literature is to say what a period thinks of itself. The age of literature, from Sade to Céline, does not project an ideological message which demands to be believed on the basis of the actual evidence. If taken literally, the message seems to be patently inconsistent and incoherent. It projects an outline sketch of its own limits, and that sketch is inseparable from the introduction of a relativist perspective. What, from this point of view, is the philosophical contribution of literature? It makes it possible to relocate all the discourse of philosophy, in its accredited forms, within the historical element which makes them the results of chance and circumstances, the products of a pathetic and magnificent throw of the dice" (*Object of Literature,* 234).

2. Stathis Gourgouris, *Does Literature Think? Literature as Theory for an Antimythical Era* (Stanford: Stanford University Press, 2003), 2.

3. Ibid., 30.

4. Ibid., 2.

5. Walter Kaufman, *The Theological Imagination: Constructing the Concept of God* (Philadelphia: Westminster Press, 1981), 53.

6. Ibid.

7. Ibid.

8. Ibid., 55.

9. James N. Comas, *Between Politics and Ethics: Toward a Vocative History of English Studies* (Carbondale: Southern Illinois University Press, 2006), 67.

10. René Wellek, *Concepts of Criticism,* ed. Stephen G. Nichols (New Haven: Yale University Press, 1963), 20.

11. René Wellek, "The New Nihilism," in *Aesthetics and the Literature of Ideas: Essays in Honor of A. Owen Aidridge,* ed. Francois Jost (Newark: University of Delaware Press, 1991).

12. J. Hillis Miller, "Critic as Host," 443.

13. Jean-Michel Rabaté, *The Future of Theory* (Oxford: Blackwell Publishers, 2002). In this work Rabaté provides a passage from Roland Barthes on "literature as mathesis": "Reading classical texts (from *The Golden Ass* to Proust), he is always amazed by the sum of knowledge amassed and aired by the literary work. . . . Literature is *mathesis,* an order, a system, a structured field of knowledge. But this field is not infinite: on the one hand, literature cannot transcend the knowledge of its period; and, on the other, it cannot say everything: as language, as *finite* generality, it cannot account for objects, spectacles, events which would surprise

it to the point of stupefying it; that is what Brecht sees when he says: 'The events of Auschwitz, of the Warsaw ghetto, of Buchenwald certainly would not tolerate a description of literary character. Literature was not prepared for such events, and has not given itself the means to account for them'" (117–18).

14. Ibid., 8.

15. "I think that all of this has to do with the latent hysteria contained in Theory. The central question of hysteria in Lacan's account is ultimately something like: 'Am I a man or a woman?' Here is one of the questions that Theory should start asking of us. Not just because I'm interested in gender theory, but because one can take Judith Butler, who is emblematic of a certain discourse of gender theory when it tries to go elsewhere, although not necessarily further. When Judith Butler continues writing Theory while denouncing Theory, or pretending that she is beyond Theory—then I see her doing Theory, but 'shaved.' In other words, to use a musical image, we seem to be always between *Le Nozze de Figaro* and the reprise of the *Figaro* theme ('Se vuol ballare . . .'), which is curiously heard at the end of Don Giovanni. My idea of the hysterization that Theory engenders takes its cue in Lacan. My starting point is Lacanian, although *The Future of Theory* is not a Lacanian book, strictly speaking. I have been interested in the theory of the 'Four discourses' in Lacan, and I was trying to see why Theory, as it has been famously or infamously displayed, or produced, had to face the discourse of the university while, at the same time, never quite being reducible to the discourse of the university.

"Since I have started shaving in front of you, I can confess more. Most of this book—it may not be obvious—is autobiographical. When I came to Penn in ninety-two, the first local star who was mentioned to me was Camille Paglia. I never heard of the name but she was the most famous anti-theoretician living in the U.S. at that time. One day, an acquaintance suggested that I should invite her to my seminar because she had 'kicked Derrida in the ass!' My response was: 'Oh really? That might be interesting.' Then I heard Camille Paglia talk a few times and loved the way she kept contradicting herself without any qualms—indeed, it was an hysterical reaction to Theory's hystericizing discourse. She was the living proof that Theory could antagonize or hystericize, thus produce effects that, for better or worse, are similar to those of classical hysteria. This led me back to the discourse of the Surrealists who, in 1928, published a praise of hysteria. My gesture in the opening pages of the book was simply to take passages from this manifesto for hysteria written by Breton and his friends, and whenever the word 'hysteria' was used, I replaced it with the word 'theory.' And it works!" (Jean-Michel Rabaté, "Conversation on *The Future of Theory* with Gregg Lambert," *Journal for Cultural and Religious Theory* 4, no. 2 [2003]: 119).

16. Ibid., 118–19.

17. Ibid., 121.

18. Jacques Derrida, *Acts of Literature*, ed. Derek Attridge (London/New York: Routledge, 1992), 36.

19. Ibid., 37.

20. Maurice Blanchot, *The Space of Literature*, trans. Ann Smock (Lincoln: University of Nebraska Press, 1982), 272.

21. Ibid., 42.

22. Ibid.

23. Ibid., 38.

24. Pope, *Essay on Man*, 442.

25. Blanchot, *Space of Literature*, 272.

26. Paul Tillich, "Aspects of a Religious Analysis of Culture," in *Theology of Culture* (Oxford: Oxford University Press, 1959), 41.

27. Ibid., 47–48.

28. Charles E. Winquist, *Epiphanies of Darkness: Deconstruction in Theology* (Aurora, CO: Davies Group, 1998), 82.

29. Ibid., 89.

30. Ibid., 49.

31. Ibid., 84.

32. Ibid., 85.

33. Ibid.

34. Ibid.

35. Jacques Derrida, *Writing and Difference*, trans. Alan Bass (Chicago: University of Chicago Press, 1978), 67.

36. Ibid., 75–76.

37. Winquist, *Desiring Theology*, 133.

38. In referring to the Baroque painters Tintoretto and El Greco, Deleuze describes the visual fold, a division of space calling attention to an indefinite separating line: "The severing of the inside from the outside in this way refers to the distinction between two levels, but the latter refers to the Fold that is actualized in the intimate folds that the soul encloses on the upper level, and effected along the creases that matter brings to life always on the outside, on the lower level. Hence the ideal fold is the *Zweifalt*, a fold that differentiates and is differentiated (Gilles Deleuze, *The Fold: Leibniz and the Baroque*, trans. Tom Conley [Minneapolis: University of Minnesota Press, 1993], 30).

39. Charles E. Winquist, *The Surface of the Deep* (Aurora, CO.: Davies Group, 2003), 175.

40. Ibid., 168.

41. Ibid., 165.

42. See Gregg Lambert, "On the Uses (and Abuses) of Literature for Life," in *The Non-Philosophy of Gilles Deleuze* (London: Continuum, 2002).

43. Leo Tolstoy, *The Gospel in Brief*, trans. Isabel Hapgood (Lincoln: University

of Nebraska Press, 1997), 21. Leo Tolstoy (1829–1910, excommunicated 1901) was a Russian novelist who wrote a series of literary texts addressing religious belief. *The Gospel in Brief* and *Confession* represent his move to an existential Christianity.

44. Ibid., 23.

45. Ray Monk, in *Ludwig Wittgenstein: The Duty of Genius* (New York: Penguin, 1991), recounts the significance of Tolstoy's text in existential terms. Wittgenstein's celebration, however, includes an element of philosophical-linguistic admiration insofar as *The Gospel in Brief* enacts much of the linguistic theory informing the *Tractatus.*

46. Tolstoy, *Gospel in Brief,* 21.

47. Ibid., 23.

48. Ibid., 16.

49. Ibid., 17.

50. Ibid., 19. Tolstoy's subtitles for each of the twelve chapters are as follows: "1. Man is the son of an infinite source: a son of that Father not by the flesh but by the spirit. 2. Therefore man should serve that source in spirit. 3. The life of all men has a divine origin. It alone is holy. 4. Therefore man should serve that source in the life of all men. Such is the will of the Father. 5. The service of the will of that Father of life gives life. 6. Therefore the gratification of one's own will is not necessary for life. 7. Temporal life is food for the true life. 8. Therefore the true life is independent of time: it is in the present. 9. Time is an illusion of life; life in the past and in the future conceals from men the true life of the present. 10. Therefore man should strive to destroy the illusion of the temporal life of the past and future. 11. True life is life in the present, common to all men and manifesting itself in love. 12. Therefore, he who lives by love in the present, through the common life of all men, unites with the Father, the source and foundation of life."

51. Ibid.

52. Ibid.

53. Ibid., 19–20.

54. Ibid., 23.

55. Ibid., 81.

56. Ibid.

57. Ibid.

58. Gilles Deleuze, *The Logic of Sense,* trans. Mark Lester (New York: Columbia University Press, 1990), 1.

59. Tolstoy, *Gospel in Brief,* 215.

60. See Victor E. Taylor, "Theography: Signs of God in a Postmodern Age," in *Secular Theology: American Radical Theological Thought,* ed. Clayton Crockett (New York/London: Routledge, 2001).

61. Deleuze, *Essays Critical and Clinical,* 157.

62. Réda Bensmaïa, foreword, *Kafka: Toward a Minor Literature,* by Gilles De-

leuze and Félix Guattari, trans. Dana Polan (Minneapolis: University of Minnesota Press, 1986), ix.

63. Gustav Janouch, "Conversations with Kafka," in Juan Insua, *The City of K.: Franz Kafka and Prague* (Barcelona: Centre de Cultura Contemporània, 2002), 12.

64. Ibid., 48.

65. Ibid., 52.

66. Ibid., 172–79.

67. Ibid., 70.

68. Ibid., 112.

69. Ibid, 127.

70. Žižek, *Parallax View*, 114.

71. Franz Kafka, "The Cares of a Family Man," in *Complete Stories*, 427–28.

72. Insua, *City of K.*, 95.

73. Žižek, *Parallax View*, 115.

74. Ibid.

75. Gilles Deleuze, *Difference and Repetition*, trans. Paul Patton (New York: Columbia University Press, 1994), 276.

76. Sara Mack, *Ovid* (New Haven: Yale University Press, 1988), 164.

77. Mack, *Ovid*, 163.

78. Ovid, *The Metamorphoses of Ovid*, trans. Mary M. Innes (New York: Penguin Books, 1971), 29.

79. Ibid.

80. Ibid.

81. Walter Pater, *Greek Studies: A Series of Essays* (New York: MacMillan Company, 1901), 3.

82. Rainer Maria Rilke, *Selected Works: II*, trans. J. B. Leishman (New York: New Directions, 1967), 244.

83. John Dominic Crossan, *The Dark Interval: Towards a Theology of the Story* (Sonoma: Polebridge Press, 1988), 2.

84. Crossan, *Dark Interval*, 2

85. Crossan seems to suggest that God is either "inside" narratives (an imaginative idol) or "outside" narratives (a transcendent unknowable). This choice results in a default, quasi-transcendental experience on the "edge of language." It is worth noting that even though God is removed from narrative, Crossan proceeds to offer "parable" as a means of "experiencing" God (*Dark Interval*).

86. Winquist, *Desiring Theology*, 138.

87. Ibid., 7.

88. Ibid., 129.

89. Ibid.

90. Paul Tillich, *The Shaking of the Foundations* (New York: Scribner's Sons, 1948), 52.

91. Ibid., 53.

92. Ibid.

93. Carl A. Raschke, *End of Theology* (Aurora, CO: Davies Group, 2000), 101.

94. Winquist, *Desiring Theology,* 138.

95. Ibid., 139.

96. Ibid., 138.

97. Carl A. Raschke, *Fire and Roses: Postmodernity and the Thought of the Body* (New York: SUNY Press, 1996), 36.

98. The aesthetic, historical, philosophical, and political crises of a postmodern age are exquisitely explored and further exacerbated in Christoph Ransmayr's novels. His works are deeply postmodern, as he spent his early days as a student of philosophy at the University of Vienna, where he studied the social and aesthetic theories of the Frankfurt School, which served as the rich intellectual mise-en-scène of his literary style.

99. Christoph Ransmayr, *The Last World* (New York: Grove Press, 1996), 38. *The Metamorphoses* ends with Ovid's declaration of his own immortality: "My work is complete: a work which neither Jove's anger, nor fire nor sword shall destroy, nor yet the gnawing tooth of time. That day which has power over nothing but my body may, when it pleases, put an end to my uncertain span of years. Yet with my better part I shall soar, undying, far above the stars, and my name will be imperishable. Wherever Roman power extends over the lands Rome has subdued, people will read my verse. If there be any such poets' prophecies, I shall live to all eternity, immortalized by fame" (357).

100. Ovid, *The Metamorphoses,* 219.

101. Ibid.

102. In this context *overdetermination* is not in reference to (post)-Althusserian ideology critique in which economic laws "determine" the meaning of events; instead, I am using the term to suggest an epistemological inability to decide a "last instance" along a signifying chain.

103. Franz Kafka, *Parables and Paradoxes* (New York: Schocken Books, 1975), 25.

104. Ibid.

105. Ibid.

106. Ibid.

107. Ibid., 27.

108. Ibid.

109. I wish to thank my colleague Dr. Mary Boldt for her assistance with translation.

INDEX